BY DAVID J. DALLIN

Soviet Russia's Foreign Policy, 1939–1942

Russia and Postwar Europe

The Real Soviet Russia

The Big Three. The United States, Britain, and Russia

FORCED LABOR

IN

SOVIET RUSSIA

BY

DAVID J. DALLIN

AND

BORIS I. NICOLAEVSKY

NEW HAVEN

YALE UNIVERSITY PRESS

1947

Contents

Contents

Maps and Documents

Preface

To understand Russia it is not enough to be able to enumerate her rivers and mountain ranges, her nationalities and races, her leaders and laws, her theories and traditions. To tell the story of ancient Rome without referring to her slaves would show profound ignorance. To tell the story of Germany during the last decade without mentioning the fate of the Jews would be outright dishonesty. A picture of Russia today which does not include a description of the system of labor camps and exile is not a true picture; often it is deliberately misleading.

The forced labor system of Soviet Russia is not the invention of a diabolic mind; neither is it a temporary anomaly nor a tumor on the body easily removed. The system is an *organic* element, a normal component, of the social structure. To understand this phenomenon is an imperative for every intelligent man. This book seeks to present the *natural history* of forced labor in Soviet Russia: the first feeble experiments, the successes and failures, the gradual development of the widely ramified system; the early ideas, and the mutations in ideology from humanitarianism to mercilessness.

At first every ugly incident of the past appears striking to the point of being unbelievable; so it has been with the medieval Inquisition, the head-hunt, and the ovens of Maidanek. Only when considered in their evolution, from the small beginnings to the massive culmination, do these phenomena assume perspective and find their proper place in the sequence of historical formations.

In the face of a resurgence of slavery in Stalin's Russia the world remains ignorant or skeptical, and usually silent. It knows of purges and mock trials, mass persecutions and executions, but it has not as yet realized the extent and significance of the use of forced labor in the Soviet Union. It is high time to become aware of the new social system which has arisen in the east during the last seventeen years—a social system with novel and surprising features, and which is as far removed from capitalist society as it is from the Socialist pattern professed by the early builders of Soviet Russia. What has emerged is a hierarchical society of several distinct classes and a multitude of intermediate castes. The entire structure, however, rests on a new foundation: the huge class of forced laborers, a segment of mankind degraded to the level of beasts of burden. It is this class which constitutes the lower level of the social structure. Like a taproot, it conveys sap to the higher layers of the edifice. Its individual cells perish with terrible speed, and much of the government's energy goes into filling the gaps with a continuous supply of fresh human material.

This new type of society is the natural product of its basic elements; no other outcome was possible. A chemical synthesis of coal, hydrogen, sulphur, and chlorine produces the poisonous mustard gas, which bears no resemblance to any of its elements. A historical synthesis of unlimited state power, a universal state economy, and militant proselytism has produced the new type of Soviet society. The former process is governed by laws of natural science, the latter by laws of sociology.

There are people who believe that the Soviet state, while depriving the individual of political rights, assures him "economic democracy" and security and to that extent represents a "progressive" form of social organization. How much mischief has been wrought with this concept of "economic democracy"! True, unemployment does not exist in Russia, and every citizen has a job. But so did the serf and the slave. Unemployment was virtually nonexistent in Hitler's Germany. If the Soviet system of forced labor is progress, what is reaction? If the Soviet system is "economic democracy," what is slavery?

The successful extension of the Soviet sphere of influence to include other nations of Europe and Asia marks the transplantation of this new set of social relationships into these countries. As soon as a nation is brought into political dependence on Moscow, the giant from the east moves the complex pattern of its own society across the border to serve as a model for the remolding of its new satellite.

Forced labor as a major economic institution developed in Russia as a combination of two elements—concentration camps and compulsory labor. Throughout the ages, in a multitude of countries, both elements have existed independently of one another. When combined and increased in extent, however, they invariably produce the phenomenon which has now matured in the Soviet Union. We can observe the two elements arising, merging, and growing in all the nations which have fallen into one of the Soviet spheres of influence. Here concentration camps are being expanded to make room for all "socially dangerous" groups of the population, and compulsory labor is being introduced in each and every one of these countries. Unless the process is checked, it cannot be long before in these countries, too, the synchronized and synthesized elements will grow into a monolithic system of slave labor on a grand scale.

ONE of the main reasons why the "iron curtain" is essential to the Soviet state, is the existence of the forced labor system. To demand the removal of the "curtain" is to indulge in wishful thinking. It would be easier for a camel to get through a needle's eye than for Stalin's government to tear down the curtain. Soviet Russia cannot afford to open the gates by abolishing control over foreign correspondents and permitting them to mix with the population, travel, observe, and report freely.

Nor is the average citizen within Russia well informed about the labor camps and the system of exile. Every individual in the Soviet Union lives within a series of curtains. Only minor items pertaining to his own life are known to him—scattered details which never permit of generalization and the drawing of meaningful conclusions. A recent arrival from Russia in this country asked us to tell him "what is going on in Russia—for we don't know anything." How could he? His newspapers and radio are masterpieces of political drapery.

The Soviet press has never so much as mentioned the process of compulsory "migration" of millions of men to the east and north, although every citizen of Russia has friends or relatives who have been a part of it. The authorities cannot afford to publish population statistics giving detailed data for the various regions of the country: they would permit drawing significant conclusions. Over-all numbers of workers, rarely as they are published, are never subdivided into free and unfree labor. Enthusiastic reports from new industrial areas, where new construction is in progress, never explain what kind of human labor is being used. Russia is the only nation where mortality rates are a well-guarded state secret. If mortality rates by districts were divulged and elaborated upon, one of the most opaque of the curtains would be lifted. Nor are total figures or reports of individual acts of suicide ever released in Soviet Russia.

The press monopoly—this system of a myriad internal curtains —is necessary precisely because these and many other developments simply cannot be revealed. The heavy taxes are never discussed in the press, nor is the level of wages and salaries ever indicated. The fixing of prices is another secret. Reports concerning free markets, both legal and illegal, are taboo. The rationing and distribution of available food and other goods may not be discussed publicly. "Human interest" stories are viewed with suspicion and therefore banned. Railroad wrecks, thefts and burglaries, and homeless children do not exist, to judge from the papers of the perfect democracy. The press is considered as fulfilling mainly the function of defense attorney, arguing on behalf of the government. An attorney does not mention *all* the facts, but only those favorable to his client; he is not bound to tell the whole truth, nor even, always, the partial truth; he omits whatever he considers convenient to omit. Only if he is contradicted will the real state of affairs be revealed. In the Soviet Union the press is never contradicted.

Where every citizen is surrounded by curtains, the foreign correspondent is at a loss. He is reduced to reporting parades, industrial plans, a fictitious constitution; he must collect stories about Stalin and count the hairs of his moustache. The great issues of present-day Russia—the forced labor system among

them—are beyond his horizon. Let us not expect him to pierce
the iron curtain with his fountain pen!

It should be the duty of educational institutions and serious
scientific studies to tell the truth, the whole truth, and nothing
but the truth about Soviet Russia. But sometimes a political bias
prevails which prevents criticism of Soviet policy and makes impossible objective study and presentation of basic issues, such as
that of forced labor. The latter is rarely mentioned, despite the
fact that knowledge of it is essential to an understanding of
Russia's political and economic system. No wonder that so many
Americans must struggle with apparently insoluble enigmas of
Russian policy. As a matter of fact, Russian policy is no more
mysterious or puzzling than any other, and the surprises and sen-
sations occasioned by revelations concerning Russian affairs are
but the products of vast misinformation and amazing ignorance.

One example of the apologist attitude toward Russia is found
in a recent book by former Vice-President Henry A. Wallace,
entitled *Soviet Asia Mission*, which contains a report on a trip
which he made to the Far East in the summer of 1944. Traveling
by air, Mr. Wallace visited Magadan, the newly erected capital
of the Far Eastern prison camps, Seimchan, one of the centers of
the widespread punitive gold-mining camps of eastern Siberia,
and Berelyakh. He should have been aware of the fact that every
yard of the ground of these cities and towns was drenched with
the blood of Russian "common men"; and that the "corrective
labor camps" located in this, one of the coldest regions of the
globe, are the most cruel and murderous institutions of our inhuman world. Yet Mr. Wallace did not even mention these
camps and their inmates. To him the development of the region
is a magnificent industrial achievement. He tells the story of the
gold-mining operations there but does not hint at the price in
human lives and suffering that the achievement cost. He poses for
a photograph with Ivan Nikishov, chief of NKVD and actual
dictator of the Far Eastern slave empire, but he speaks of him
only as an "industrial boss." And as a climax of bewilderment or

misinformation, he delivers a public address in Irkutsk and tells his listeners that "men born in wide, free spaces will not brook injustice and tyranny. They will not even temporarily live in slavery."

Actually they *do* live in slavery. They have been torn out of life and society, deprived of everything including hope, and nothing is left to them but their chains . . .

Nothing but their chains! Exactly a century ago Karl Marx and Friedrich Engels appealed to the workers of the world to unite —"you have nothing to lose but your chains." It is under this slogan that the great Soviet experiment has been carried out. It is under this slogan that "wage slavery" has been replaced with a degree of coercion of labor never heretofore attained. After three decades a new class has emerged, a class degraded and condemned to new slavery, a class of workers who have certainly nothing to lose but their chains.

THE organization of the book, the sequence of its chapters, and the distribution of material are always a problem in the preparation of an historico-political work; it was not absent in connection with the preparation of this volume. The division of the book into "Present" (Part I) and "Past" (Part II), is, of course, somewhat artificial; many references to history were necessarily incorporated into the first part of the book, while the second brings the narrative up to the present time. It seemed, however, sensible to concentrate, in the first part of the book, the most important data relating to the situation in the 'forties and to supplement them with accounts and descriptions of the most important forced labor camps.

In preparing this book we were able to draw on a number of first-hand reports concerning the Soviet punitive institutions, written by men and women who have had a record of sad personal experience. For obvious reasons some of them must, at least for the time being, appear under assumed names. Chapter I, which is a narrative of life in the prison camps, was written by Ernst Tallgren, who is of Estonian origin and who was, before the war, a professor at an eastern European university. Boris

Sapir, a former prisoner of the Solovki camps on the White Sea, has written of his experiences in Chapter VIII. Mrs. Anna Falk, Lieutenant Colonel Sergei Malakhov, and Dr. E. Felix prepared the shorter reports which have been incorporated in Chapters II and III. Boris I. Nicolaevsky is the author of Chapter VI, dealing with the labor camps of the Far East; the rest of the book was written by David J. Dallin.

Thanks are due to F. K. Lawrence for editing; to Lieutenant Sylvester Mora for permission to reproduce his map of the labor camps; to Alexander Dallin for research work as well as for the translation of documents used in this book, and to Jean Zallinger for the redrawing of maps.

PART I
IN OUR TIME

I

The Corrective Labor Camps[1]

A corrective labor camp in the Soviet Union is the latest variety of a concentration camp, adapted to suit the current needs and policies of the government. It is a large enclosure, varying in size, surrounded by barbed-wire fences, with high towers for the guards at each corner. From the towers one can overlook the multitude of flat buildings, among which a few better houses serve as offices and homes for the administration, and the rest—an agglomeration of rudimentary huts and barracks—house the hundreds, thousands, and sometimes hundreds of thousands of prisoners.

A multitude of smaller camps are spread all over the country, while the larger camps, integrated into huge clusters, are located mainly in the eastern and northern regions of Russia. Some of them cover an area of hundreds of square miles.

Each camp is assigned its economic task. In the Komi Republic, for instance, the Sevzheldor Camp is in charge of the construction and maintenance of the railway line linking Kotlas with Vorkuta. The near-by Ustvym Camp fells timber, cuts planks, and makes sleepers for railroad cars. The Ukhtizhm Camp has the job of lumbering and of operating mines and oil fields as well. At Vorkuta the principal task is coal mining. In the Kolyma area gold mining is the major job. The part played by forced labor camps in the construction of great canals and highways is well known. Other groups of camps carry on extensive industrial enterprises, such as the manufacture of shoes for the Soviet Army. One camp in the Krasnodar region is noted for its large-scale manufacture of canned meat.

1. This chapter was written by Professor Ernst Tallgren, a prisoner in the Soviet labor camps in 1940-42.

Certain camps act as construction crews of large industrial establishments. They put up the buildings, then move on to put up more somewhere else.

NUMBER AND CLASSIFICATION OF PRISONERS

There are three distinct groups of prisoners in the labor camps: (1) professional criminals; (2) *bytoviks;* [2] (3) political offenders.

Professional criminals: thieves, burglars, murderers, etc. A decided minority, they form the only organized group within the camps. Because of their solidarity they usually get along better in the labor camps than other prisoners. They are better fed and better clothed. They influence camp life much more than their number would seem to justify. Most of them continue to practice their criminal trades, stealing anything they can get their hands on, especially food. Frequently they organize assaults on their fellow prisoners. During the winter of 1941-42, in some of the camps in the north, I saw the criminals openly snatch bread from the other prisoners as the rations were being distributed. Their victims had no defense but to try to gulp down their food as fast as possible. "The only safe place to keep your bread is in your stomach," they would say. In spite of this wisdom, bread would often be seized while a prisoner was eating it. This struggle between hungry people for a 500 gram (1.1 lb.) loaf of bread might have been a scene out of Dante. The camp authorities, though claiming a desire to suppress criminality, shut their eyes to most of these practices, and are sometimes in silent accord with the criminals.

Bytoviks: mostly officials in public institutions found guilty of abuses. As all life in the Soviet Union is state controlled, even the man who sells lemonade at a soft-drink stand is a state official. These state employees are badly underpaid,

2. The closest one can come to this word in translation is "offenders against the mode of life."

and in order to support themselves and their families they often resort to various kinds of speculation. Among this group are also sexual offenders, people engaged in illegal business, and similar cases.

The bytoviks are often given posts in the administration of the camp or in the "cultural and educational department." They are proud of their distinct character and position of preference over the "enemies of the people," or political offenders.

The category of political offenders consists of several subgroups:

1. Peasants suspected of individualistic tendencies and thus undesirable on the collective farms. The most numerous among these are the Ukrainian farmers; the Russian farmers come next; and then follow a host of dissenting farmers from among the national minorities: Kazakhs, Uzbeks, Kirghiz, Mordovians, Caucasians, and so on. They are usually without political convictions except for a wholehearted hatred of the Soviet system. As they are used to heavy physical labor, they constitute the bulk of the work brigades.

2. Persons who have been abroad, or have members of their families abroad with whom they communicate. Here the percentage of Jews is disproportionately high, as almost every Jewish family in Russia had relatives living in Poland or Rumania. This group also includes foreign Communists: Germans, Austrians, Hungarians, etc., who fled the persecution of their own governments. Nearly all of them were arrested in 1937, when Yezhov was Commissar of the Interior, under a charge of espionage. Today these prisoners are referred to in the camps as "men of the 1937 class." Like the peasants, the majority of them are sentenced not by a court but simply by some agency of the secret police.

3. Former inhabitants of the borderlands. These are primarily Russian Poles who lived along the western frontier of

the Soviet Union, and Chinese and Koreans who lived along the eastern border. Many of them were deported into the interior before 1937, and during the mass arrests that year were sent from their new homes straight to labor camps.

4. People condemned for their religious beliefs: Catholics, Baptists, members of the Ukrainian Orthodox Church, and others. They are distinguished by their high moral standards and the firm strength of their convictions. Against the background of demoralization and mutual enmity prevalent in the camps, these people shine like beacons in the dark.

5. Middle or high state officials sentenced for various political offenses. Many belong to the Communist party. A large number are civil engineers and technicians convicted chiefly on suspicion of sabotage. This group is slightly better off than the rest of the political prisoners; they usually manage to get administrative posts which ensure easier living conditions.

6. People condemned for specific Soviet wartime crimes: collaboration with the enemy under the occupation; prisoners of war; men and women dragged to Germany and found guilty of voluntary ties with the enemy; and nationals of countries occupied at the end of the war.

MATERIAL CONDITIONS

Work. Every prisoner is required to work. What he does depends on his qualifications as well as his physical ability.

The prisoners are classified as follows: (1) fit for any kind of labor; (2) for labor demanding moderate effort; (3) for light labor only; (4) invalid, first class; (5) invalid, second class. They are assigned accordingly to any work, moderate work, or light work. In practice, the camp authorities pay little attention to the distinction among the first three classifications. To be listed as an invalid means to be put on a starvation diet which is often tantamount to slow death. There are instances, however, where the transfer of a prisoner to the class of invalids has the opposite effect. This is true in the case of intellectuals, qualified for office work rather than physical labor. When listed as invalids, they are often assigned to administrative work and thus manage to survive.

The prisoners are organized in brigades of 20 to 30 men. Each brigade has its leader named from among the prisoners. During work the brigade is supervised by a foreman ("team surveyor"), also a prisoner. At the end of the day the team surveyor records the amount of work done by his brigade. The "brigade leader" and the team surveyor together fill out work certificates for each prisoner. These go to "norm determiners," who figure out, according to a system of percentages, how much each prisoner has produced as compared with the daily norm prescribed for him. The certificates then go to the food-supply department and serve as the basis for determining what rations each will receive the next day.

The minimum norms are continually being raised, compelling the prisoner to strain more and more to attain his 100 per cent norm. The desire for more food drives some men to complete exhaustion, since the nourishment from the larger ration does not supply the extra energy they expend to get it.

To get the prisoners out to work is the job of the foreman. He is usually a man of marked brutality and ruthlessness. About half an hour before the time to set out (5 or 6 A.M.) the foreman appears in the barracks and starts to drive the prisoners to the gates, pulling them off their bunks if necessary. Naturally this does not occur without blows. Prisoners who have been long in the camps say that trained dogs have sometimes been used for this purpose.

In spite of this, some prisoners succeed in evading work. They are called "refusers" and are punished. A "refuser" receives "punitive" food consisting of a very thin soup in the morning and 250 grams (about .5 lb.) of bread in the evening. Moreover, he is usually put in an "isolator" (solitary confinement cell). If a prisoner has several refusals against him, his case is referred to a court, and the usual sentence is death. The execution of the sentence is made known to all the prisoners. Falling below 30 per cent of the average work norm is often also treated as a refusal and punished by the same measures.

Nevertheless there are many "refusers," especially in winter. The most frequent type is a totally exhausted man who has become indifferent to everything. He has but one wish: to lie quietly on his bunk, in a passably warm corner, so as to feel as little as possible the gradual ebbing of energy and life. In camp jargon this is called "dying away."

Another type is the cunning fellow who calculates that if he stays all day within the camp zone and manages to escape the isolator he may be lucky enough to steal something, or by services to the cook, the barber, or the head of the supply department, obtain some food. Such a trickster is often better fed than the worker who achieves more than the 100 per cent norm.

The third type is less numerous but more interesting: those who refuse to work on principle. They are usually mystics, and they believe that Russia has been conquered by Satan; that Satan directly controls everything in the country. They are haunted by the thought of the antichrist. To work in any Soviet institution is, to them, working for Satan. Their lot in the camps is very hard. They are victims of violence and mockery from both the camp authorities and their fellow prisoners. Their usual end is a death sentence.

In theory work is paid for in money. Formerly this was of some consequence, and there were prisoners who even saved a little. But now the pay is so small that the best workers get for a month's work little more than the equivalent of 1–2 kgs. (2.2–4.4 lbs.) of bread on the camp's black market. Prisoners who belong to the technical staff of the camp receive better salaries.

Camp Zone. The prisoners live in "zones." A zone is an area enclosed on all sides by a fence of wood planks and barbed wire, and guarded from watchtowers. Within the zone are the camp offices, kitchens, baths, hospital, and prisoners' barracks. The living quarters of the free members of the staff, some of the stores, the bakeries, workshops, stables, cattle sheds, tool sheds, etc., are usually outside the zone.

Within the zone the prisoners have liberty of movement; they are not, however, allowed to go outside. A few whose work requires it receive individual passes. Otherwise, the prisoners leave the zone only in work brigades and with a military guard.

The military guard of the camp is on hand to watch the prisoners at all times. Its members are wholly independent of the camp authorities, and there is often conflict between the two. The authorities may want to disperse the brigades over a wider territory, whereas the guard objects that it would make its task too difficult. Or the guard may refuse to allow the sawing and chopping of wood for fuel within the zone because the saws and axes are potential weapons. In these matters the military guard overrules all others.

Food. The food given to the prisoners is far from uniform. There have been times when the rations were so appalling that hundreds died of starvation. In 1938–39 a change for the better occurred in most of the camps. In 1940 the situation became worse again, and after the outbreak of the Soviet-German War in 1941 famine became the normal condition in many camps. The prisoners would dig out rotting cabbage from rubbish heaps, and roast rats. This naturally resulted in increased mortality.

The general food policy in the camps is to keep the men in a state of semistarvation, and by holding out hopes of slightly better food give them an incentive for doing more work. Thus for an additional roll and a piece of fish after the day's work the prisoners strain to the last limit of their strength. Generally speaking, the food is somewhat better in the camps of the north, worse in those of the Temperate Zone. The better food supplies, I have been told, go to the camps beyond the

Arctic Circle, where the prisoners receive additional polar rations. Food is also better in the camps engaged in industry and mining; it is worse in the lumber camps.

All camps ration out food according to a "cauldron" system. Based on the principle that quantity and quality of food must correspond to the efficiency of labor, this "cauldron system" varies, however, considerably from camp to camp. Here, for instance, is the ration allotment in one of the camps in the north of European Russia during the winter of 1941–42:

1st cauldron (for those who failed to achieve the full norm; the day laborers within the zone; and invalids, second class): thin soup twice a day and 400 grams (about 14 oz.) of bread.

2d cauldron (the full-norm and office workers): thin soup twice a day, 700 grams (about 1.54 lb.) of bread, and buckwheat in the evening.

3d cauldron (for those achieving 15 or 25 per cent above the norm): soup twice a day, 900 grams (2 lbs.) of bread, buckwheat and a small piece of meat or fish in the evening.

4th cauldron (the governing staff): 750 grams (about 1.65 lb.) of bread, and a meal twice a day containing some meat or fats.

5th cauldron (sick food): a meal three times a day, which contained fats (usually vegetable fat), and 700 grams (about 1.5 lb.) of bread. The quantity was quite insufficient and the quality mostly not appropriate for the sick.

Prisoners achieving more than 25 per cent above the norm were allowed to buy an extra 200 to 300 grams of bread, and the very few who attained 100 per cent above the norm 50 grams of bacon besides.

The prisoners are fed between 4 and 5 A.M. before leaving for work, and after their return between 5 and 7 P.M. Occasionally the full-norm workers are brought half a liter of thin, fatless soup at midday. But as a rule the prisoners receive no food during their 12 hours of work.

On this diet they soon become exhausted, particularly on the march back to the zone after a day's work. Some are so fatigued they can scarcely move and they advance painfully, driven by the shouts of the guards. Only when exhaustion becomes widespread and seriously curtails the camp's output, and mortality reaches alarming proportions, is anything done about this. A commission is appointed to examine the prisoners' living and working conditions. The slogan "regenerate the people" is adopted, and the food improves for a time. This took place in some camps during the winter of 1940–41, and on a wider scale in the winter of 1941–42.

In general, however, the prisoners are convinced they can survive only if they are lucky enough to be employed within the zone itself. Here it is possible to form "connections" with the cook, or various officials. This so-called *blat*, or personal "pull" enables them to obtain extra food. Moreover, it is easier to endure hunger indoors at a soft job than at hard labor. A serious organic disease entitling the sufferer to be classified as an invalid is a blessing that often saves his life.

Clothes and shoes. Shoes and gloves are a great problem. Leather shoes are almost nonexistent; those that are available are of extremely poor quality and made of pigskin, which is highly permeable to water and soon wears out. The supply of *valenki* (shoes made of sheepskin, cowhide, and horsehide combined) is likewise inadequate. The prisoners are given instead rubber boots which are heavy, hurt the feet, are insufferably hot in summer, and hold no warmth in winter. Cases of frozen feet and consequent amputation of the toes are therefore frequent.

Clothing is old and much worn. Each prisoner has a long-sleeved waistcoat lined with wadding, which is worn over a summer blouse, and a jerkin also lined with wadding. In winter he receives, in addition, wadded trousers. After a few weeks of use all this clothing becomes a heap of worn and torn rags.

Living Quarters. Within the zone the prisoners live in wooden barracks or tents. They sleep on double-decker bunks, usually with no other bed covering than their clothes. Only for the most efficient workers, as well as for the governing staff, the barracks are fitted out a little better. Here the cracks in the walls are stuffed with wadding, and instead of bunks there are sleeping partitions (also double-decker) resembling those in a third-class railroad car. Good workers may also have straw mattresses and blankets. Sometimes they even have bed linen.

The most acute problem is heating. Each barrack has iron stoves, but these heat a radius of only five to six yards, leaving the rest of the building cold. In the north this is especially painful. It is made worse by the constant fuel shortage. Even in camps situated in the taiga, surrounded by forests abounding in fuel, the men in the barracks shiver from cold—a characteristic Soviet paradox.

Such a paradox is brought about chiefly because the camps must carry out a production plan. All efforts are bent to that end, and the fuel supply for the camps is neglected. Furthermore, the military guard refuses the extra escort necessary to send a few men into the woods to cut firewood. Thus every log that comes within the zone is literally fought over by men from the different barracks.

Sanitary conditions and medical facilities. These come under a special department whose head is nearly always a free man. The doctors, medical assistants, and sanitary workers are all answerable to him. There is certainly a desire to maintain satisfactory sanitary conditions in the camps, but the appalling state of the barracks makes this impossible. I myself know that in the camps in the north there was no soap for either bathing or laundry.

The doctors are mostly prisoners. They are in charge of the

dispensary and the hospital. A doctor's powers are rather far reaching, as he can grant a dispensation from work. On the whole the doctors use their powers to make camp life easier for the prisoners. But their opportunities are limited. For one thing, they are under the constant control of camp authorities. And for another, they have almost no medical supplies.

Much disease is caused simply by the climatic conditions of various camps. Vitamin deficiency in the north brings on scurvy and pellagra. Natural resistance to illness among the prisoners is low. In the winter of 1941–42 pneumonia was fatal in 90 per cent of the cases. Undernourishment produces swelling of the feet and face, and, in its final and lethal stage, swelling of the abdomen. The women in the camps show greater endurance than the men; mortality among them in periods of little food is not so great as among men.

To prevent the illnesses caused by vitamin deficiency, the doctors often prescribe an antiscurvy ration of sauerkraut. A drink made from fir needles is supposed to have a high vitamin C potency and is accessible to all prisoners. The doctors claim that the vitamin deficiency could be remedied if enough berries were gathered and stored in the camps. Berries are plentiful in all the forests of the north. Here again, however, the camp authorities are unwilling to spare prisoners from their regular jobs for this work. This only means, of course, increased losses in production during the winter because of lack of vitamins.

KVCH AND MVD

Cultural and Educational Department (KVCh). A Communist party member usually runs this department with the help of a staff that includes both free men and prisoners. The KVCh has a library and a reading room; it lends newspapers to the barracks, organizes amateur shows, moving pictures, concerts, etc. It is supposed, further, to perform the more subtle task of looking after the atmosphere of the camp, censoring the prisoners' correspondence, receiving their requests to be submitted to higher authorities, and similar matters.

The library usually contains a few score of books. Prisoners engaged in "general labor" are, for the most part, too exhausted to think of anything but food and sleep. To them the books mean nothing. But those employed in the camp offices and the invalids have more leisure to use the library. Besides, there are certain advantages to be gained from active participation in the KVCh, such as temporary release from work, and food "connections."

The closest assistants of the KVCh director are the KVCh inspector and the educator. These posts are occupied by free citizens, often young people 18 to 20. They get up talks as well as entertainment, which are intended to inspire the workers to more intensive work. All the educators I met in all the camps were half literate.

Bands are also used as a part of this endeavor to make the prisoners more enthusiastic about their work. These musical treats occur at rather incongruous hours. Imagine for a moment that it is five o'clock in the morning of a gray, rainy, autumn day; the foremen are driving out the hungry men, drenched and angry, clothed in rags and torn boots, many of them hardly able to move their feet from exhaustion; and there on the platform near the gates a band is playing a lively march tune.

The MVD Plenipotentiary. Every camp has its representative of the MVD,[3] who is always a particularly trusted party member. It is his duty to guard the interests of the Soviet regime, to be its eyes and ears. He is everywhere, controls everything, and is feared by everybody. Among other things, he is supposed to be constantly on the lookout for any abuse, any

3. In 1934 the functions of the OGPU were transferred to the new Commissariat for Internal Affairs—the NKVD. In 1941 its tasks were split with the Commissariat of State Security. They were reunited after the outbreak of war but again divided in 1945. In 1946, finally, the two Commissariats were renamed ministries—MVD and MGB. For purposes of simplicity the functions of both are listed below under MVD and NKVD. Throughout this book both designations—MVD and NKVD—are used according to chronology.

manifestation of incompetence or ill will in either camp authorities or prisoners. When he detects such offenses, he is the examining magistrate.

In order to fulfill his duties adequately he keeps a network of agents planted among the prisoners. Their reports frequently result in trials for antigovernmental activities or sabotage. These trials, especially during the war with Germany, have usually ended in a death sentence.

Prisoners convicted of serious political offenses are more closely watched than the others. Knowing this, they live in continual fear lest they say anything which may be interpreted as an indication of antigovernment feeling.

RELATIONS AMONG THE PRISONERS

The relations of the prisoners to each other are a sad commentary on mankind. There is neither solidarity nor comradeship among them. A prisoner can sooner count on the aid and sympathy of the administrative authorities than of his fellows.

This lack of sympathy is symptomatic of a state of mind prevailing throughout Russia today. Like all manifestations of a collective psychology it is difficult to analyze. There can be no doubt, however, that it has its roots in the government's policy of suppressing all collective action or thought outside the officially defined framework. The MVD's treatment of the prisoners carries this to an extreme. If husband and wife are both sentenced to forced labor, they are never sent to the same camp, or to the same region, where they might have some chance of meeting accidentally. This rule applies equally to parents and grown-up children, friends, and men sentenced for the same offense. There is also a tendency to separate prisoners who have been working together for some time. Hence a practice of continual transference from brigade to brigade and from camp to camp.

Soviet Russia is a country covered from end to end with a monstrous network of agents and informers. In the time of the tsars informing was regarded by all Russians as contemptible.

Even the supporters of the regime would not shake hands with one of the tsar's informers. But today the youth of Russia is being brought up to reverence the agent and the informer. In all kinds of quarrels people threaten to report each other to the MVD. There are men in the camps who have been betrayed by their own children, relatives, friends, by people to whom they have been kind. It is not surprising, therefore, that the basic attitude of people toward each other —in the country as a whole, and in the camps in particular— is one of distrust.

Within the camps this distrust turns into enmity. There is mutual hostility—hostility of each against each. Of course there are exceptions. There are people full of kindness and sympathy toward their fellow sufferers. They remain, however, only exceptions, and they cannot alter the general tenor of personal relations in the camps.

Russia has always been a country of expert cursing, but the terms of abuse now used in the camps surpass anything heretofore known. This brutality of speech and manner is directed even against the weak and the sick. Blows inflicted for no reason are far more frequent than a helping hand. When a strong man sees someone in obvious ill health, he will ask him: "When are you going to kick off?" The sick are usually forced to take the worst place on the bunks and often have to lie on the floor.

Some modification of this attitude is found within each national group. The camps are towers of Babel. Besides the Russians, there are many Ukrainians, Germans, Poles, Georgians, Armenians, Caucasians, Tatars, Uzbeks, Kazakhs, Chinese, Koreans, etc. Within each national group there develops a certain amount of sympathy and readiness to help. Among the prisoners of all other nationalities there is a marked hostility toward Russians—often plain hatred. Often, too, Russianism and the Communist regime are identified as being one and the same thing. In this the camps mirror a feeling which prevails to a considerable extent outside them. Nationalistic tendencies are a decentralizing influence in the Soviet Union.

Sexual Life. Prisoners engaged in heavy labor scarcely feel any sexual needs, even when they are relatively well fed. It is otherwise, however, with prisoners not employed at hard labor and better nourished—that is, those who are in technical or administrative positions, such as cooks, barbers, and sanitary workers. They often fix their attention on some woman interned in the camp. Sometimes two or three prisoners belonging to the engineering or administrative staff and living together in one room agree to have the same woman. They provide her with better food; she in return looks after them, mends their clothes, and keeps the room tidy. It is a sordid caricature of a family. But even in this degenerate form people can find some illusion of domestic life. Officially sexual intercourse is forbidden to prisoners; however, the camp authorities shut their eyes to infractions of this rule. Often a woman, asked where her husband is, answers: "Which one? The camp one or the free one?" The term "camp wife" is in general use.

There are relatively few women among the prisoners—generally less than 10 per cent—and most of them belong to the criminal group. Among the political offenders are women sentenced because they failed to report to the MVD the alleged counterrevolutionary activities of their husbands, fathers, or brothers. In Soviet Russia, family members are expressly bound to report any counterrevolutionary activities or plans of their parents and relatives. The punishment for not doing so may be ten years at hard labor. The prisoners call one paragraph of the Criminal Law "The Ladies' Paragraph," because most of the women political prisoners are sentenced on the basis of it. Moreover, many women are sentenced for carrying on anti-Soviet conversations.

Generally, any woman in the camp soon becomes a prostitute. The question of food plays a great part in this. Only those prisoners who have sufficient position and influence to receive supplementary food can keep a woman. In conversations about sexual intercourse the women are as cynical as the men, and as immodest in their language. They use, without the slightest embarrassment, the same expletives and obscenities.

FREE MEN AND PRISONERS

In every camp a number of nonprisoners are employed. Among them are the heads of the various departments of the camp administration, members of the military guard, and similar people. Sometimes these free employees work under prisoner experts. A free assistant surgeon, for instance, might be subordinate to the prisoner doctor. Among these free workers are to be found many ex-prisoners who, after serving their sentences, remained in the camps. Even the directors of the camps are sometimes ex-prisoners. Their situation is not bad. They are much better provided for than many people in normal Soviet life. Various considerations may induce a prisoner to stay on in the camp after the expiration of his sentence. After the many years in prison he frequently feels quite lonely and at a loss; neither his family nor his friends would welcome him back home. Meanwhile the camp has become his world, in which every detail is of interest to him. Finally, the comparatively good pay of free employees in the camps is a factor of importance.

In this setting of the free versus the condemned the idea arises that the prisoners are lower beings, belonging to an inferior class of people, and that mere contact with them is an insult to a free man. It is considered inadmissible for a nonprisoner to eat the same food as a prisoner, to sleep under the same roof, or have any friendly relations with him. Sometimes this distinction verges on the ridiculous. I once saw a free mechanic, employed in the camp's electric power plant, bring his shirt to the disinfecting chamber to be deloused. It was put in with the prisoners' clothes. Later the man in charge of the disinfecting chamber was admonished by the head of the camp for having dared to mix the garment of a nonprisoner with those of prisoners.

The administration of the camps is a vast bureaucratic machine which leaves to the individual directors little scope for initiative. When the head of a camp works his men into a state of complete exhaustion by forcing them to their maximum productive effort, it is mainly because higher authorities demand that he fulfill certain norms. If he fails, he is in danger of becoming a prisoner himself. I have seen the workers in a sawmill driven until they could hardly stand on their feet, yet the head of the camp and the manager of the sawmill were both called to account for the nonfulfillment of their quota.

It is a seriously demoralizing circumstance that only those survive the hardships of camp life who are tricky enough to escape being taken for general labor, who obtain some position within the zone, find means of getting extra food, etc. Each day is a struggle for bare existence, and those win out who have no moral scruples. This produces a general view among the prisoners that there is room in life only for those who are not troubled by virtues.

The labor camps are places of boundless physical and moral suffering. Hundreds of thousands and millions of people perish in them from starvation, cold, and exhaustion. They constitute a system which has no respect whatever for man as an individual, a system impregnated with absolute contempt for human life.

II

Eye-Witnesses Report on Forced Labor

A lieutenant colonel in the Soviet Army, Sergei Malakhov,[1] relates the following about the Russian labor camps and the position they occupy in the people's life and in public opinion:

The population is well aware of the great issue of forced labor and "corrective" camps. But the attitude of the Russian people is not easy to describe. Since the millions of inmates of the labor camps are officially labeled "enemies of the people," not even the slightest sympathy toward them may be expressed either in public or in private circles. It is only rarely that the problem is even mentioned in conversation. When something occurs which calls attention to the labor camps, people generally express their disapproval of the "people's enemies" in order not to be suspected of criticism, or of compassion for the convicts.

In the late 'thirties and during the war some prisoners who had served their terms were released from exile and from camps, and a few were even permitted to return home. Their lives became so burdened that they sometimes felt impelled to end them by suicide.

I was acquainted, for example, with the case of a professor of mathematics at the University of Moscow who returned from a labor camp in 1938. He had been accused of conspiracy against the government, sentenced to ten years in a corrective labor camp, but was released after eight years when it turned out that he was innocent. When he arrived in Moscow, he found nobody at home in his apartment. His little daughter was playing in the yard. When they saw him, the neighbors appeared confused and stared

1. Colonel Malakhov, now in the United States, left Russia after the second World War. His book on internal conditions in Russia is scheduled for early publication in this country.

at him silently, while his daughter ran off in tears, crying, "My father is an enemy of the people. I don't want to see him." He tried to catch her, but she disappeared. At nine o'clock that evening his wife came home from work. She told him that during his absence she had remarried, that she had burned his belongings and that he could not enter the apartment. Meanwhile, the second husband appeared and asked him to leave immediately, threatening to call the militia (police). The professor spent the night in the yard. One of the neighbors called a policeman, who checked his papers and found out that he was permitted only to pass through Moscow and could not stay there longer than 24 hours. The professor again knocked at the door of his wife's apartment, but once more she refused to let him in. When she left the house in the morning, he tried to open the door with a master key, whereupon he was forcibly put on a train leaving Moscow. While the train was running at full speed, he jumped off and was killed.

I knew a construction engineer, a member of the Communist party, an interesting, lively man of great energy and will power. He had never taken part in any "conspiracy," but was accused of friendship with a Communist leader who was convicted during the "great purge." He was arrested and sentenced to a term of 15 years. He was placed in a lumber camp, where he worked under the most severe conditions. After a year and a half he was released, but not until the camp administrators themselves had been executed by the NKVD for excessive cruelty. Now he was declared innocent, given 2,000 rubles, and sent home. At first his wife refused to have anything to do with him, but he produced his documents showing that he had not escaped but had been released and rehabilitated. He has been a broken man since. He is frightened and jumpy, reluctant to talk, and exceedingly nervous. He mistreats and shouts at his child, whom he used to love very much. He has not changed since his release, and whether he will ever fully recover is doubtful.

I know a barber in the Ukraine who, under Lavrenti Beria, was released from a labor camp when the reaction against the sweeping terror under Yezhov set in. He had previously been a mechanic in a flour mill. He was accused of wrecking equipment and of causing stoppages. He was arrested, cruelly beaten up, and made to "confess." Sentenced to ten years, he was sent off to Siberia, where he managed to become a camp barber. Because his work was comparatively easy he managed to survive. In the labor camp there he met Alexander Kosariov, the former boss of the Communist Youth League, a political leader of high standing who had had good prospects of advancement to the highest level of government. Kosariov had been arrested during the purge and sent to a labor camp, where he was lucky enough to become a bathhouse attendant. When Beria became head of the NKVD, the barber was released, having signed a pledge never to reveal conditions in the labor camps under penalty of death. He returned home, was even permitted to join a trade union, but was not allowed to work as a mechanic.

In 1945, a friend of mine, as an assignment from his superiors, visited the labor camp at Rybinsk. It was to this camp that so many artists, writers, and actors were deported. In the women's section of the camp Natalia Satz was a prisoner. She was the famous founder and director of the First Children's Theater. She lived under fairly good conditions and was even permitted to visit other camps as a member of an actors' troupe. The only accusation leveled against her was that she had been the wife of Mikhail Tukhachevski, the well-known marshal, who was executed in 1938.

In the same camp, the popular singer, Kozin—the Russian Sinatra—was a prisoner; another was Leonid Utiosov, the leader of the best-known jazz band, a gay man of 55, full of humor and enterprise. The fame of his band had been so great that it was often invited to play at soirées in the Kremlin. Utiosov was accused of having tried to escape abroad while on a tour in Vladivostok. He was released in 1938, later obtained permission to go to the front, and there earned the title of "People's Artist." Among other prisoners of the Rybinsk Camp were the actors Borisov, of the Vakhtangov Theater, and Shirin, of the Lenin Collective Theater. Shirin was sentenced to the labor camp for once having exclaimed, "Don't feed us Soviet straw; let's play the classics!"

The famous theatrical director, Vsevolod Meyerhold, died in a labor camp a few years ago. A member of the Communist party, he had been under suspicion since 1935, but so long as Stanislavski, the noted director and head of the Art Theater, was alive, Meyerhold was left at liberty. In 1937 Stanislavski died. Soon afterward Meyerhold's wife was killed in her home; her husband's letters and papers were found strewn around the apartment. Meyerhold himself was arrested the same day and deported to a labor camp in the east. There he died in 1941.

Early in 1942, during the retreat of the Red Army, the arrival of Finnish or German armies was anxiously awaited in more than one labor camp near the Finnish border. In one camp near Archangel the inmates overpowered the guards, seized arms from the supply depot, moved to the front and attacked the Soviet troops from the rear. Special troops of the NKVD were dispatched to quell the uprising. Most of the insurgents were annihilated, but a few managed to reach the enemy lines and later joined General Vlasov's army fighting under German command.

In a number of instances, during the war, wives of men deported to forced labor camps refused to be evacuated during the Soviet retreat, preferring to remain under German occupation.

A GERMAN COMMUNIST IN SOVIET EXILE

The wife of a German Communist, herself a well-known Communist leader, was arrested in Moscow in June, 1938, about a year after her husband was arrested and disappeared. Because she had belonged to an anti-Stalinist faction of the party in Germany back in 1931–32, the NKVD now accused her of counterrevolution and sentenced her to five years of corrective labor. She was deported to the Karaganda region in Kazakhstan. Here is her story: [2]

After a trip of several weeks, during which we were crowded together like cattle, I landed in Karaganda Camp in the Kazakhstan steppe. We convicts had the honor of cultivating the steppe, for the first time since the creation of the world, I presume. I had previously read of this in newspapers, which described it as a manifestation of socialist progress.

We lived in clay huts with thousands of lice, bugs, and fleas, fully on the level of the Kazakh nomad but without his mutton steak and koumiss; we spent the short hours of the night lying on wooden boards or on the ground, without straw sacks, without blankets, only to line up for work at sunrise. Our work, which

2. *Deutsche Blätter* (Santiago de Chile, October, 1946), No. 33, pp. 31–33.

lasted till sunset, was rewarded with 600 grams [1.3 lbs.] of bread but only if the full quota of work was fulfilled (such as digging out 3,000 meters of sunflower beds that had been sown by machine, and clearing the furrow on both sides). How one learns to hate the pitiless Siberian sun, to hate every morning that it rises and that begins with yelling and profanity!

You take your sack and put it on your shoulder, carry your *kotelok* (tin can), and wearily walk out into the steppe under guard of the soldiers' bayonets. There is nothing more desolate than the steppe. No tree, not the least shrub, all through the summer the same yellow-brownish arid land. And then the endless sky, which only heightens your despair.

I spent almost the entire term of my sentence in Siberia in the camp's penal cell because, Western idiot that I was, during the first 14 days of my stay in section "Burma" of the Karaganda Concentration Camp I had written a postcard to my grandmother in Germany and a letter to the Supreme Court of the Soviet Union protesting my five years of forced labor. The convicts in the penal cell are assigned to the hardest tasks and receive the worst food. There are five different levels of food rations in the camp. A camp section (*raion*) has four to five subsections, located some 40 to 50 kilometers from one another. I could not determine how many subsections there were in Karaganda; the camp seemed to be the size of Brandenburg Province or even larger.

We were split up into brigades and were shipped from one subsection to another to perform our tasks, such as cleaning out infested sheep stables. A devastating epidemic of brucelosis prevails, which fells sheep and cattle and which is contagious for humans through manure and milk. Once you are infected, recovery is out of the question under the circumstances. The prevalent symptoms are a permanent fever and paralysis.

We were supposed to dig up about two feet of soil around the stables, haul it out into the steppe, and "burn" it. Since I pretended to be a specialist in oxen, I hauled the dirt and drove it out into the steppe with my two favorite oxen, Vasya and Mishka.

I spent my best time in the El-Maryi section at the foot of the Ural Mountains. I was assigned to haul water. There was a spring there in a hole in a small, narrow valley. Yelling "Tsobi-Tsop" (right—left) and employing all the Russian oaths at my disposal I encouraged my little oxen to toil their way slowly up the mountain . . . Then down the steps to the water with a pail, slowly filling up the two barrels on my cart. This was my job from sunrise to sunset. Our main occupation was carrying bags, baking bricks; there were no days off; we could only celebrate if mother nature showed sympathy with us and presented us with a sandstorm or, in winter, with a snowstorm . . .

Months and months went by like this. In the fall of 1939 I fell sick. Brucelosis, they told me; when I began to spit blood, I got into a hospital. For the first time a bed, a bedsheet! Though with bedbugs and lice, still . . . My life was saved by a Russian doctor, a convict, who made up for the lack of medicine with exemplary care for the sick. Supplied with a note, "No longer fit for hard labor," I returned to my penal cell after several weeks.

In January, 1940, there came an order from the central point of the camp ordering me to move immediately to the collection point. After a touching parting from my comrades, and supplied with a little bag of salted fish and bread for the trip—perhaps to a far-off camp—I was driven to the nearest railroad station through the icy Siberian night. After a few days at the transit point, I and two other Germans were returned to Moscow.

In prison there I met Roberta Gropper, Zensl Muehsam, Carola Neher, Wally Adler, Hilde Hausschild, and many others. All together we were 25 German women who had all been returned from prisons and penal camps. We did not know what was to happen. They always called out two or three women at a time. We only learned our fate when about three weeks later Betty Olberg and I were loaded on a prison train in Byelorussia and left in the direction of the Polish border. In Brest-Litovsk the GPU turned us over to the Gestapo. We were taken to Lublin prison, where there were already 150 Germans, including 17 women. Thirty-nine men and I were arrested by the Gestapo and taken to Berlin.

The author of this report spent the next five years in the Nazi concentration camp of Ravensbrück in northern Germany and was liberated only at the end of the war when the German resistance collapsed.

THE UKHTIZHM CAMP

Dr. E. Felix, released from a labor camp, and now in this country, will relate his experiences in another book scheduled for early publication. In an outline of that volume he says:

Even if you are a student of Russia's punitive institutions and if you have heard much and read everything available on the labor camps, you will never be able to understand the horror of them. I shall never be able to forget the smallest detail of my experiences there.

. . . It was very cold when I arrived in the camp of Ukhtizhm in December. After three weeks of travel we were given but one day of respite—and then to work. My walking shoes were torn and my felt shoes were in poor condition, too. After roll call next morning I was ordered to join a "brigade" leaving for the woods. I complained about my shoes and was asked to wait until the chief appeared. In a few minutes he showed up, looked at my shoes, laughed, and said, "The shoes are in excellent condition, and you're probably just a shirker. Get on to work!" In the meanwhile the brigade had left and I did not know where to look for it. I was immediately declared a shirker and was sent to a penal cell for 36 hours. It was an ordinary cell but it was unheated. The cold was biting, and for hours I kept moving around the cell to keep from freezing. Later another prisoner was thrown into the cell; we lay down and tried to warm each other by the heat of our bodies.

But if you ask me what is the worst aspect of the prisoners' life I would not know whether it is the administration or the criminal fellow prisoners and overseers. Of course the whole system is run according to the whims and orders of the local bosses. All hardships, including the rule by criminals, emanate from them. But so long as you, as a prisoner, have committed no particular offense, remain in good health and able to work, you still suffer from the acts of the bandits surrounding you even more than from the administrative officials. They steal your belongings, they take your place in the barracks, they push you around at work, and there is no force prepared or able to protect you. They play cards with your shoes as the stakes. If the card shark has bad luck, you may be sure that the next morning your shoes will be gone. More than once you will be asked to make a gift to one of the bandits around you—a valuable gift, such as a warm coat. If you decline, you will be persecuted and will be sorry that you did not follow his "advice"; if you comply with his "suggestion," you have his protection, but you run the risk of freezing at work.

One cold winter day we were at work in the forest. The criminals started a fire and warmed themselves for half an hour. They sat around the fire while we, the "politicals," had to stand in the second circle. I had a piece of frozen bread in my pocket; I asked permission to place it near the fire for a moment in order to unfreeze it. The permission was granted, but I never saw my bread again.

For a while I had to work in Chibyu-Ukhta. One day it was announced that a quantity of cosmetics would be distributed among the prisoners. A few hundred of them lined up after work. Women who were unable to get soap to wash themselves or combs to comb their hair appeared with little bottles of perfume, which they poured on themselves. They did not smell any better, however, than the rest of us dirty prisoners who always gave off stench. The men, too, lined up for eau de cologne; they simply drank it. The explanation of this strange gift was that a certain department in Moscow was ordered to distribute the available supply of cosmetics and had simply gone down the list and divided it among the large and small cities, and our settlement had got its share in the usual bureaucratic way.

The same system of distributing goods was behind another tragi-comic feature of prison life. When we had to line up to get our so-called soup, most of us appeared with old rusty cans. A few people, however, proudly stepped up with chamber pots in hand. How they had managed to get them, I don't exactly know. But how proud they were of their "civilized" acquisition!

THE PECHORA CAMP CLUSTER

Leonid Shchekach, a Polish newspaperman arrested in September, 1940, and transferred from the Kharkov prison to the Pechora Camps in the spring of 1941, gives the following account of prison life: [3]

3. *Sotsialisticheski vestnik* (The Socialist Courier) (New York, 1946), No. 9.

. . . We went by foot, walking along the tracks of a railroad line under construction. Day and night we were driven on. After a few days we could no longer distinguish between the days and nights because the aurora borealis made the nights appear as bright as day. We had long lost track of the calendar and our lives had come to resemble a cattle-like existence.

Crossing the forests we encountered throngs of people carrying cut trees on their backs. In three different groups which we met I saw several hundred women carrying these heavy logs; farther along the tracks we came across women carrying rails on their backs. . . .

We walked in this fashion through the taiga for an unknown number of days and nights, inadequately fed, receiving even insufficient amounts of drinking water, sleeping in clothing drenched by rain and permeated by sweat, exhausted, broken physically and morally. We were in a state of complete stupor and indifference to our fate.

As we passed by different camps, the administrators would come out and select groups of convicts—from 50 to several hundred at a time. Through one of these selections our convoy lost the only physician among us. . . .

When, with some 700 others, I finally reached my destination after this long and unbearably strenuous forced march, I could not believe my eyes. A few primitive barracks stood in the small, dirty, unpaved yard, where the rain puddles had not dried. Low narrow cots made of round logs were our sleeping accommodations. There were neither straw mattresses nor blankets nor pillows. There was no running water, no sewerage, no light in the barracks. A tiny squad room, three quarters under ground, without any equipment—a hut which resembled a dog house—served as *sanpunkt* [dispensary]. . . .

There was so little space on our cots that we had to sleep in a tightly packed row. Some of us could not even find that much room. Our roommates told us, "When we go to work you'll be able to sleep on our cots."

The first day I was ordered to dig a hole of 12 cubic yards and haul the soil some 12 yards away—all this during one night shift. During my shift I managed to dig only 4 cubic yards. Even the Stakhanovites were never able to dig more than 6 to 8. The term katorga [penal servitude] is utterly inadequate to describe this kind of slave labor. . . .

We were awakened at 4 A.M. We would wash quickly in the open; there was no special building or plumbing available. Depending on the water supply, we would wet our faces or just our eyes, drying them with our sleeves or shirttails. There was no water in the camp itself; water was brought in in barrels and frequently we were altogether without water.

About 5 A.M. everybody, even the sick, was chased out of the barracks for roll call, which was attended by the chiefs of the camp. Roll call always took a long time; for some reason the count never came out right and had to be done over several times. When roll call was over the brigadiers would collect their brigades and we would leave for work.

Our work was very strenuous, demanding superhuman effort. When digging we often ran up against hard soil which could not be broken up with our shovels. Still worse was the appearance of water and the flooding of places we had already dug out. In either case it meant extra work at that spot, while the overseers threatened to punish such "sabotage" by sending us to a disciplinary camp. The administration was naturally very much concerned about output. By producing a large output it could prove to the higher-ups that the administration and organization were in reliable hands. . . .

To this day I cannot understand how we survived. We worked so hard and ate so little, resting only a few hours a day and living in filth that defies description. We made constant and conscious efforts not to succumb to moral depression. It grieved us to realize that we, the victims of Hitlerism, were fated to be slave laborers in the Soviet Union, and to suffer privation and humiliation. We were bitterly disappointed in Soviet Russia.

A ZIONIST LEADER IN THE LABOR CAMPS

Dr. Julius Margolin, a Zionist leader and before the war a writer in Poland, belonged to that sizable group of "liberals" who believed in the "progressive" character of the Soviet state and avoided all criticism of Stalin's policies. Then his own experiences began. When he was finally released from Russia in 1946, he wrote the following on board a ship taking him to Palestine:

I have lived in the Soviet Union for almost seven years, from the fall of 1939 to the summer of 1946. I spent five years at hard labor in Soviet corrective labor camps. There I came to understand the secret of Soviet strength and stability. The last year I spent in a small town in the Altai region as a released and legalized Soviet citizen, taking part in the gray, workaday life of the Soviet people.

I think that I am entitled to speak about and judge of that country. Tolstoy wrote that "no one who has not sat in prison knows what the state is like." This anarchist aphorism certainly applies to the Soviet Union. No one who has not passed through Soviet prisons can say that he knows Soviet Russia.

Until the fall of 1939 I had assumed a position of "benevolent neutrality" toward the USSR; this was the characteristic attitude of the progressive and radical sections of the European intelligentsia. "It is true," we would say to ourselves, "that their system is no good for us in Europe. But it appears that it is a regime that suits the wishes of the Russian people. It's their business, they have asked for it. For us Europeans it is valuable as a great social experiment, and all of us can learn many important and valuable things from the Soviet Union. For instance, the solution of the problem of nationalities; or planned economy; or the new role of the woman. Let them live and work in good health! Let's wish them the best of luck."

Such was my view until 1939. When I used to read the prewar press of the Russian émigrés, I could not rid myself of a disagreeable impression, and I thanked my stars that I was beyond narrowness and petty criticism and could view the Soviet reality with due objectivity. I could not stand violent "reactionary" criticism of the Soviet regime. In my book, *The Zionist Idea*, which appeared before the war, there was no trace of hostility toward the Soviet Union. . . .

The last seven years have made of me a convinced and ardent foe of the Soviet system. I hate this system with all the strength of my heart and all the power of my mind. What I have seen there has filled me with horror and disgust, which will last to the end of my days. . . .

. . . My task is to speak the truth, a truth which so many people dare not, will not, cannot, or simply fear to know. I write with the emotion of a man who feels that he has but one day left to live—and in that day he must say what is most essential, the faster the better, for tomorrow may be too late.

Millions of men are perishing in the camps of the Soviet Union.

Russia is indeed divided into two parts: one part, the "free" Russia, is accessible to the visiting foreigner, so far as foreigners are at all permitted into the Soviet Union; there are show places, such as the Moscow subway, with brilliant façades, and dirty courtyards which are at least in theory accessible to the foreigner.

The other Russia—the second Russia, behind barbed wire—is the thousands, endless thousands of camps, places of compulsory labor, where millions of people are interned. Deprived of citizenship, these people are excluded from Soviet society and are in the literal meaning of the word the state's slaves. After the completion of their ten-year sentence (and recently a new category of 15- and 20-year convicts has been established), they are commonly transferred to the status of "special migrants," not being permitted to return home and often forced to remain in the locality where they have just served their punishment. Millions of slaves colonize the far-off peripheries of the Soviet north. And, in general, there is no corner in this huge land where there is not a camp surrounded by high fences, with the four standard guard towers, one at each corner.

This second Russia is a huge dump, a gigantic heap on which are deposited, whenever desirable, entire groups and classes of the population. This "invisible" Russia is genuine hell, a diabolic invention, scientifically organized according to the latest police technique. It is hard to say just how many people are in it. The inmates mention fantastic figures. I think that in some years the camps housed from 10 to 15 million people. During the war a considerable number died out. Now new herds of men are sent there again. To mention them aloud or to speak of them is impossible in Russia. Soviet literature shamefacedly keeps silent. At one time foreign correspondents were even permitted to visit Hitler's concentration camps, but no one has been permitted into those of the Soviet; the only way journalists have found their way there is as prisoners. And this explains why up to the war the world knew so little about them. The terror and secrecy in which these camps are veiled are indescribable. As in a Russian fairy tale, you talk to people one day—the next day they have disappeared. The bad wolf has eaten them. You are no longer supposed to concern yourself about them. If they write to you, you will seek in vain in their letters any clue to their mode of existence. They will ask for parcels and assure you that they are in good health. Their names have been crossed out of the book of life; their wives will divorce them, and their Komsomol children will not write to them.

The Soviet state is the only one in this world where people live under continual threat, as if at the muzzle of a cocked revolver. In the camps of the BBK—the White Sea–Baltic Sea Canal—alone, there were about 500,000 people, and the 50,000 Poles sent there easily dissolved in the total mass. All of Russia is covered with camps as if with a mysterious rash; and the infinite cynicism of officialdom, well aware of its own actions, is expressed in the hermetic isolation of these camps from all foreign visitors. This enabled the subservient rascals among the cultural élite of Soviet society to deny the very existence of this unprecedented system before the war. After my liberation I held in my hands the official textbook of *Political Economy*, a collective work published in Moscow under the editorship of Professor Mitin, in which one erudite scoundrel calls the assertion that slave labor exists in the USSR "bourgeois calumny."

It is ridiculous to suppose that all these millions of prisoners are guilty. How can half a million Poles (most of them Jews) who were sent to the camps in the summer of 1940 be criminals? A government which does not hesitate to keep millions of its citizens in a state of slavery as a measure of pacification and strengthening the regime; a government that continually tears pieces of live flesh from the body of the most unfortunate people in the world; a government that sends masses of innocent and intimidated people through the sieve of the NKVD, without trial and without cause, without pity or regard, into the labor camps (and the local staffs of the NKVD, in turn, themselves operate under terror and fear)—such a government is the most monstrous phenomenon of our contemporary world.

It is true that in comparison with the death factories of Oswiecim and Maidanek the Soviet camps may pass for humane. But Hitlerism has been beaten, while the Soviet camps continue to exist.

There are no more crematoriums; but the camps where I spent the best years of my life continue to be ignored by the people; and the cot I once occupied is now taken by my comrade. Since they came into being, the Soviet camps have swallowed more people, have exacted more victims, than all other camps—Hitler's and others—together, and this lethal engine continues to operate full-blast. . . .

An entire generation of Zionists has died in Soviet prisons, camps, and exile. We were never able to come to their rescue, not only because it was difficult but above all because we had lost all heartfelt, spiritual contact with them. We did not care about them. I do not remember seeing a single article about them in the prewar press, not the least effort to mobilize public opinion and alleviate their fate. . . . My most shocking encounters in the Soviet camps were meetings with people who had been sentenced solely for having been Zionists in their youth. Before me were old men and women, broken, without hope or faith. They asked me to give their regards to their people and their country, as if to holy symbols that would never again become a reality for them. People with many achievements to their credit, people whom their countrymen must certainly remember—they asked me not to mention their names in the press abroad, because this might be fatal for them or their children, for their families living in freedom, in Soviet "freedom," that is. I keep silent about them. But there are other names that I shall list without hesitation because they are public knowledge, and not I but others should long ago have raised the question of their fate.

M. Kulbak, a brilliant and talented Yiddish poet, suddenly "disappeared" in Soviet Russia. Kulbak was no Zionist. He was a friend of the USSR and had gone there to live and work in the "fatherland of all toilers." He wrote two notable books there: *Messiah ben Efraim* and a novel, *Zelmenianer*. Kulbak had the same idea of Communism as many others who have lived in a world of phantasy. But he was careless enough to settle not in Paris but in Moscow. Now his books are on the index, his works are forbidden, and he himself is listed as "missing" . . .

Every Lithuanian Jew and every Zionist knows the name of Benjamin Berger, before the war President of Zionist Organizations in Lithuania. I bow my head before this man, who saved my life, saving me from . . . starvation. In the Kotlas Camp, where we met as prisoners, he slowly and patiently literally put me on my feet. I know of no man more wonderful, more noble, purer than Dr. Berger. His silvery hair and his tired, intelligent eyes have the imprint of divine humaneness. All of his life—he is 66 years old now—has been filled with unselfish service to fellow men, to science, and to his people. There is no man in the world whom Dr. Berger ever harmed; and there are legions who owe him their lives. Dr. Berger did not fail to help a suffering human being whenever he could, and in the prison camp, into which he has been thrown, he remains a living personification of warmth and care, attention and compassion, moral support and paternal love for all the unfortunate, humiliated and crushed people who for six years now constitute his only environment.

There is something savage and irrationally unnatural in the fact that people like Dr. Berger—obvious heroes of human fraternity—are classified as "antisocial elements" and as criminals in the Soviet Union. After the occupation of Lithuania Dr. Berger was arrested and deported in 1941. For belonging to an organization as "reactionary" as the Zionists he was sentenced to ten years of hard labor. For a person of his age and health (he has a serious heart condition), ten years are tantamount to a death sentence. . . .

Berger's case is the case of all the Jews who had dedicated their lives to Zionism and who, living in Poland and the Baltic States before the war, had no truck with the Soviet Union. Now they are considered Soviet citizens—and the Soviet land finds no better use for them than slavery.

LIFE IN THE LABOR CAMPS

Hundreds of reports were written by Polish prisoners released in 1941–42 and published in *La Justice soviétique*.[4] A few reports from this source are reproduced below.

In the middle of a deserted, muddy plot of land, surrounded by a fence with guard towers at each corner, there stood cages, into which groups of men were put as they arrived. There the prisoners spent several days. But at night the cage barracks could not hold more than 20 per cent of the prisoners. The others wal-

4. Sylvestre Mora and Pierre Zwierniak (Rome, Magi-Spinetti, 1945), pp. 268–314.

lowed in the mire, exposed to the cold and rain. They lit fires, pulling the barracks apart for wood. Now and then club-swinging guards chased the men from one cage into another, hitting them indiscriminately and without any reason. Twice a day the prisoners received one third of a liter of soup, and once a day about half a kilogram of bread. Drinking water was drawn from canals, ditches, and puddles. In these camps bands of thieves had the upper hand; they organized assaults against whole groups of prisoners and robbed them of their belongings, especially clothes. The harassed prisoners, under the threat of clubs, merely let themselves be robbed in the night.

. . . In the labor camp we were put in with Soviet thieves, dregs of the dregs. Those that I knew were indeed human beasts. Homosexuality was common among them and was practised openly. These offenders were let loose on every new contingent of Poles arriving in the camp. They pilfered whatever the newcomers possessed. Several of them would attack a single person, grab all he had, and run away, while the guard looked on with amusement. Prisoners thrown into isolation cells with them were tormented by these convict supervisors, sometimes to the point of death by starvation. . . . There was no defense against them since the guards winked at all this, and sometimes even incited it. . . . Wounding or killing a man bothered them no more than would killing a fly. They were in charge of everything, and it was their business to determine the quantity of work allotted to each prisoner.

Half naked, barefoot, and nearly dead, we reached a place in the deserted, terrible, frozen "tundra" where a post bore the sign "Lagpunkt No. 228." With almost superhuman effort we dug *zemlyankas*, i.e., pits filled with mud and barely covered with branches and earth. Our nourishment was rye flour (raw) kneaded with water. In the night men crowded in the zemlyanka sleep on branches thrown over the mud, warming themselves by contact with one another's bodies. Moans, curses, cries, and threats resound during the night. The men irritate and hate one another. At 4 A.M. the *naryadchik* [chief] sounds reveille by hitting the blade of a saw with the haft of some instrument. There is no need of dressing, since no one ever undresses. Breakfast consists of the second half of the flour portion received the evening before, provided it has not been stolen and eaten during the night. At 5 A.M. the second "gong" signifies "To the *razvod*." [5] Slowly, one after another, the men emerge from the zemlyanka, tattered, filthy, shivering from cold, half dead, and fall into line four abreast. But only half of the men present themselves. Then the naryadchik and the *lekpom* (medical assistant), armed with clubs, enter the pit. The chief asks the first man he sees why he does not come out. "I am sick," is the answer. The lekpom feels his pulse and pronounces him all right. Then blows shower upon the man and he is kicked out into the open. "Why don't you go to work?" the chief asks the next man. "I am sick," is the stubborn answer. The day before, this prisoner went to see the lekpom and gave him his last dirty louse-infested shirt. The lekpom feels his pulse and finds high fever. He is released from work. A third man replies that he has neither clothes nor shoes. "Take the clothes and shoes of the sick one," the chief rules sententiously. The sick one refuses, whereupon his things are taken off him by force. When the man who has no clothes refuses to put on someone else's, he is pushed outside, where the temperature is —40° [F.], and the sick man's clothes are thrown out after him. "You will get dressed there all right," the chief says with a sneer. This business being disposed of, the soldier takes charge of the men, counts them off in fours, and leads them off to work. The work is construction of a road running parallel to the near-by railroad. Snow has to be removed with spades; the deeply imbedded brakes of the tundra and other plants have to be uprooted and the soil leveled off. The quota is 20 square meters per worker. With limbs stiffened by the frightful cold, one has to keep moving and working in order to avoid freezing.

In the evening the aurora borealis sheds its rays over the country. We return from work. We receive the flour, eat half of it, and go to sleep as on the night before. Only half the quotas have been fulfilled. By the light of smoky birchbark torches the administrative personnel anxiously calculate and sum up the results of the day's work. At six o'clock in the morning a report has to be sent to the higher administration, and woe to the personnel if the total accomplishment is less than 80 per cent of the quota; in that

5. Assembling of groups of workers for the assignment of various kinds of work.

case they will have to go to work, along with the others, and for-
feit their privileges . . . Consequently, calculations have to be
manipulated to show good results, a procedure referred to in the
USSR as *tufta* ["chiseling"].

Sometimes the following scene could be observed near the
kitchen: numerous prisoners would be squatting expectantly outside the door. Suddenly the cook would appear and throw out
the slop and remnants. Everybody would rush, push, fight, and
rummage in the garbage for some putrid food. If someone had the
luck to find a good piece, he would run away to avoid having it
taken away from him, sit down at a safe distance, and devour his
loot. In an instant, not a trace of food would be left. And the men,
who were no longer men, would return to their former position
and wait, with their eyes fixed on the kitchen door.

. . . The working conditions were almost always deadly for
us. We were forced to work in temperatures of —40° [F.]. Only
when the cold was even more intense than this were the men sent
back to their barracks. Rain and snow storms were disregarded.
We had to cut trees in the forests even when the snow was waist
deep. Falling trees would hit the workers, who were unable to
escape in the deep snow. In the summer, while mowing in this
marshland, the men had to stand knee deep in water or mud for
10 or 12 hours. The same thing happened in the turf pits. At
night the clothes of the men, drenched with snow or mud, were
hung around the stove. The nauseating evaporation polluted the
air in the barracks, and the clothes never dried out properly. In
the morning most prisoners had to don damp tatters. No wonder
they constantly fell ill. Influenza, bronchitis, pneumonia, tuberculosis (the consumptives were not isolated, nor were they relieved of work unless their temperatures rose above 37.5
[99.5 F.]), malaria, and other illnesses decimated our ranks.
Scurvy was widespread, wounds opened, and abscesses suppurated.
Gangrene was frequent, often necessitating amputation of fingers,
hands, and feet. The men continually had frozen extremities and
amputation due to frostbite was common. Sickness was considered
fortunate if it led to hospitalization. The prisoners often mutilated
themselves to avoid working. Cases of cutting fingers, hands, or
even feet became frequent. The men were compelled to work by

force. Those who resisted were put in jail (in unheated cells, without clothes, and with a food ration of 300 grams of bread and a bowl of soup once a day). Flat refusal to work entailed a death sentence. Such sentences were often read to us. But before recording a refusal, the camp authorities would force the prisoners to work by beating, kicking, dragging them by their feet through mud and snow, setting dogs on them, hitting them with rifle butts, and by threatening them with revolvers and bayonets.

The climate alone was enough to kill the southerners. Convoys of hundreds of Mongols, Circassians, Georgians, Uzbeks, etc., would arrive in the camp. After a year or two only a few of them were alive. The work killed even the strongest among them. For a year or a year and a half a "hero" prisoner would do Stakhanovite work and accomplish 120 or 150 per cent of his quota. Then one night he would die in his sleep, without a moan, of a heart attack, and in the morning his companions would find beside them a "healthy corpse"—healthy, because he had died suddenly without having been ill.

. . . In the 17th camp the rate of mortality was very high. After a few weeks the daily toll of death would be one or two persons, sometimes more. The men died in the camp hospital, in the barracks, in the woods, as a result of accidents, and on their way to the hospital. There were many cases of suicide. In September of 1940 in the barrack where I lived a Viennese Jew, Frischhof, hanged himself from his cot. The Germans had held him in Dachau for 11 months; he had endured that imprisonment but could not stand this one. Another case was that of a man who, driven to despair, threw himself into a well and was drowned.

I shall relate an authentic story which I heard in prison, and which throws light on the fate of the Trotskyites. Several dozen of the most important among them were deported to Vorkuta. While they were still together, they decided to eternalize their memory by a last manifestation of their inflexible will, and thus remain victorious, even if sent to hard labor.

They presented a list of demands, claiming the right (1) . . . to be isolated from common criminals; (2) to be employed only for work corresponding to their professions, i.e., intellectual work; (3) never to be separated from one another.

They implemented these demands by a threat of a hunger strike until victory or death. The NKVD of course turned down their demands. The Trotskyites then started a hunger strike which lasted for 120 days without interruption. During this time the camp authorities forcibly administered artificial nourishment. In spite of this many died. When all efforts to break their spirit proved ineffective, the Trotskyites were separated with the help of a pack of fierce dogs unleashed in their barracks.

The sick men were carried out by the soldiers. They were sent in various directions and, after a while, nobody ever mentioned them. It is pretty certain that they were shot, since no one of them has ever been seen since.

III

Milder Forms of Forced Labor

While the corrective labor camps constitute a revival of the old Russian system of penal servitude, two milder forms of punishment have been reintroduced which are reminiscent of the prerevolutionary practice of exile. These "milder" methods, however, have attained such proportions and been applied with so much severity that actually no parallel can be drawn between the old and the new systems of exile.

Basically "exile" means the assignment of a certain locality for residence to a sentenced person; more often than not, such a locality is a small town in a distant region. But the exile may move freely around the town; no barbed wire surrounds his residence; and he works as a wage earner, not as a prisoner. In effect, however, the ancient system of exile has undergone such a profound change in the last two decades that it is sometimes quite akin to penal labor.

Banishment and exile have been applied by Soviet courts and the OGPU since the early 'twenties. Banishment from one or several areas (usually "minus six," i.e., from the six biggest cities) left to the exiled person the choice of his residence and occupation anywhere else within the country. Exile, on the other hand, meant compulsory residence in a certain locality. But before 1930 both of these measures were tantamount to real exile, that is to say, they permitted a certain degree of individual freedom within a prescribed locality. In January, 1930, the attempt was made, by means of a new law, to introduce greater severity and provide that places of deportation be located in distant, unsettled regions. The law also established a new form of punishment—"exile combined with corrective labor." As it turned out, this new kind of punishment was not often imposed. The courts, and particularly the GPU, preferred to sentence persons directly to corrective labor camps.[1]

Meanwhile another kind of exile was becoming prevalent, soon reaching enormous proportions and evolving, along with the corrective labor camps, into a standard type of forced labor, although of a somewhat milder form. This was the forcible "resettlement" of great masses of the population who were considered either inimical or dangerous where they originally lived.

In the early 'thirties, when hundreds of thousands of kulaks and "wreckers" were sentenced to labor camps, this milder method of deportation was often employed against their families in order to "eradicate" every vestige of the kulak in the village. This group was called "settlers," or sometimes even "voluntary migrants." The aim was twofold: to purge the villages of the breed of kulaks and simultaneously populate the vast empty spaces of Russia. The total number of people deported between 1930 and 1933 goes into the millions.

Thereafter, whenever the "socialist offensive" was intensified, streams of new "settlers" arrived in the north and east. Members of "suspicious" nationalities or inhabitants of border areas were moved great distances. After the outbreak of war in 1939, deportations assumed tremendous proportions. A minority of these people were sentenced to terms in corrective labor camps; the others were resettled in remote regions as "special migrants." In 1943–45, four national territorial units were liquidated and part of their population deported, made "special migrants," and resettled as such on the peripheries of the Soviet Union.

Only in exceptional cases were these migrants allowed to settle in cities, where they might intermingle with the population and live in comparative freedom. As a rule they were obliged to build their own new settlements or, at the outset, to use the abandoned buildings in the slums where some other

1. B. Utevski, *Sovetskaya ispravitelno-trudovaya politika* (Soviet Corrective Labor Policy) (Moscow, 1935), p. 51.

working colony had formerly toiled. Over such groups of exiles a representative of the NKVD—the commandant, who embraced the functions of both mayor and employer—was the sole boss. Sometimes the local head of a state economic unit, for example, of an agricultural unit (sovkhoz), where the exiles have been assigned to work, became their overseer; he had to follow instructions given him by the NKVD. Often the influx of deportees was so large and rapid that their settlements were not ready for occupancy; in such cases thousands of deportees had to start their new life in the open, in the sands of Central Asia, in the Siberian taiga or the forests of the north, in the endless stretches between the Urals and the Finnish border.

MIGRANTS AND SETTLERS

A description of living conditions of these migrants has been given more than once, although the non-Russian world seems to be almost unaware of this great problem and to know even less about the migrants than it does about "corrective labor."

Olaf Feldheim, a Finnish prisoner deported in the early 'thirties to a labor camp in the region beyond Kuznetsk in western Siberia, reported:

The railroad cut directly through the mountains; on the fresh cuts of the cliffs distinct layers were clearly visible: *chernoziom* [fertile black soil], clay , coal. At the foot of many slopes something had been dug that looked from a distance like garbage dumps and black furrows. Out of them black beings emerged, adults and children, it seemed, and followed us with their eyes.

"What are they? Human beings?" I stupidly asked. Our rabble broke into laughter and obscenity.

"These are called *spetspereselentsy*—special migrants," our new authority on local affairs began to explain. "There are thousands of them, many thousands. For the most part they are forgotten. They are sent here as voluntary deportees. They won't let them into the camps or barracks. If you want to eat, you've got to work; if you don't want to, you might just as well dig yourself into the earth. There is little difference. But it's all voluntary; as you please. Of course you have to live in the ground. The soil is warm. You dig a hole, cover it with some boards, if you can get them, and there you live. The work? You get it from the GPU, whatever they want. The women work, too . . ." [2]

The life of special migrants in other regions of Russia has not been much different from that around Kuznetsk. From northern Russia it was reported by prisoners in 1933–34:

People eat the bark of trees and grasses. Children, women and old men run and grovel around in the forest and feed like animals or wild beasts. . . .

* * *

The workers [from a near-by prison camp] . . . met coming through the forest two children of ten and twelve years of age, who were both utterly exhausted. They said they were just wandering. Their mother had died at R—— and their father at Y——. They could get no more bread where they had come from, so they had left to go just anywhere. They were already in the depths of the forest, far away from any roads. There are many berries in the forest now, blackberries among them, so they may manage to keep alive on these. The workmen gave them all the food they had left. . . .

* * *

We are kept here like slaves and the treatment up to now has been very bad. We have to work beyond our strength and there is very little to eat. . . .

* * *

I have now been here five days and have looked around me. May the Lord have pity on this misery! Children of 13 and 14 must work norms just to receive a tiny piece of bread, this being quite insufficient to still their hunger; and they are also being tortured by all kinds of vermin in the swamps. [3]

One important attribute of the general wage system was adopted in the migrant colonies—the differential in food rations in accordance with the individual labor accomplishment

2. *Sovremennyye zapiski* (Contemporary Notes) (Paris, 1937), Vol. LXVIII.
3. *Out of the Deep: Letters from Soviet Timber Camps* (London, G. Bles, 1933), pp. 16, 57, 90, 93.

as well as the allowance of extremely low rations for those unfit or unable to work. The consequences have frequently been a very high mortality rate in these settlements, and the settlers themselves often considered it highly improbable that they would live to see the day of their liberation if their sentences ran to five years or more. Alexander Schwarz, a Volga-German sent to the Vyatka forests along with 246 other kulaks during the first period of collectivization, has given a detailed account of "Settlement No. 513" in a book published in Germany in the late 'thirties. All persons fit to work were obliged to do lumbering. The working day lasted nine hours. The daily food ration for men and women unable to work amounted to 350 grams (13 oz.) of bread. Working settlers received a pound of bread, 20 grams of fat, and 10 grams of sugar daily. Since these rations, too, were entirely insufficient in view of the hard forest work, the settlers bartered clothing and their rings for food in the neighboring Zyrian villages. Their "stocks" of exchangeable goods were soon exhausted, however. Illness occurred with ever-increasing frequency. Deaths were frequent. Children who had been deported along with their mothers were always hungry and rapidly starved to death. The author himself tried to escape, even reached Leningrad, but was caught and returned to the settlement. After three years a great many of the original settlers were dead.[4]

LIFE IN EXILE

In the 'forties, during and after the war, "special migration" again developed on a large scale and snared hundreds of thousands of new laborers. During the 12 to 15 years that have passed since the beginning of this system living conditions have not changed appreciably. They were somewhat better in the late 'thirties but rapidly deteriorated during the war years.

Firsthand reports concerning these conditions are numerous.

4. Alexander Schwarz, *In Wologda's weissen Wäldern* (Altona, 1937).

Mrs. Anna Falk, until recently an exile in western Siberia, writes us:

When our group arrived, we were summoned to a meeting, at which the local officer of the NKVD told us:

"There is one thing you must get out of your heads: the idea that you can return to any other part of the country. You must reconcile yourselves to the idea that you are here for good. There has been no case of an exile who has left our settlement. Some of us are successful, some even lucky. But for you, success is possible only here."

He reiterated this as often as he could. He met a group of us in the street and began all over again:

"If you are diligent at work you will be granted a piece of land. If you work well you will get a cow. You will be well off. But never will you leave this place."

This hopelessness was even worse than hunger and cold. The outer world gradually ceased to exist. News from Russia proper reached us rarely and in distorted fragments. One day the commandant—not a bad man at all—came into our hut and we started to talk about returning to civilization. He called me to the window and said, "Look to the left. You see Potapov's home. It is the finest in the whole village. If you do good work you can come to possess just as good a home as Potapov. But to leave this place will be forever impossible. Rid yourself of this thought, the sooner the better!"

How little the system of mass exile changed during the 'thirties is obvious from reports and letters dated 1940 and 1941, which strikingly resemble those of 1930–34. "We live in a hole in the ground," a new arrival in exile writes from Kazakhstan in 1940.

It is quite a large hole, and wooden poles support the turf walls which are covered with dry clay and manure. We have a stove but it fills our hole with smoke. Yesterday two of us fainted. Our ceiling is so low that we can touch it with our hands and we have to crawl to go in and out. We are sometimes shaken with laughter at the way we are living; and then afterwards we weep. There are so many bugs and fleas we sleep with cotton in our ears.

There is no permanent work here. W—— has been working in the stables. Mother and S—— and I have been embroidering linen. We worked all day for three weeks and earned enough to buy a pood [about 36 pounds] of potatoes. The Kirghiz are very wild looking, but some of them are kind to us. In all this village there are only two houses made of wood. Everyone lives in mud huts.

Another letter read:

. . . we were brought to the Kirghiz steppe where there is nothing but grey emptiness. We live in a hut. The sun burns terribly; when it rains the hut leaks, all of our things are wet. We sleep on the ground; we have no beds, no tables, no chairs. We work all day till we fall. Then we cannot sleep for the bugs. We have been forced to work on the dungheaps, as that is the main work here, mixing dung by hand with fertilizer eight hours a day, even during the worst heat. The only reward once every ten days is a kilo of black, sour flour.[5]

One of the first to present a systematic report about actual conditions in Soviet exile was Olga Kochanska, the American-born widow of the famous violinist. With thousands of others, she was arrested in Lvov in July, 1940. She described her deportation from Lvov; the 16-day journey in a dirty car, the filth and lice; a woman gone mad; the arrival at the Sosva River in the Tobolsk region of western Siberia; and, finally, the settlement, Wintertown (Zimni Gorodok), in which the settlers were to remain forever. It was obviously an old settlement that had been abandoned by its former inhabitants, with about 200 cabins, a half-ruined sawmill, and a burnt-out electric light plant. Endless forests surrounded Wintertown.

The new settlers consisted of 600 men and women, among them 40 children from 6 to 16 years old. Husbands and families were in this case allowed to live together (this was the great advantage of certain "special migrants" settlements over the labor camps). There was, however, no municipal administration; as in the case of the corrective labor camps, an officer

5. Lilian T. Mowrer, *Arrest and Exile* (New York, William Morrow & Co. 1941), pp. 139–141.

of the NKVD with the title of commandant had complete authority over the new population.

"Those who work will eat," the commandant declared, and promised each worker an income of five rubles a day. Actually men were able to earn 40 rubles a month, women about 20. Only meager "advances" were paid out against these earnings. The settlers had to pay for their food, which consisted of watery soup and sour bread; they were "always hungry." For every minor infraction of the rules they were fined. For lateness at work they were fined only a few rubles, but the real punishment consisted in compelling the culprit to walk to the offices of the NKVD, some 60 miles away. He lost ten working days on the round trip. For persistent refusal to work, or for walking around in the woods during working hours, "settlers" were imprisoned in a special jail, a cabin with iron bars.

A few psychological observations of Mrs. Kochanska have a significance that extends beyond the limits of little Wintertown. She relates how the population of the settlement gradually revised its former political convictions in favor of Germany and even of Hitler. The revision went so far that a Polish Jew, Dr. Altberg, declared: "We did wrong in ever opposing Hitler. Poland should never have fought. Nothing could have been worse than our plight here."

Other remarks in the same vein make clear how unproductive and inefficient forced labor is even when compensation, wages, and food are correlated to the output of the laborers. When the women gathered potatoes in the settlement fields, a great many potatoes rotted and nobody cared. When valuable vegetable oil was spilled, nobody cared. And, in general, everyone came to the same conclusion:

". . . what I don't do today I can do tomorrow. And anyhow, they'll probably let the hay rot here, so what little I do will be so much wasted effort."[6]

6. Mowrer, *op. cit.*, pp. 80–81, 121. Another interesting report about the Poles in Soviet exile is Ada Halpern's *Conducted Tour* (New York, Sheed & Ward, 1945.)

The Soviet exile does not strike the imagination as sharply as do the people of the labor camps. The deported are not confined in large prisons; they get wages for their work; their living conditions sometimes approximate those of the native population, particularly in the poverty-stricken regions of the east. In many cases, however, the "freedoms" in which they live include the freedom of the state not to care for its exiles, and hence systematic starvation. The exiles undoubtedly constitute a section of the forced labor class experiencing most of the harsh features of compulsory labor—a mass of humanity, whose exact numbers at present, while not known, certainly reach into the millions.

IV

How Many Camps and Prisoners?

The more forced labor has developed since 1930, the denser has become the official fog that shrouded this institution in mystery. No foreign correspondents have been allowed to visit the labor camps, and not one of the few who have had permission to move about unrestrictedly in Russia has obtained access to the camps or talked to its inmates. In the middle 'thirties, when the flow of books and speeches on the advantages of the Soviet penal system ceased, the last of the prisons and camps still under control of the Department of Justice were turned over to the silent NKVD; escapes abroad became nearly impossible after a number of camps near the border were closed down. Apparently all gaps, leaks, and loopholes of information had been tightly stopped up.

The authorities took pains to prevent the spread of even indirect information, and unusual measures were resorted to in order to accomplish this. Statistical abstracts, which, as in the rest of the civilized world, had been published in Russia for a long time, had contained figures on trials, prisons, and prisoners. In the early 'thirties publication of the statistical yearbooks stopped altogether. A few economic yearbooks appeared irregularly but they contained no data on the actual composition of the labor force.

Most unusual was the handling of the 1939 census figures. The statistical agency announced with pride that, unlike their slow-working capitalist colleagues, Russian statisticians would complete the compilation of all the data derived from the 1939 census within one year. They actually managed to finish the job in 16 months, ending it in May, 1940. What was more extraordinary than the speed of the compiling, however, was the fact that except for a few summary tables and unconnected figures nothing was published. After the previous census, that of 1926, voluminous statistics had been published in addition to interpretative material. The census of 1939 is much more secretive. Military considerations were not decisive in determining this attitude. Even Hitler's government, while systematically preparing for war and suppressing information on certain problems, still found it possible to make public many valuable figures on Germany's population and economy. Among the reasons that motivated a different attitude on the part of the Soviet Government was the fact that population statistics would reveal too much about the prevalence of forced labor.

A statistical analysis of popular balloting can often serve as a substitute for a population census. But again the Soviet Government, while emphasizing the fair and democratic way in which elections are conducted in Russia, did not publish a summary of election results by districts or regions. Only overall figures for each of the Union republics were announced after the election held in February, 1946, and again in February, 1947.

How embarrassing it would have been for the Soviet Government if the complete statistical data in its possession were revealed is obvious if one considers, for example, the widely publicized figures on the spectacular growth of the urban population of the Soviet Union. From about 26 million in 1926 the urban population rose to 55.9 million in 1939. To achieve this increase it was necessary to move not less than 23 million peasants to the towns and cities in the course of a 12-year period—a phenomenon unknown elsewhere, even in the United States during the period of the most rapid development of American cities. In this Soviet achievement the Five-Year Plans and industrialization programs played an important role. However, another factor remains concealed in official rhetoric. For the purposes of the census, a settlement is either rural or urban. Any forced labor camp with a population exceeding 3,000 or 5,000 constitutes a town. The deportation of millions of kulaks to labor camps was thus reflected in the census figures as a rapid growth of towns; and, in general, the expansion of labor camps is an element of the proud growth of "cities" evidenced in Soviet statistics. How great is the significance of this factor may be judged from the fact that the statistical "migration from the villages to the cities" in the 'thirties followed the ups and downs of repressions against kulaks and other suspicious elements of the population.[1]

It is also significant that the fastest growth of "towns" occurred not in the industrial areas of Russia but in those regions of the far north and east where most of the large labor camps are situated. While the urban population of the Soviet Union increased by 100 per cent in the period between 1926 and 1939, the greatest increase—558 per cent—was in the Karelo-Murmansk region (between the Arctic Ocean and the Gulf of Finland); in the northeastern regions (which include a number of great camps) the urban population increased by 335 per cent; in eastern Siberia by 384 per cent; and in the Far East by 329 per cent.[2]

THE GROWTH OF THE LABOR CAMPS

In spite of the reticence of the government, an abundance of information on the amount of forced labor is available, al-

1. According to Professor Frank Lorimer (*The Population of the Soviet Union* [Princeton, 1946], p. 150), the migration to towns and cities between the two censuses began with the comparatively low figure of 800,000 in 1927; in 1928 it was still only 1,062,000. From 1929 on (with the deportations getting under way) it rose rapidly, reaching 4,100,000 in 1931. This was the apex of both the anti-kulak campaign and the urbanization. From 1936 to 1938 the migration to towns and cities was held to an average level of 1,500,000 a year. The admirers of Stalin's industrialization and modernization of Russia would do well to give a thought to these figures.

2. In Karelo-Murmansk, according to Professor Lorimer, "the increase was concentrated in the extreme northern districts. The total (urban and rural) population of the Murmansk district grew ninefold." The cities of eastern Siberia "held only 891,000 in 1926, but these cities *and the new ones* founded during the next twelve years received over two million additional persons in the inter-census period, giving a total urban population of 2,978,000 in 1939."

though it is neither exact nor complete. The main sources of information are four:

First, memoirs and reports of former officials of the NKVD, particularly those previously assigned to labor camps.

Second, those fugitives who had been employed in the camp administrative offices and had access to official correspondence and communication with Moscow and other camps.

Third, items in the Soviet press, which inadvertently throw light on the labor camp system.

Fourth, since 1943, the many thousands of former prisoners who were released and permitted to leave, particularly Polish citizens freed as a result of the Sikorski amnesty of 1941 and Polish Jews released from Russia in 1945–46.

On the basis of all available information the numerical development of the labor camps seems to have taken the following course (also depicted on the accompanying maps).

1928–1930

Kiseliov-Gromov, himself a former GPU official in the northern labor camps, states that in 1928 only 30,000 men were detained in the camps. By 1930 the following six camps were in existence:

> Solovetski Islands
> Kond Island (in Onega Bay)
> Myag Island (in Onega Bay)
> Karelia, between Petrozavodsk and Murmansk
> In the Archangel region
> In Turkestan (Kazakh SSR) [3]

The total number of prisoners in the entire network of camps in 1930 he gives as 662,257. This figure should be considered approximate, since the author was writing from memory rather than quoting official documents.

A GPU official who escaped to Finland in 1930 said in a

3. N. I. Kiseliov-Gromov, *Lageri smerti v SSSR* (The Death Camps in the USSR) (Shanghai, 1936).

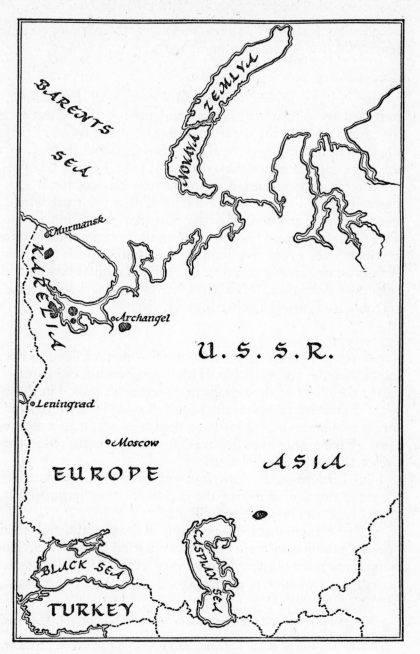

The Corrective Labor Camps, 1930.

sworn statement that "734,000 prisoners were employed under the OGPU in the autumn of 1929." [4]

1931–1932

The volume, *From Prisons to Educational Institutions*, compiled by a panel of authors and published in Moscow, contains the following data: D. Stelmakh states (p. 171) that all places of detention of the Russian Soviet Republic received 294,015 copies of various newspapers in 1931. For the Ukraine the corresponding figure is approximately 60,000; for Byelorussia, 11,713. For the entire Soviet Union the total would thus approach 400,000. Miss A. Shestakova, writing in the same volume, reports (p. 259) that on the average there is one newspaper for every five inmates. Combining these two sets of figures, one arrives at a total of nearly 2 million men in the "places of detention." [5] This number of prisoners for 1931 is corroborated through other sources.

1933–1935

For 1933–35 only approximate totals—neither detailed nor substantiated—are available. This vagueness of estimates is partly the result of the zigzags in government policy in those years. Extensive persecutions were followed by a short-lived spring of liberalism, which gave way once again to a severe purge. Each zigzag in policy was immediately reflected in the size of the camps' population.

John Littlepage, an American engineer, reported hearing the camp population during the middle 'thirties "estimated at anywhere from one to five millions." [6]

A French engineer, back from Russia, estimated that "nearly 5 million men are currently interned in concentration camps, and their number grows every year." [7] Equally vague

4. Duchess of Atholl, M. P., *Conscription of a People* (New York, Columbia University Press, 1931), p. 65.

5. This figure would also embrace the prison inmates.

6. John D. Littlepage and Demaree Bess, *In Search of Soviet Gold* (Harcourt, Brace & Co., 1937), p. 135.

7. XXX, "Les Camps de concentration de l'URSS," *Etudes* (Paris, March 20, 1934).

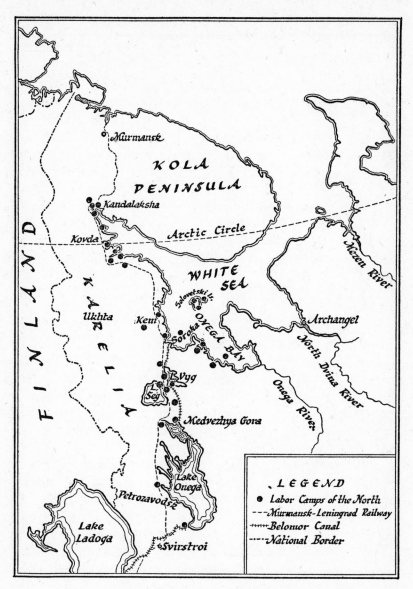

The Network of Corrective Labor Camps, 1932.

LEGEND
- Labor Camps of the North
- Murmansk-Leningrad Railway
- Belomor Canal
- National Border

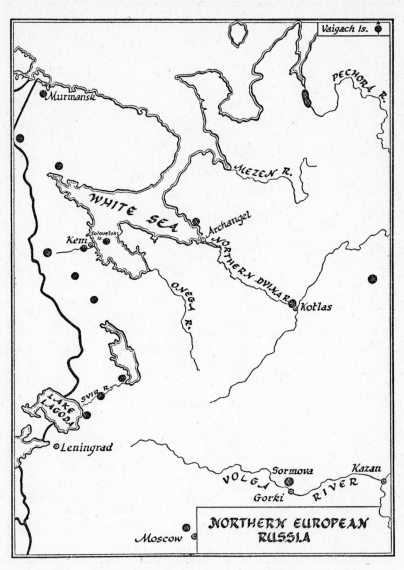

The Network of Corrective Labor Camps, 1936.

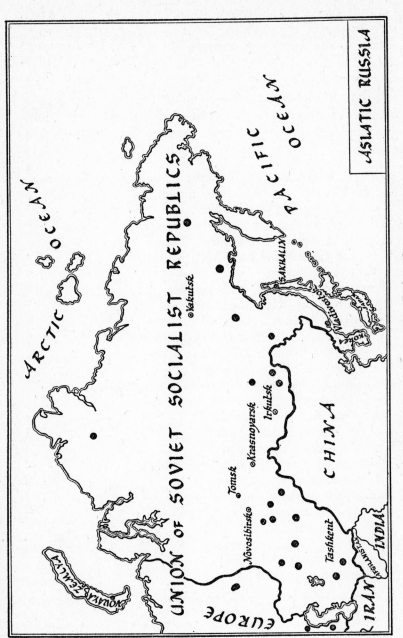

The Network of Corrective Labor Camps, 1936.

and uncertain are the estimates given by I. Solonevich, a former prisoner, for the year 1934: "The total of inmates in all the camps is not less than 5 million." [8]

1935–1937

Nikonov-Smorodin, another Russian fugitive from a labor camp, gave an estimate of 5 to 6 million for 1935–37. He compiled a map (see pp. 56–57) and a detailed list of the camps as follows:

1. Solovetski Islands: peat, brickyards, workshops, farming.
2. Belomor Canal: lumber, construction, chemical plants.
3. Nevastroy: hydroelectric power.
4. Svir River: lumber, hydroelectric power.
5. Karelia: lumber (Petrozavodsk).
6. Northern Camps: lumber (Archangel).
7. Volkhov: aluminum.
8. Ukhta-Pechora: canal, roads, lumber.
9. Khibinsk: roads, mining, phosphorus.
10. Murmansk: harbor, fishing, cattle.
11. Novaya Zemlya: hunting, fishing, farming.
12. Vaigach Island: hunting, farming, fishing.
13. Kem: lumber, fishing, farming.
14. Dmitrovo (Moscow Canal): canal construction.
15. Sormovo: port construction.
16. Kotlas: railroad construction.
17. Vishera: chemical plants, lumber.
18. Kungur: mining, metallurgy.
19. Northern Caucasus: farming, vegetables.
20. Astrakhan: fishing.
21. Karaganda: cattle.
22. Karkaraminsk: grain.
23. Kuznetsk: mining.
24. Chardzhuy: cotton and textiles.
25. Tashkent: cotton and textiles.
26. Siblag: coal mines and ores.

8. Ivan L. Solonevich, *Rossiya v kontslagere* (Russia in Chains) (Sofia, 1936), p. 8. In his *Prisoner of the OGPU* (Longmans, Green & Co., 1935) (pp. 335–336) George Kitchin included a list of the camps known to him. These 13 camps had about 450,000 prisoners. Kitchin's list, however, was far from complete.

27. Lena: gold mines (Bodaibo).
28. Igarka: port construction, lumber.
29. Narym: lumber.
30. Shilka: mining, roads.
31. Sretensk: mining and plants.
32. Sakhalin Island: fishing.
33. Baikal-Amur: railroad construction.
34. Yurga: cattle and farming.
35. Ridder: mining.[9]

1940–1942

Professor Ernst Tallgren, one of the contributors to this book, who was himself a prisoner in the labor camps in the early 'forties, says:

"I have heard many people, well acquainted with the internal conditions prevalent in Russia today, estimate the number of prisoners at anywhere from 8 to 20 millions. The true figure probably lies somewhere between the two estimates. In any event it can be assumed that the number of people confined to the camps exceeds 10 million." This statement relates to 1940–42.

On the basis of a multitude of reports by former prisoners, assembled in a collective work, a group of Polish officers in Italy compiled a list of labor camps and their population in the initial war years: [10]

1. Soroklag: [11] mining, construction, electric power plants, brickyards, quarries, etc.
2. Severonikel: aluminum, nickel, copper, lead, and zinc.
3. Baltic–White Sea Canal: construction and maintenance of the canal.
4. Volgastroy: construction and maintenance of Volga–White Sea Canal, railroad construction, lumbering, quarries.

9. M. Z. Nikonov-Smorodin, *Krasnaya katorga* (Red Katorga) (Sofia, 1938) pp. 111–113.
10. Mora and Zwierniak, *La Justice soviétique*, pp. 120–124.
11. The suffix -lag is the Russian abbreviation for *lager*, i.e., camp. In some cases this ending cannot be used for linguistic reasons; in that case, the abbreviation "ITL," Russian for corrective labor camps, is used. The suffix -stroy is the abbreviation for *stroitel'stvo*, i.e., project, construction.

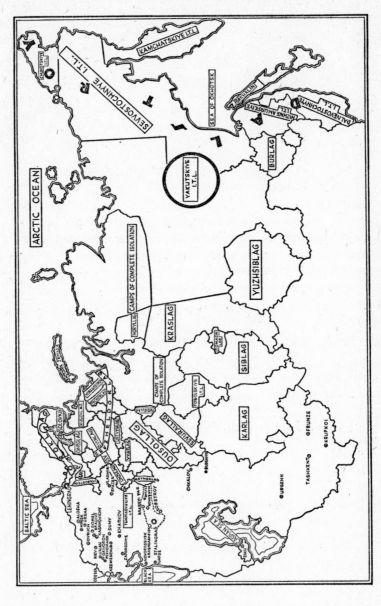

The Corrective Labor Camps, 1942.
(*After Mora and Zwierniak, La Justice Soviétique.*)

5. Oneglag: lumbering, agriculture, construction.
6. Kargopollag: lumbering, agriculture, construction.
7. Sevdvinlag: lumbering and paper industry, construction.
8. Kuloilag: lumbering.
9. Ukhtizhmlag: oil, iron, coal deposits, cement.
10. Ustvymlag: brickyards, lumbering, road construction.
11. Pechorlag: railroad and airdrome construction, etc.
12. Vorkutstroy: coal industry, road and railroad construction.
13. Sevzheldorlag: Kotlas–Vorkuta railroad.
14. Unzhlag: railroad construction, lumbering, brickyards.
15. Temnikovskiye ITL: lumbering, agriculture, workshops.
16. Samarlag (Bezymenlag): construction, quarries, etc.
17. Osobstroy: war industry construction.
18. Yuzhlag: Lenkoran–Salani railroad construction (Caucasus).
19. Vyatlag: lumbering, construction.
20. Usollag: lumbering, construction.
21. Sevurallag: iron, metal, coal deposits, metal industry.
22. Ivdellag: lumbering, road construction.
23. Karlag: coal, ore deposits, construction, etc.
24. Tobolsk ITL: coal and metal deposits, quarries, etc.
25. Siblag: iron mines, quarries, brickyards, etc.
26. Tomasinlag: lumbering, road construction.
27. Kraslag: coal mines, lumbering, railroad construction.
28. Norillag: coal mines, lumbering, railroad construction.
29. Yuzhsiblag: road and railroad construction, quarries, etc.
30. Novaya Zemlya ITL: coal mines, fisheries.
31. Burlag: coal mines, construction, quarries.
32. Nizhne–Amur ITL: construction, fortifications, etc.
33. Dalnevostochnyye ITL: road and railroad construction.
34. Yakut ITL ⎤
35. Sevvostochnyye ITL ⎟ gold, platinum, lead mines,
36. Chukotskiye ITL ⎬ construction of roads and airdromes,
37. Kamchatskiye ITL ⎟ lumbering, quarries, fisheries.
38. Sakhalin ITL ⎦

(Camps 31 through 38 belong to the Dalstroy.)

Concerning the number of inmates, this Polish study says:

A camp usually houses 1,200 persons; in most regions there are ten camps, and in each cluster 20 regions:

$$1,200 \times 10 \times 20 = 240,000.$$

This is a conservative calculation. We know, for instance, that in 1941, 300,000 prisoners were kept at Bezymenlag, that in Yuzhlag 200,000 prisoners were working on the construction of a railroad, and that there are at least two million on the Kolyma. Let us assume for the sake of caution that the normal population of a cluster consists of only 250,000. Then the total number of prisoners in the above-listed clusters alone would amount to 9,500,000.

To this figure must be added the inmates of hundreds of camps outside of these clusters, and all persons under arrest or held for investigation.

We are convinced that for the years 1940–42, 15,000,000 is a conservative estimate.

The grand total of 15 million, although based on a wide range of information and personal testimony of inmates, cannot be considered definitive. Other sources estimated the total prisoner population at from 8 to 12 million in 1942.

1945–1947

For 1945–47 information is on hand concerning a further group of camps which were unknown to the authors of previous descriptions, memoirs, and estimates. The attached maps (pp. 64–65), compiled on the basis of the information obtained from all available sources, indicates the situation after the end of the war and includes the following labor camps: [12]

RUSSIA IN EUROPE

1. Northwestern Russia

1. North Dvina Camps (*Sevdvinlag*), with headquarters at Kotlas: timber and paper industry, also railway construction;
2. Kotlas Camp (Archangel region): lumbering and railway construction;

12. Groups of camps located in the same region are frequently part of the same system, or clusters, of camps. Since the exact borders of these cluster regions are not known and in order to avoid arbitrary classification, no attempt has been made to group the camps listed below by clusters and systems.

3. Onega Camps, with headquarters at Plesetsk: timber work, railway construction, farming;
4. Soroka Camps (*Soroklag*), with headquarters at Soroka: mining, lumbering, light metal industry, quarries, brick-yards, railway construction;
5. Archangel Port Camps: lumbering, railway construction, port construction and work at Archangel;
6. Molotovsk Camp (Archangel region), connected with the North Dvina Camp cluster: railway construction, stevedore work at Archangel;
7. Yagry Camp (Archangel region): mining, construction work;
8. Kargopol Camps (Archangel region), with headquarters at Kargopol: timber industry and farming;
9. Kuloi Camps (Archangel region): lumbering at the mouth of the Kuloi and Mezen Rivers;
10. Solovetski Camps (islands in the White Sea);
11. Franz-Josef Land (islands in the Arctic Ocean, north of 80th parallel);
12. Murmansk Camps (Kola Peninsula): iron and nickel mining;
13. Kandalaksha Camps (Kola Peninsula): aluminum, nickel, and zinc mining; work for *Severonikel Kombinat;*
14. Monchegorsk Camp (Kola Peninsula): nickel, tin, and tungsten mining;
15a. Volkhov Camp (Leningrad region): maintenance of Volkhov water works and mining;
15b. Svir River Camps (Leningrad region): maintenance of Svir Canal;
16. Belomor Camps (Stalin Canal or *BBK*, Leningrad region and Karelo–Finnish SSR), with headquarters at Belomorsk: maintenance of White Sea–Baltic Sea Canal;
17. Khibinsk Camps (Karelo–Finnish SSR): phosphorus mining, construction work;
18. Ladoga Camps (Karelo–Finnish SSR): lumbering and construction work;
19. Vytegra Camp (*Vytlag*): iron and other mining.
20. Vanzlag (Karelo–Finnish SSR): lumbering and construction work on Lake Vanz; a women's camp;

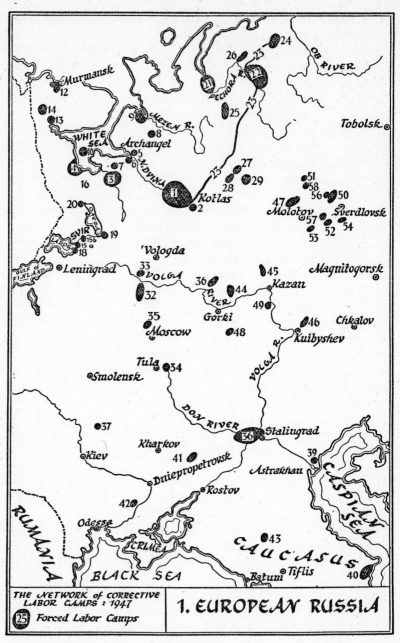

1. EUROPEAN RUSSIA

The Network of Corrective Labor Camps, 1947.

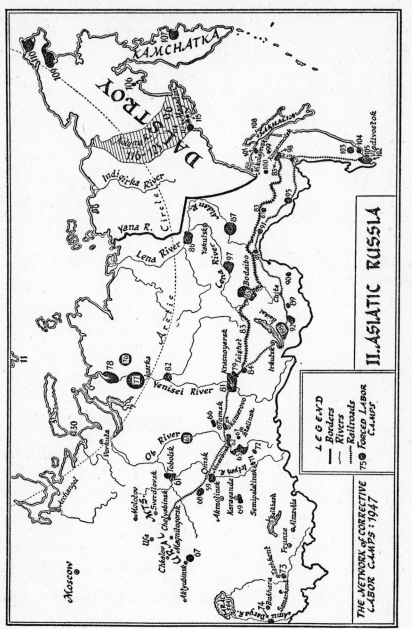

The Network of Corrective Labor Camps, 1947.

II. ASIATIC RUSSIA

THE NETWORK of CORRECTIVE
LABOR CAMPS : 1947

LEGEND
Borders
Rivers
Railroads
75 ⊙ FORCED LABOR
CAMPS.

II. Northeastern Russia

21. Northern Pechora Camps (Archangel region), with head-quarters at Naryan-Mar: railway construction, mining, quarries;
22. Pechora Camps (Komi SSR), with headquarters at Ust-Kozhva: railway construction and mining;
23. Northern Railroad Camps (*Sevzheldorlag*), with headquarters at Knyazhipogost (Archangel region and Komi SSR): in charge of Vorkuta–Kotlas Railroad;
24. Vorkuta Camps (Komi SSR), with headquarters at Vorkuta: coal mining, road and railway construction;
25. Ukhtizhm Camps (Komi SSR), with headquarters at Ust-Ukhta, consisting of Ukhta and Izhma Camps, connected with the Pechora Camp cluster: coal, iron, copper mining; oil wells;
26. Ust-Usa (Komi SSR), connected with the Vorkuta Camp cluster: coal mining, fishing, turf;
27. Ust-Vym Camps ⎫
28. Vychegda Camps ⎬ (Komi SSR): mining and lumbering;
29. Vishera Camps ⎭
30. Vaigach Island (in the Kara Sea): lead, zinc, fluorite, and other mining;
31. Novaya Zemlya Island Camps (in the Barents Sea): copper and other mining, construction work.

III. Central European Russia

32. Volga Camps (Yaroslavl region), with headquarters at Rybinsk: maintenance and construction of Volga canals, waterway expansion, and canal construction;
33. Rybinsk Camp (Yaroslavl region): peat extraction;
34. Stalinogorsk (Moscow region): Tula coal and iron mines;
35. Dmitrov Camp (Moscow region): canal maintenance;
36. Unzha Camps (*Unzhlag*) (Ivanovo region), with headquarters at Sukhobezvodnaya: railway construction, lumbering, brickyards;
37. Starodub Camp (Orel region): hard labor camp for child convicts;

IV. Southern European Russia

38. Stalingrad Camps (*Osobstroy*), with headquarters at Stalingrad: work in industrial plants;
39. Prorvinsk Camp (Astrakhan region): railway construction, fishing, oil fields;
40. Caucasus Camps (*Yuzhlag*), with headquarters at Baku: railroad and airfield construction;
41. Starobelsk (Ukraine): iron and coal mining; also an indeterminate number of camps in the Don Basin;
42. Nikopol Camps (Ukraine): industrial work, mining;
43. Nalchik (Kabardin ASSR): construction work and oil wells;

V. Eastern European Russia

44. Vetluga Camps (*Vetlag*) (Gorky region): lumbering;
45. Vyatka Camps (*Vyatlag*) (Kirov region), with headquarters at Volosnitsa: lumbering, road and railroad construction;
46. Bezymennaya Camps (Kuibyshev region), with headquarters at Bezymenka: quarries, brickyards, underground airfields;
47. Usol Camps (*Usollag*) (Molotov region), with headquarters at Solikamsk: lumbering, oil fields, railroad construction;
48. Temnikov Camp cluster (Mordva ASSR), with headquarters at Potma and Yavas: timber industry, wood finishing, farming, textile works;
49. Tetyushi Camp (Tatar ASSR): lumbering and coal mining.

VI. Ural Region

50. Northern Ural Camps (*Sevurallag*), with headquarters at Sosva: mining of iron ore, coal, light-weight metals and precious metals; metallurgical plants, quarries, lumbering;
51. Ivdel Camps (Sverdlovsk region), with headquarters at Ivdel: lumbering, mining, road construction;
52. Revda Camps (Sverdlovsk region), with headquarters at Revda: lumbering and mining;

53. Kungur Camps (Sverdlovsk region): silver and other mining;
54. Nadezhdinsk Camp (Sverdlovsk region): peat extraction, iron-ore mining, and metallurgical plants;
55. Chusovaya Camp (Sverdlovsk region): hydroelectric power;
56. Lobva Camps (Sverdlovsk region), with headquarters at Novaya Lyalya: mining;
57. Pervouralsk Camp (Sverdlovsk region): mining and metallurgical work;
58. Samarovo Camp (Sverdlovsk region): lumbering and farming.

RUSSIA IN ASIA

I. Western Siberia

59. Omsk Camp (Omsk region): lumbering and construction work;
60. Asir Camp (Omsk region);
61. Tobolsk Camps (Omsk region): coal and ore mining, road construction;
62. Novosibirsk Camp (Novosibirsk region): mining and building industry;
63. Narym Camps (Novosibirsk region): lumbering and peat extraction;
64. Kemerovo Camps (Kemerovo region): industrial construction;
65. Siberian Camp cluster (*Siblag*) (Novosibirsk region): iron-ore mining, textile mills, timber industry, farming, tanning;
66. Tomsk-Asino Camps (*Tomasinlag*) (Novosibirsk region), with headquarters at Tomsk: lumbering and road construction.
67. Barnaul Camp (Altai region): building industry and transportation.

II. Central Asia

68. Petropavlovsk Camps (northern Kazakhstan), with headquarters at Petropavlovsk: mining and road construction;
69. Karaganda Camp cluster (*Karlag*) (Kazakh SSR), with headquarters at Karaganda, Dolinskoye, and Spask: coal and

light-weight metal mining, factory construction, road and railroad construction;

70. Aktyubinsk Camp (west Kazakhstan): lumbering and construction;
71. Semipalatinsk Camp (east Kazakhstan): light-weight metal mining;
72. Leninogorsk Camp (east Kazakhstan): light-weight metal mining, metallurgical plants, road construction;
73. Tashkent Camps (Uzbek SSR), with subcamp at Yangi-Yul: industrial and construction work;
74. Chardzhuy Camps (Uzbek SSR): oil fields;
75. Sukhobezvodny Camp (Uzbek SSR): oil fields.

III. *North Central Siberia* (Krasnoyarsk region)

76. Norilsk Camps (*Norillag*), with headquarters at Norilsk: road and railroad construction, coal mining;
77. Igarka Camps, with headquarters at Igarka: lumbering, logging on Yenisei River;
78. Yenisei Camps, at Yenisei estuary; lumbering and construction work;
79. Ingash Camp;
80. Absagachev Camps;
81. Krasnoyarsk Camp cluster (*Kraslag*), with headquarters at Kansk: coal mining, lumbering, railroad construction, building industry;
82. Turukhansk Camp: lumbering and farming.

IV. *Eastern Siberia and the Far East*

83. Baikal–Amur Railroad Construction Camp system (*BAM*), with administrative centers at Taishet and Svobodny (Irkutsk, Chita, and Buryat–Mongol regions): construction of Taishet–Komsomolsk Railroad;
84. Taishet Camp, terminal of Baikal–Amur Railroad: mining, road and railroad construction;
85. Upper Lena Camps (Irkutsk region), with headquarters at Bodaibo: gold mining and lumbering;
86. Lower Lena Camps (Yakut ASSR): lumbering and logging;
87. Aldan Camps (Yakut ASSR): gold mining and lumbering;

88. Dzhido Camp cluster (Chita region): gold, iron, tin, tungsten mining;
89. Gubarevo Camp (Chita region): gold, iron, tin mining;
90. Dermidonovka Camp (Chita region): iron and gold mining;
91. Magdagachi Camps (Chita region): cobalt and iron mining;
92. Zakamensk Camps (Chita region): molybdenum and lightweight metal mining; industrial plants;
93. Yerofei-Pavlovich Camps (Chita region): railroad construction;
94. Olekminsk Camp (Yakut ASSR): lumbering and mining;
95. Bureya Camp cluster (*Burlag*) (Khabarovsk region), with headquarters at Izvestkovaya: railroad construction work;
96. Northeastern Camp cluster of the Far East (*Sevvostlag*), with headquarters at Magadan (Khabarovsk region): gold, lead, and platinum mining, construction and communication work (cf. below);
97. Kolyma Camp cluster (Khabarovsk region): gold, platinum, and lead mining, fishing, road and railroad construction, building industry, transportation (cf. below);
98. Lower Amur Camp cluster (*Nizhneamursk*), with headquarters at Komsomolsk: construction and mining;
99. Novotambovsk Camp (Khabarovsk region), connected with Lower Amur Camp cluster;
100. Polovinka Camp (Khabarovsk region): mining;
101. Nikolayevsk Camps (Khabarovsk region): iron and gold mining, road and railway construction;
102. Vladivostok Camp cluster (Maritime region): transportation, communication, building industry;
103. Suchan Camp (Maritime region): mining;
104. Port Nakhodka (Maritime region): stevedore work;
105. Askold Island (Maritime region): gold mining;
106. Gizhiga Camps (Khabarovsk region): road construction and lumbering;
107. Kamchatka Camp cluster: construction, fishing, oil fields;
108. Sakhalin Island: road construction, oil fields, mining;
109. Chukotka Camps (extreme northeast), with headquarters at Chukotka: mining and building industry;
110. Bering Camps (on Bering Straits, facing Alaska): mining and building industry;
111. Verkhoyansk Camp;

112. Arman Camp (Kolyma cluster): port work and building industry, a women's camp;
113. Piostraya Dresva Camp (Kolyma cluster): gold mining, transportation, road construction;
114. Magadan Camp: Kolyma cluster headquarters camps;
115. Nagayevo Camp: port work and fisheries for Kolyma cluster;
116. Seimchan Camps: communications and transportation for Kolyma cluster, building industry, gold mining;
117. Srednikan (Kolyma cluster): building industry, mining;
118. Maldyak Camp
119. Berelyakh Camp
120. Ytyryk Camps
121. Verkhnekolymsk Camps
122. Srednekolymsk Camps
123. Shaivinsk ("Valley of Death")
124. Talon Camp
125. Chai-Urya Camps

gold mining, agriculture, building industry, transportation in the Kolyma cluster of the Dalstroy

This list of over 100 labor camps [13] is far from complete; a great many small camps all over European Russia could not be included.

The most important of the camps, or rather of the camp systems or clusters, are these five:

1. The Dalstroy Camps of the Far East, including the numerous gold mining camps on the Kolyma River, described in detail in Chapter VI. Their population is estimated variously from 300,000 to a million.

2. A group of camps in eastern Siberia to the north and east of Lake Baikal, occupied in construction of the new Taishet–Komsomolsk (Baikal–Amur) Railroad, in mining, etc. The population of this cluster of camps is estimated at about 500,000.

13. In addition the following labor camps have previously been reported in existence. There is no confirmation, however, of their operation at present; some of them may well have closed down. Petrozavodsk Camp (Karelo-Finnish SSR): lumbering; Sormovo Camp (central European Russia): construction; North Caucasian Camp cluster: agriculture; Karkaraminsk (Central Asia): agriculture; Shilka and Sretensk (Chita region): mining and construction; and Yurga (Omsk region): agriculture.

3. The Pechora Camps, with from 900,000 to 1,100,000 prisoners. This system of camps was in charge of the construction of the long railroad from Kotlas to Vorkuta. Since its completion the prisoners are employed in coal mining, oil drilling, and lumbering.

4. The Yagry and adjoining camps in the Archangel region, with an aggregate population of nearly 500,000 men and women. These camps were of particular importance during the war since their prisoners were engaged in widening the White Sea port facilities, building airfields and railroad branches. A new town, Molotovsk, has sprung up here in the vicinity of Archangel. The Yagry Women's Camp is known for its hard living conditions.

5. The Karaganda Camps, with about 150,000 internees employed at copper, silver, iron, and particularly coal mining. To obtain their food supply these camps operate their own farms and have their own cattle and camels. Among the political prisoners in the Women's Camp here there is a sizable group of wives and widows of former Communist leaders "purged" in the late 'thirties. This camp is commonly referred to as "the Wives' Camp."

Several camps are known for particularly bad living conditions and cruel treatment of prisoners:

1. The Dzhido cluster of eastern Siberia has a particularly high rate of attempted escapes because of insufficient food and harsh treatment. In order to stem these attempts the administration now chains captured fugitives for the remainder of their sentences.

2. At least two punitive camps (for special punishment of prisoners from other camps) are known to exist in the Far East: one on the Kolyma River, the other on the lower Yenisei near the estuary on the Arctic Ocean. The mortality rate there is reported to exceed 30 per cent per year. No correspondence of the prisoners with their relatives and friends is permitted.

3. The Stalinogorsk Women's Camp is known for ex-

tremely severe living conditions, harsh punishment, and bad food. The women work in the iron and coal mines of the Tula region.

4. The Vorkuta Camps have among their internees thousands of men sentenced for treason and desertion during the war. The extremely high mortality rate is notorious.

5. A camp near Komsomolsk in the Far East is labeled "Traitors' Camp." Here are interned men and women condemned for disloyalty to the Soviet Union. Their sentences go up to 25 years at penal servitude. The internees of this camp are engaged in building a railroad line to the Tartar Bay. The food is bad, the punishment severe, and the death toll extremely high.

6. The Prorvinsk Camp on the Caspian Sea has among its inmates thousands of natives of Central Asia who refused to do military service in the Red Army.

7. In certain camps of the Pechora Camp cluster corporal punishment, officially abolished in 1917–18, has been reintroduced.

8. The Krasnoyarsk Camps, with about 10,000 prisoners, are conspicuous for their lack of medical facilities and hospitals.

In the camps on the lower Yenisei in north Siberia rumors circulate about a mysterious camp on the shore of the Arctic Ocean. These rumors have it that a few thousand men work there in mines under the floor of the ocean, extracting precious minerals. They reportedly not only work but also live underground. Deportation to this camp is a sentence to slow death; not one of the inmates has ever come out alive. Every day the great elevator brings up a number of corpses for burial. It is impossible to check and verify these reports; more often than not, however, persistent rumors about conditions in Soviet labor camps have proved to be based on facts.

Among the other camps two are noteworthy: that near Rybinsk (on the Leningrad–Moscow Railroad) is reported to have a group of women sentenced to five years at forced labor for cannibalism during the German siege of Leningrad

DOCUMENTS FROM 32 CORRECTIVE LABOR CAMPS

"USSR-NKVD
Volga Corrective Labor Camp
—Perebory, Rybinsk Region."

"USSR-NKVD
Administration of Unzha Corrective Labor Camp."

"Administration of Northern Ural Camps of the NKVD: Vasil'yev."

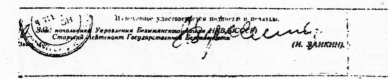

"USSR-NKVD

Bureya Railroad Construction Camp—Izvestkovaya, Far Eastern Railroad."

"USSR-NKVD-GULAG

Bezymyansk Corrective Labor Camp—Second Section—Kuibyshev."

"Deputy Chief of Administration of Bezymyansk Camp of the NKVD of the USSR—Senior Lieutenant of State Security: I. Zaikin."

"USSR-NKVD
Administration of Vorkutstroy
—Second Section."

"USSR-NKVD
Administration of Usol Corrective Labor Camp—Second Section—Solikamsk."

"Chief of Administration of *Kraslag*—NKVD
Captain of State Security: Pochtarev.
Chief of Second Section of *Kraslag*—NKVD
Junior Lieutenant of State Security: Aronson."

"USSR-NKVD
Administration of Krasnoyarsk
Corrective Labor Camp—Kansk,
Krasnoyarsk Region."

"USSR-NKVD
Norilsk Corrective Labor Camp
—Norilsk, Taimyr National
District."

LABOR CAMPS OF THE FAR EAST

С. С. С. Р.
НАРОДНЫЙ КОМИССАРИАТ
ВНУТРЕННИХ ДЕЛ

УПРАВЛЕНИЕ
НИЖНЕ-АМУРСКОГО
ИСПРАВИТЕЛЬНО-ТРУДОВОГО
ЛАГЕРЯ НКВД

25 августа 1941 г.
№ 1-5545 х

г. Комсомольск, Хабаровского края.

НКВД СССР
УПРАВЛЕНИЕ
СЕВЕРО-ВОСТОЧНЫХ
ИСПРАВИТЕЛЬНО-ТРУДОВЫХ
ЛАГЕРЕЙ
№ 1051

18 сентября 1911

г. Магадан Хабаровского края

"USSR-NKVD
Administration of Lower-Amur
Corrective Labor Camps of the
NKVD—Komsomolsk, Khaba-
rovsk Region."

"NKVD-USSR
Administration of the North-
eastern Corrective Labor
Camps—Magadan, Khabarovsk
Region."

Начальник Управления Севвостлагерей
Дальстроя НКВД СССР—
батальонный комиссар Драбкин (Драбкин)

"Chief of Administration of Northeastern Camps of the Dalstroy of the
NKVD-USSR—Battalion Commissar DRABKIN."

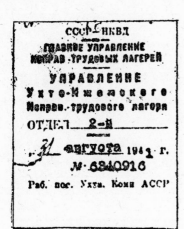 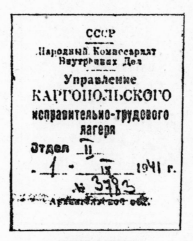

"USSR-NKVD
G U L A G
Administration of Ukht-Izhma
Corrective Labor Camp.
Komi ASSR."

"USSR-NKVD
Administration of Kargopol
Corrective Labor Camp—Section II. Archangel Region."

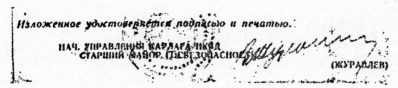

"Chief of Administration of *Karlag* of the NKVD—
Senior Major of State Security: Zhuravlev."

"USSR-NKVD
Administration of Karaganda
Corrective Labor Camp."

"USSR-NKVD
Administration of Railroad
Construction and Soroka
Corrective Labor Camp,
Belomorsk, KFSSR."

"Deputy Chief of Administration of UNZHLAG of the NKVD—
Senior Lieutenant of State Security: GOLOV
Acting Chief of Second Section: GALAT."

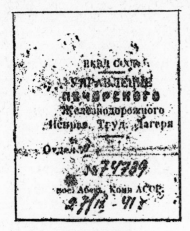

"NKVD-USSR

Administration of Pechora
Railroad Corrective Labor
Camp, Komi ASSR."

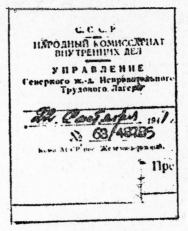

"USSR-NKVD

Administration of Northern
Railroad Corrective Labor
Camp, Komi ASSR."

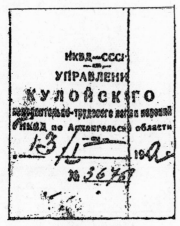

"NKVD-USSR

Administration of Kuloi Cor-
rective Labor Camp of the
NKVD in the Archangel
Region."

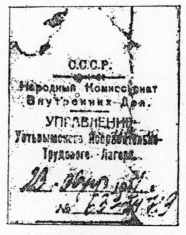

"USSR-NKVD

Administration of Ustvym
Corrective Labor Camp."

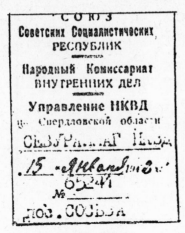

"USSR-NKVD
Administration of the NKVD
for Sverdlovsk Region:
Sevurallag NKVD, Sos'va."

"USSR-NKVD
Administration of the Novo-
Tambovsk Corrective Labor
Camp—Komsomolsk."

"USSR-NKVD
Onega Corrective Labor Camp
—Plesetskaya, Northern Rail-
road."

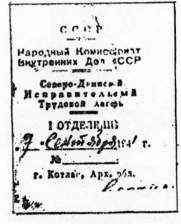

"USSR-NKVD
Northern Dvina Corrective
Labor Camp—Kotlas,
Archangel Region."

"USSR-NKVD
Administration of Vyatka
Corrective Labor Camp—
Volosnitsa, Kirov Region."

"USSR-NKVD
Administration of Vytegra
Camp of the NKVD."

"Deputy Chief of Norilsk Kombinat and Camp of the NKVD—
Junior Lieutenant of State Security: YEREMEYEV."

in 1942–43; and the Zakamensk Camp in eastern Siberia has a considerable number of children from the Moscow region among its internees, boys and girls sentenced for criminal offenses. They work in mines and near-by industrial plants.

Finally, a few camps are remarkable for their speedy migration eastward during the war and subsequent return after the liberation of their original areas. Among these are the Belomorsk Camp near the Finnish border, the Dmitrov Camp in the Moscow region, and the Svir River Camps near Leningrad.

THE NUMBER OF PRISONERS

How many prisoners are there at present being kept in Russia's "corrective institutions"? There is no definitive answer to this question; there are only estimates and guesses of varying degrees of reliability.

In Russia itself the number of prisoners in all kinds of forced labor institutions is generally estimated to be very high. Guesses go up to 15, 20, even 30, million men. In his book, *I Chose Freedom*, Victor Kravchenko reports on forced labor during the war:

. . . our industry became more and more dependent upon the vast armies of prisoners, their ranks now swelled to unprecedented size by war arrests. In official circles twenty millions became the accepted estimate of this labor reservoir. The estimate did not include the boys and girls from 14 to 16 forcibly torn away from their parents and assigned to regions and industries in which manpower shortages were sharpest.

The war industries of the U.S.S.R., like those of Germany, rested primarily on slave labor.[14]

Brooks Atkinson reported after his return from Moscow: "No one knows how many million political prisoners are now living in jail or in exile. The estimates run all the way from 10,000,000 to 15,000,000." [15] Vasili Petukhov, a former Red

14. Victor Kravchenko, *I Chose Freedom* (Scribner, 1946), p. 104.
15. *New York Times*, July 7, 1946.

Army man, a native of Siberia, who is now in this country, stated in the press that "by the end of 1943 not only common people in Siberia but even the administration mentioned a figure of 24 millions in the camps, in addition to the prison population." [16] Another refugee states that "the number of prisoners—political and others—in Soviet Russia is estimated at 20 million by the Russians themselves." [17]

Mora and Zwierniak report that

the Russian prisoners say that in 1937, in the "Yezhov Reign," [Yezhov's rule of the NKVD has become proverbially synonymous with terror] there were over 40 million persons detained in Russia. This figure is certainly exaggerated. It is, however, interesting to note that the Polish prisoners, deported to Russia in 1939 and later, were told by the prison guards who were boasting of Russia's power and bigness: "Poland has scarcely 35 million inhabitants. In our country, we have that many prisoners alone!" [18]

These figures appear to be highly exaggerated. The exaggeration is in itself, however, indicative of the huge scope of forced labor in Russia and of the horror of the population in the face of this institution. The Soviet Government, by never mentioning forced labor or even giving a hint of its real proportions, is responsible for the frequent acceptance of estimates—inside Russia as well as abroad—which picture the Soviet Union in even gloomier colors than it actually deserves. The world is shocked by both the dimensions of slavery in a modern state and the utter silence maintained by its government on this subject.

There is another reason why guesses and estimates vary so greatly. Of the millions of deportees, one part are settlers, special migrants, and similar groups who enjoy a modicum of fictitious liberty; while the rest are inmates of labor camps. Therefore both kinds of estimates—the higher and the lower ones—may be accurate, depending on whether migrants and settlers are taken into consideration.

16. *Novoye russkoye slovo* (New York), August 1, 1946.
17. *New York Times*, March 23, 1946.
18. Mora and Zwierniak, *op. cit.*, pp. 126–127.

Finally, the rapid fluctuation in the slave population further contributes to the wide differences in estimates, which are therefore not necessarily contradictory. Within a year the population of the camps may increase or decrease by millions.

The mass of new prisoners from Poland, the Baltic States, and Bessarabia caught up by the forced labor network totaled over one million in 1940. In 1942 and 1943 heavy mortality and, to some extent, conscriptions into the Red Army considerably depleted the forced labor population. Then the influx of prisoners of war and the deportation of members of "disloyal nationalities" to new settlements suddenly began to boost the number. Finally, the repatriation of Soviet military and civilian personnel from abroad served to fill the gaps in the forced labor population.

A few years ago this writer estimated the forced labor class at from 7 to 12 million.[19] It appears that this figure was approximately correct.

German documents which fell into the hands of the Allies reveal with how great an interest the German Government observed and studied the Soviet system of forced labor. When the Soviet-German Pact of 1939 went into effect, a multitude of German economic and other commissions visited Moscow and traveled through Russia. On the basis of their reports, and probably also of those of the German Embassy in Moscow, it was estimated in Berlin that on the eve of the German attack on Russia forced labor in the Soviet Union embraced 9,600,-000 persons.[20]

Professor Sergei Prokopovich, a noted and cautious economist, has stated:

However much we may want to reduce the possible estimates (for purposes of comforting ourselves and in order to reduce the shameful blot on the new Russia), be it only five to seven million, one thing remains clear beyond any doubt: in the Union of Soviet

19. D. J. Dallin, *The Real Soviet Russia* (Yale University Press, 1944) p. 96.
20. These unpublished German estimates are valuable whereas the "reports" and "statistics" prefabricated in Joseph Goebbels' offices for publication were, of course, propaganda.

Socialist Republics we have a class of slaves of *many millions*, whose living and working conditions are infinitely worse than those of the American Negroes in the Southern states. It is horrible to realize that for them, the Russian slaves, the life of the American Negroes represents the ideal of well-being.[21]

Our generation is so accustomed to deal with huge figures—millions and billions—that we fail to realize immediately the full significance of seven, ten, or fifteen million human beings living in prison, exile, and penal servitude. Our feelings have been dulled and blunted. Would it help to remind ourselves that the biggest of the American states—New York—has an adult population of about eight millions; that, assuming the prison population of Russia to be ten to twelve millions, it is greater than the total adult population of Canada?

All sources agree that 85 to 90 per cent of the population of prisons and labor camps consists of males. In 1940 the adult population of males (over 18 years of age) in the Soviet Union, in its prewar borders, amounted to 47 million. War casualties have considerably decreased this figure. It has been officially stated that the war cost the Soviet Union seven million lives; the real number of dead is often estimated to be considerably higher. At any rate, the total adult male population today amounts to less than 40 million. The eight or ten or twelve millions of forced laborers (minus the women) represent at least 16 per cent of all adult Soviet males.

This is why forced labor must be considered one of the main classes in Soviet Russia's social structure—a class more numerous and economically no less important than that of free workers in industry.

21. S. Prokopovich, "*O samom glavnom,*" *Novoye russkoye slovo*, September 14, 1946.

In his *Soviet Politics at Home and Abroad* (New York, 1946), Professor Frederick L. Schuman tries to minimize the problem of forced labor in Russia, as well as the number of prisoners involved. According to him, "200,000 prisoners with long-term sentences would be proportionate to the situation in the U.S."; and he is willing to throw in "a comparable number of political prisoners in penal camps." These figures are without any foundation and entirely misleading.

V

The Essence of Forced Labor

Forced labor in Soviet Russia, like any kind of slave labor, is cheap, and therein lies its first and foremost virtue. Soviet authorities have never indicated precisely how great the cost differential is as between free and forced labor. It has been officially stated, however, that in 1932–33 "the cost of upkeep per prisoner was over 500 rubles a year." During the same period the average wage in the Soviet Union, according to official statistics, amounted to 1,496 rubles a year.[1] This differential, multiplied by the millions of prison workers and the years of work, is an important element of the government's industrialization fund. General workers' wages rose 174 per cent between 1926 and 1933 (due in part to the inflationary rise of prices); during the same period the cost of food per prisoner increased by only 90 per cent.[2] The quantity of available "consumer goods," and especially of clothing, housing, and food, was extremely small in the 'thirties and, of course, in the 'forties, too. The economies achieved as the result of use of forced labor enabled the government to increase the supply of these goods for the benefit of the other, especially the higher, strata of the population. This feature of forced labor in Russia is the source of huge profits realized by the NKVD in certain of its enterprises—profits never made in other fields of Soviet economy. It is for this reason that Soviet publications never present complete reports or statistical data concerning the profits of such industrial units. From the very

1. *Baltiisko–Belomorski Kanal*, p. 53, and *Sotsialisticheskoye stroitel'stvo* (1936), p. 512.
2. Andrei Vyshinski, ed., *Ot Tyurem k vospitatel'nym uchrezhdeniyam* (From Prisons to Educational Institutions), p. 437.

beginning of the labor camp system these profits have been its great advantage and one of the government's motives behind its expansion. The works erected by forced labor during the last 15 years cost a negligible sum compared with similar structures that might be built by free labor in Russia or abroad.

NO CAPITAL NEEDED

Just as important is the second virtue of forced labor—the possibility of employing prisoners almost entirely without investment of capital. Industrial equipment to a great extent had to be bought abroad at a time when export opportunities were limited by the small amount of *valuta* on hand. Forced labor was largely manual labor and did not require modern industrial equipment. This important feature of Soviet forced labor has remained unaltered to this day. Soviet reports sometimes contain eloquent stories about the manual laborers, reminiscent of those of the slave labor that erected the Egyptian pyramids. During the initial stage of the construction of a large canal, built by forced labor in 1931–33, a commission of Soviet engineers, themselves prisoners working under the GPU, were shocked by the fact that no machinery was supplied and that huge rocks had to be moved by hand. "If we could only have machinery!" the engineers dreamed aloud. One of them, Mogilko, said, "We have to cut down on the number of men. . . . Men are more precious than machines."

"Men are more precious than machines." Engineer Mogilko did not understand the intrinsic meaning of the forced labor system. He had in mind the Dnieprostroy, popularized and advertised throughout the world. To erect the Dnieper dams highly expensive equipment had to be imported from the United States. Mogilko was reprimanded by one of the chiefs of the GPU, who told him:

"This is no Dnieprostroy, which we were given a long time to complete and for which we were given foreign exchange. The White Sea–Baltic Sea Canal was assigned to the GPU, and the GPU was told: 'Not one kopek of foreign exchange.' " [3]

Hence, men had to be used instead of machines.

After the early period of the labor camps prison labor was also employed in the sea fisheries. The results, from a pecuniary viewpoint, were brilliant:

The invested capital was negligible, the cost of production unusually low, and the profits enormous. With a catch of 700 tons, and the purchase of a similar quantity from fishermen,—a total of 1400 tons—the *Ribprom* [State Fishing Agency employing prison labor] had earned in 1930 a net profit of one million roubles. Compare this with the record of the North State Fishing Trust [employing free labor] which in 1928, with a catch of 48,000 tons, earned a profit of less than one million roubles. [4]

Forced labor is therefore being used in those branches of Russian economy where simple manual labor, involving no expenditures for modern machinery, can be profitably employed, for example, in forestry, in canal and highway construction, in rudimentary building industries. In striking contrast with the almost mystical Soviet adoration of modern techniques and machines, the little publicized forced labor marks a return to those ancient times of Rome and Egypt when roads, aqueducts, and pyramids were erected by hand and when food was raised by thousands of slaves. Summarizing the experience of the first years of labor camps, the authorities issued the following instructions:

The following should be chosen as objects of mass labor best fitted for the realization of the purposes of corrective labor: large-scale industrial construction (factories, dams, dikes, blast-furnaces, railroads, etc.) . . . ; irrigation work; highway construction to make possible the motorization of the country. [5]

3. *Baltiisko–Belomorski Kanal*, pp. 112 ff.
4. V. Tchernavin, *I Speak for the Silent* (Ralph T. Hale & Co., 1935), p. 281.
5. *Sovetskaya yustitsiya* (1934), No. 15.

DISCIPLINE

The third useful feature of forced labor, as compared with free labor, is the strict discipline that can be imposed upon the personnel, both technical staff and workers.

Despite all the Soviet laws, regulation, and pressure, it has never been possible completely to overcome the difficulties with free workers in industry. Absenteeism has been consistently high; lateness is a constant source of trouble; at times the turnover among workers has deprived industries of stability and of any assurance of being able to accomplish planned tasks. It has been difficult to prevent women, burdened with household tasks in addition to their factory work, from leaving their jobs. It has been of no avail to punish workers by dismissing them, since the great demand for labor made it possible for every dismissed worker to find a better position. During the entire period of the Five-Year Plans, from 1928 to the present time, this has been one of the most important problems of Soviet economics. Neither the hundreds of decrees and instructions nor summary punishment has succeeded in entirely solving it.

Under the system of forced labor these problems do not exist. The maintenance of discipline within the prison is already taken care of. The director of a labor camp, who is simultaneously general manager of a great industrial enterprise, knows precisely the size of his labor force; and the system of a camp is in itself a guarantee that the inmates will show up for work. Working hours are no problem in a forced labor camp, nor is Sunday work, when necessary. Even an insufficient food supply does not prevent the prisoners from reporting for work and staying at it as long as ordered.

A component of this system of discipline, never even approximated in the rest of the Soviet economy, has been the ability to transfer thousands of workers, like armies, to remote areas in a short space of time. When they have completed the construction of a highway or a plant, the working prisoners

are immediately shipped to some other region of Russia to begin work on a new project. On arrival, the prisoners themselves construct barracks, barbed-wire fences, and watchtowers for the guards, while the bulk of the labor force
immediately attacks its major assignment. This mobility of the
labor force has been of great advantage, especially during the
war years. Many military projects were constructed by special detachments of prison laborers. Deadlines fixed by the
military command were always met.

Against these apparent economic advantages, the forced
labor system—essentially slave labor—has its ominous features which become obvious as the system attains importance
in the life and history of a great nation.

SLAVERY IN RUSSIA AND ABROAD

We are assisted in this classification of the Soviet forced labor system as a form of slavery by the scientists and jurists
of Soviet Russia herself. In a multitude of printed works they
have pointed to the slave character of prison work, directing
this criticism at the capitalist world. Labor in prisons, they
have repeatedly emphasized, is organized as slave labor. They
deny this only in regard to the Soviet network of prison labor,
but present no logical arguments to prove the distinction.

In every instance where slavery has existed as a widespread
economic system it has possessed certain distinguishing attributes. Slavery in ancient Greece differed from Roman slavery.
The system of slavery in the United States varied considerably from that of the ancient world. The enslavement of foreign laborers in Hitler's empire was again quite a distinct type.
And the slave system in the Soviet Union differs greatly from
its historical predecessors. But all these systems possess a common denominator, common features which make them species
of the same genus. Each marks a phase in the continuous historical development of slavery.

In one of his speeches Stalin gave his conception of the sequence of social orders in history—a conception which to a

certain degree he had taken over from his teachers. Slavery, he said, was the first phase of exploitation of the lower classes. Then "the revolution of slaves abolished the slave owners as well as the slave exploitation of the toilers." This phase was succeeded by another form of exploitation—serfdom—which, in turn, was abolished, and capitalism developed. Now, Stalin says, the Soviet state has succeeded in ending all forms of exploitation.[6] In this outline slavery appeared as a hoary relic of the past, long since done away with and today almost forgotten.

It sufficed for Stalin merely to utter these words, and immediately his pupils and followers lifted them to the level of indisputable historical law. This interpretation of slavery as a specific social order chronologically preceding serfdom and therefore belonging to times long past is utterly inadequate. Slavery has appeared at different junctures of history, at various stages of civilization, under the most diverse political and economic systems. It was a component of the highly civilized culture of the ancient world; it was an important factor in the history of the United States until after the middle of the nineteenth century; and was a part of a system which Marx himself and every one of his followers considered an example of capitalist social organization. Certain elements of slavery appeared in Russia in the advanced stages of serfdom. If twentieth-century Germany was capitalistic, and if Soviet Russia is socialistic, then slavery has made its reappearance during those phases of social development which, according to Stalin, are the most advanced.

THE ESSENCE OF SLAVE LABOR

The economic prerequisite of slavery is the ability of a man to produce more than the minimum he requires for living. At the dawn of history slavery did not exist; it was impossible: there would have been no sense in converting prisoners or fellow citizens into slaves as long as their labor merely sufficed to

6. Speech before kolkhoz peasants, February 19, 1933.

keep them alive. Defeated enemies were usually killed, not enslaved. Only in a societal development which was on a comparatively high level did a surplus beyond the minimum required for life become a normal economic phenomenon. So long as this surplus continues to exist and grow, the economic possibility of slavery is present; whether slavery actually develops as an important factor in society depends on political, cultural, and ideological conditions.

War served as the most important impetus to the institution of slave labor in the ancient world. Millions of prisoners were enslaved in Greece and Rome. The man hunt—not real war—was another source of slaves until recent times. A third and not unimportant source was ordinary fellow citizens—debtors, those who submitted to voluntary indenture, and those produced through traffic in members of one's own family.

In Greece slavery reached its peak in the fifth and fourth centuries B.C. It is estimated that out of a population of 3 million in Greece, 1 million were slaves.[7] The status of Greek slaves was comparatively good as contrasted with that of slaves of a later period. Many a Greek slave was active as banking agent, tutor, musician, factory worker, or artisan; their lot was fortunate compared with that of the slaves of lower strata who labored in field or workshop under severe restrictions. Thus the distinction between a slave intelligentsia and plain hard physical slave labor is not an innovation of the Soviet system.

Nor is it a new idea that slaves may be owned by the community. It is important to recall that not all slaves in Greece were private property. Publicly owned slaves were employed as city officials and county clerks. In ancient Athens, at one time, 1,200 policemen were slaves; in the Greek armies slaves served as workmen. The famous Laurion silver mines in Attica belonging to the Athenian state were operated with slave labor.

Slaves who are considered the property of the community

7. Julius Beloch, *Die Bevölkerung der Griechisch-Römischen Welt*, p. 506.

have always presented a special problem. The problem has great significance in connection with contemporary Russia, where no private slave ownership exists. Whenever men have been the property of a state or of a city, members of the free community were not always entitled to do with them as they pleased. Various agencies had specified rights as to giving orders and punishing slaves, and they were obliged to feed and to house them. A written or unwritten code of regulations concerning state-owned slaves must be obeyed.

It is no new phenomenon for the best minds of a nation to approve of slavery. Maxim Gorky, with his cohorts of minor writers, had a predecessor in Greece whose stature far exceeds his own. Aristotle considered slavery a useful institution even while insisting that no Greek citizen should be enslaved.

The most extensive development of slavery may be seen in the Roman Empire. In Italy during the first century B.C. there were 2 million slaves, as compared with a free population of 2.5 million. In addition, 400,000 slaves in Sicily worked beside 350,000 free Sicilians. Under Augustus the number of slaves rose to 3 million, i.e., more than half of Italy's population at that time.[8] The characteristic of slavery in ancient Italy was the widespread use of slave labor on private estates. In certain regions the entire agricultural economy was based on slavery; workers and employees were the property of absentee landlords who resided in the towns. Along with the millions of these hard-working slaves, however, an upper class of slaves developed in the cities, particularly in Rome. They were active as physicians, teachers, and philosophers. Many great actors, librarians, and artists were the private property of citizens of Rome. A paradox duplicated in Russia was the activity of slaves as prison wardens and prison guards.

Another group of slaves were the *servi publici*, some of whom occupied positions in magistratures while others worked as ordinary public laborers, building roads, repairing

8. These estimates are Beloch's. Most historians are doubtful whether the number of slaves in Rome can be established with any degree of certainty.

aqueducts, etc., all over Italy. One important use of slaves was as gladiators. Ten thousand gladiators took part in the games under Emperor Augustus, and an equal number in those under Trajan, which lasted for several months. There were both slaves and free men among these gladiators.

The status of a slave was almost always permanent. For a slave to gain his freedom, however, was not impossible, and at times he bought his liberation with his earnings. Former slaves constituted a class of some importance in Roman society in the first centuries of our era. It is worth emphasizing, however, that, contrary to Stalin's statement, slaves rarely succeeded in freeing themselves by means of concerted political action, uprisings, or direct fighting. The most significant attempt along these lines was the famous uprising under Spartacus, who was himself a gladiator slave. He managed to lead his slave troops for two years (73 to 71 B.C.) against the armies of Rome. In the end he was defeated and his army annihilated. Other slave attempts at revolt in the ancient or modern world have rarely been successful.[9] It is not to be expected that a "class movement" of forced laborers will ever be able to attain freedom through its own power. The slaves in the United States were freed in a civil war of free men against free men. The few revolts occurring in the labor camps of Russia were easily suppressed.

The liberation of slaves is brought about only in the course of a political struggle among elements of the free population.

THE UNITED STATES

The last country in which slavery attained any considerable proportions prior to the twentieth century was the United States. The American type of slave labor, in some respects similar to earlier models, had its own peculiar earmarks. The most important was the fact that the slaves belonged to a different race from that of their masters. Another distinguishing element was the mode of supply—the great slave

9. Haiti is one of the few cases where slaves succeeded in liberating themselves.

traffic that went on for over a century. The man hunt in Africa developed into an institution, and the shipment of slaves to the American colonies became an important and regular item of foreign trade. The incidence of disease and deaths among slaves in transit was high, but since the original purchase price was very low, it was not worth while to improve conditions aboard ship. The hunt for slaves in Africa was a small-scale war conducted without great risk by the slave hunters. The relationship between war and slavery was now reversed: whereas slavery had at first been a by-product of wars fought for other ends, now war was the by-product of a slave economy, conducted with the single purpose of securing the "goods."

How considerable was the role played by slave labor in the United States is evident from the fact that no less than 2,130,-000 slaves were imported in the course of one century (1680–1786). When slavery was finally abolished, the number of slaves emancipated totaled 3,950,000.

The abolition of slavery in the United States and the simultaneous abolition of serfdom in Russia marked the temporary end of slavery in the civilized world. It has remained a feature of backward societies, however, in the uncivilized parts of the world, and here progress was slow despite public opinion and the efforts of governments. One of the goals of the League of Nations was complete abolition of slavery, but it soon became clear how difficult it was to struggle from the outside against deeply rooted and time-honored customs and traditions.

There were at least 3 million slaves in the world outside Russia up to the second World War. Slave trading was being carried on in 19 political areas, such as Abyssinia, Algeria, China, Egypt, Eritrea, Sahara, Sudan and some other border regions of the world. Other practices constitute one form or another of involuntary servitude, such as peonage and compulsory, or indentured, labor in Malaya, South Africa, the Dutch East Indies, the Congo.[10]

10. Raymond L. Buell, *"Slavery and Forced Labor,"* in *The Nation*, December 24, 1930.

GERMANY AND SOVIET RUSSIA

A new upsurge of the slave system manifested itself in Europe in the 1930's, following protracted international and civil wars. This rebirth of slavery was not only materially correlated with the wars but also a psychological result of them.

A slave system on a large-scale was in existence in Hitler's Germany of the early 'forties. Not only did prisoners of war have to perform compulsory work, but millions of civilians were dragged forcibly from the west, south, and east and conscripted for forced labor. While the employment of war prisoners for labor was a temporary phenomenon that would have had to cease after the war, the use of civilians as slaves was undoubtedly the beginning of a new system which, had there been a German victory, would have attained huge proportions. The Nazi ideology—that state of mind which regarded other peoples as inferior and predestined to serve the chosen people; the lack of manpower for an expanding German industry after the war; the planned colonization of enormous areas—all laid the groundwork for an eventual enslavement of Slav nations by Germany. The beginnings of this German slave labor system did not develop further only because of Germany's defeat in the second World War.

Since the early 'thirties, slave labor has been spreading rapidly in the Soviet Union. The economic significance of the movement is precisely the same as that of all its historical predecessors. The peculiarity of the Soviet system of slave labor as compared with the Roman lies in the fact that it comprises only *servi publici*, and private ownership of slaves is not permitted any more than other manifestations of private economy. Another peculiarity of the Russian system is the theoretical possibility that members of the compulsory labor force might regain their freedom after the expiration of their sentences. In practice, of course, prison terms have often been prolonged; and liberation from labor camps has often meant settlement in exile. In many other respects, however, the Soviet system resembles its historical predecessors. In particular, the large-scale utilization of intellectuals on economic projects of the state is reminiscent of the slave administrators and slave scientists of ancient times.

NOTHING IS IMPOSSIBLE

History and economics have stressed two important negative aspects of slave labor, namely, the lack of interest of the working slave in his work and the waste of capital invested in the slave, that is, the rapid destruction and annihilation of great masses of men.

When Soviet authorities began building up the forced labor system they were fully aware of these problems, particularly of the first. Not only Adam Smith, the father of modern political economy, but Karl Marx and Friedrich Engels, whose works they studied in detail, were explicit regarding the shadowy aspects of slavery. "The experience of all ages and nations," wrote Adam Smith,

demonstrates that the work done by slaves, though it appears to cost only their maintenance, is in the end the dearest of any. A person who can acquire no property can have no other interest but to eat as much and to labor as little as possible. Whatever work he does beyond what is sufficient to purchase his own maintenance can be squeezed out of him by violence only, and not by any interest of his own.[11]

Karl Marx had the same view: "The lowest possible wage which the slave earns appears to be a constant, independent of his work." In contrast to the free worker, "the slave obtains the means necessary to his subsistence in natural form, which is fixed both in *kind* and in *quantity*," whereas the remuneration of a free worker "is *not* independent of his own work." [12]

This lack of interest in his labor on the part of the slave appeared to Marx the main cause of the fall of the Roman Empire, whose agriculture was based on slave labor. The abolition of slavery in the United States was similarly interpreted

11. *Wealth of Nations* (1937 ed., Random House [Modern Library]), p. 365.
12. Karl Marx's manuscripts, published in *Bolshevik* (1932), Nos. 5–6.

by him as being prompted by the needs of modern capitalism. Modern capitalism, he maintained, requires diligent attention and great effort on the part of a qualified worker, and the employment of slave labor in modern industry or agriculture is clearly unprofitable. Ancient slavery was the subject of studies of the Soviet State Academy for the History of Material Culture, which published a number of volumes in a comparatively short time. Most of the contributors, Soviet professors, accepted the theory that in ancient times slavery implied a certain degree of progress; that, however, a slave system becomes detrimental to the national economy once the latter attains a higher level of development, because "the slave has no interest in raising the productivity of labor." [13]

Was this theory correct? Was compulsory labor really impossible under modern economic conditions? Is it true that a slave has not and cannot have any material interest in the results of his labor?

With truly Bolshevik audacity and dynamism, and determined to smash all traditions, those in power approached the forced labor problem resolved to solve it: If capitalist society is incompatible with slavery, does this also hold true for the new and "higher type of society" created in the Soviet Union? Cannot Soviet society find methods by which slave labor can be put to use in the operation of the Socialist economy?

A way out of this apparent impasse was found. Marx had naïvely assumed that a slave must receive the subsistence minimum of rations below which neither life nor work is possible. Now it was found that a differential could be introduced in food rations in slave labor camps and that the smallest ration, i.e., that allotted to "slackers" and "shirkers" and in general to inefficient laborers, might well fall below the minimum required for subsistence. Moreover, this deliberate undernourishment would of itself compel all in the labor camps to do their utmost for the national economy. Differentials in

13. *Izvestia Gosudarstovennoi Akademii Istorii Material'noi Kul'tury,* LXVI (1933), 11.

wages had been introduced by the government in all fields of economy. A similar system, with appropriate modifications, must be introduced in the labor camps.

"He who does not toil does not eat." This inspiring maxim of the first years of Soviet rule, borrowed from the Gospel, was unexpectedly quoted to explain and justify the peculiar innovation, this Soviet modification of the age-old system of slave labor. The GPU as well as other commissariats ordered prisons and labor camps promptly to create differentials in food rations and other living conditions, according to the productivity of each laborer. This differentiation became universal throughout Russia; the most successful forced laborers were referred to as "shock troopers" and enjoyed considerable privileges.

"How much differentiation there exists in nutrition," one Soviet author reveals,

can be judged from the contents of Camp Order No. 9 of the Administration of Dmitrevski Camp, concerning the norms of bread rations for general issue and special purchase. A camp inmate fulfilling his production norms up to 79 per cent under the increased rations (for particularly hard work) is issued 600 grams [21 oz.] of bread daily; if he fulfills from 80 to 99 per cent, 700 grams daily; from 100 to 109 per cent, 800 grams [28 oz.]; and from 110 to 124 per cent, 800 grams plus the right of obtaining 200 grams from the stalls; [14] those producing 125 per cent and above are entitled to obtain 1,000 grams and 200 grams from the stalls.[15]

"In Karelia special kitchens are organized for the feeding of shock troops," another report reads:

In the Belogorsk house of detention a separate mess hall has been opened for shock troops. In four corrective labor institutions in the Northern region, shock troops are billeted in special dormitories, which are better equipped and provided with better cul-

14. Stalls selling food independently of the kitchen.
15. I. L. Averbakh, *Ot Prestupleniya k trudu* (From Crime to Labor) (Moscow, 1936), p. 158.

tural facilities. In the Urals—in the Chusovski, Berezovski, Sverd-lovsk, and Perm colonies—special stalls have been opened for shock troopers, and they are issued shock-troop ration cards.[16]

The lowest scale of food rations for prisoners is the minimum allotment to the least efficient workers—the "shirkers" and "slackers." It is intentionally set so low as to make subsistence impossible.[17] It usually amounts to about a pound of bread a day, with rare and small additions of other foods; sometimes it falls even below this norm. The intention is obviously to compel the "shirker" to revert to efficient work.[18] On the other hand, it also means a gradual weakening of the prisoner and eventual death.

This is a new and peculiar kind of "wage" for slave labor. Many further incentives were gradually introduced; they were usually taken over from the wage system of free workers, not without certain modifications in accordance with the requirements of prison work. For example, "work by collectives" was adopted—a system by which a certain assignment is given to a group of prisoners as a unit and the remuneration is payable in accordance with the achievements of the whole group. Each man is thus compelled to concern himself with the output of his co-prisoners, to fight the "lazy" and the "shirkers" and in various respects to assume the functions of

16. *Sovetskaya yustitsiya* (1933), No. 9.
17. Official regulations never admitted, of course, that a starvation diet was prescribed for nonworking prisoners. Instead of determining this minimum, however, the decrees only provided that "rations will be fixed by the OGPU."
18. The following table (from Mora and Zwierniak's *La Justice soviétique*, pp. 102–103), gives an idea of the food values for the various classes in the camps:

	Price of Food per day (in rubles)
Military guards (*Vokhra*) in the camps and firemen in command	3.56
Administrative-technical staff (ATP)	2.25
"Fourth ration" (those producing more than 100 per cent of the norm of output)	2.09
"Third ration" (those producing between 81 and 99 per cent of the norm)	1.57
"Second ration" (75 to 80 per cent)	1.38
"First ration" (up to 74 per cent)	1.19
Sentenced "shirkers" and prisoners under investigation for offenses committed in the labor camp	.71

administration. As another incentive, the possibility of advancement to the ranks of the prison police and administration is sometimes held out to outstanding workers.

These and a great many other innovations are intended to induce the prison laborer to work better and to overcome the traditional and well-known negative aspects of slave labor. It is explained that the degrading results of compulsory labor would not appear in the Soviet land since the new system of incentives, combined with the alleged "interest of the prisoner in his work," puts the system on a higher level than its antecedents.

In fact, however, it is the old slavery plus a new system of incentives, among which the strongest is the urge to stay alive.

THE WASTE OF HUMAN BEINGS

The other negative aspect of slave labor has been the tremendous waste of human material. No means has been found by Soviet authorities to reduce this natural consequence of a slave labor system. Moreover, it is likely that in no previous instance of the utilization of slave labor has the waste of men and manpower been as great as in the case of Soviet Russia.

A private slave owner who invested capital in his slaves was concerned about their well-being and existence just as he was concerned about his animals. In a state economy, which is not required to invest money in its labor force, this motive for providing minimum care for the slaves does not exist. Nor does a state need to supply its laborers with labor-saving equipment. The man who is no longer able to work efficiently becomes a burden.

In the history of American slavery, the slave driver was not identical with the slave owner. The slave trader had to go deep into Africa and sometimes to burn villages in order to take possession of his live merchandise. In the Soviet Union the MVD performs both functions. The villages and cities from which it takes its human material are within its realm and under its control. When manpower perishes, the slave-employing agency sustains no loss of investment.

In the first stages of the development of the forced labor system the labor camps were a consequence of certain political measures resorted to by the government, such as the collectivization of agriculture. Later on, cause and effect were intermingled. In the latter 'thirties, and particularly during the war, the NKVD took certain political measures because of its need for fresh human material. There was, for example, no political necessity for sending a million men and women from eastern Poland, the Baltic countries, and Bessarabia to prison camps in 1939–40, when these regions were annexed by the Soviet Union. There was no political sense in sending to labor camps many thousands of men and women from among the small national groups whose "autonomous regions" were liquidated during the war. There is not the least doubt that whenever an important measure of suppression is being discussed and prepared, the NKVD never forgets its great economic function—to fill the perpetual need for replacements for the dwindling population of the labor camps.

An unusual disproportion exists in Russia between the number of males and females. Even before the latest war there were about 8 million more women than men in Russia. The huge mortality among males during the war has made this disproportion an alarming problem. The number of boys and girls born is almost equal. The reason for the disproportion in peacetime is the great mortality among adult males; and the existence of forced labor is one of the most important causes of this unnaturally great mortality of men in Russia, since women constitute no more than 10 to 15 per cent of the population of the camps. This state of affairs is of course well known to the Soviet Government, but everything is covered up and explained away with the hard-ridden, trivial formula of the "inevitable sacrifices in the great struggle."

THE PRICE OF SLAVERY

In its economic results, the system of forced labor appears to have been efficient in Soviet Russia. In making a summary analysis of the war, Stalin stated—and the entire press immediately echoed—that it had been a great test of the new social and political system of Soviet Russia; that victory had demonstrated the soundness of the policy of farm collectivization and industrialization, as well as of Communist domestic policies. He avoided all mention of another important factor of the war economy—the forced labor system—which contributed a great deal to the wartime economy. If it were true that the final success justified and blessed the means, it would be equally true that it constituted historical approbation of slavery in a modern state.

Actually, the efficiency of forced labor, despite incentives and compulsion, was and is on an extremely low level. The *average* efficiency of a slave laborer has certainly been below 50 per cent of that of a free Russian worker, whose productivity in turn has never been high.

In a broadcast People's Commissar Krylenko complained that in the corrective labor colonies there prevails "a careless attitude toward public property, hitches and shortcomings of various kinds, raw materials and tools lie around uncared for and are improperly utilized, and we have snags instead of a capable organization of work." He also stated that the crops grown in corrective labor colonies were 40 per cent lower than the average for the Soviet Union.[19]

"Ugly wrecking activity took place in the Armavir CLC," a report to the Conference of CLC Agronomists stated, ". . . grain was squandered in the fall and in the spring no grain was found for sowing; in the horse stables pieces of glass were mixed in with the fodder; as a result about half the horses perished." In general, "in most corrective labor colonies the

19. Broadcast of May 24, 1934.

cultivation of the soil is unsatisfactory." "Escapes," the report continued, "are a direct consequence of the bad material and cultural conditions in which the prisoners live. . . . A serious defect in the CLC's work is the poor cultivation of the land, which is responsible for the extremely low harvest in our colonies. Year after year we invest great means in our agricultural colonies; however, the results thus far have been poor. . . . As a result of poor organization of work, incompetent supervision, drift of manpower, and the distribution of manpower, the weeding campaign was worse than the sowing in a number of colonies in the northern Caucasus, and the threshing—we are ashamed to say—took place only in January." [20]

Besides being unproductive and wasteful of human material, the forced labor system has become a great cause of moral and political degradation. Deceit, theft, corruption are the natural and inevitable results of the internal conditions prevailing in the camps, and no human being could survive there if he tried to go the straight and honest way all the time. The so-called "corrective" labor camps have necessarily become corruptive labor camps. There is no spot in the world where morals have sunk so low as in the institutions of modern slavery. The effects of this alarming degradation are felt far beyond the walls of the concentration camps.

From the political aspect, the labor camps have rapidly developed into breeding centers for violently antidemocratic sentiments. There are, of course, no real political debates going on inside the barbed-wire fences, and no reliable information concerning domestic and world events is available. Resolutions have sometimes been proposed and unanimously adopted, expressing the unqualified loyalty of the camp inmates to the Soviet cause. Their value, however, is nil. The men who have succeeded in escaping abroad from labor camps did not continue to preach loyalty to the Soviet Union. Some fugitives chose another road. One of them, for instance, Ivan Solonevich, a Russian athletics instructor, escaped abroad in

20. *Sovetskaya yustitsiya* (1934), No. 6.

1934. He first joined the political group of Paul Milyukov, the leader of liberal Russian émigrés, but soon discovered that Milyukov's opposition to the Soviet regime was not violent enough; he went to Sofia, founded a newspaper, *Russia's Voice*, and became the leader of a not unimportant group of Russian pro-Nazis who eventually assisted Germany in her war against Russia. Another case was that of Nikonov-Smorodin, a former provincial peasant leader who escaped after six years in prison and labor camps and found his way into a similar political group in Sofia.

Escapes abroad have, however, been extremely rare. While a few former prisoners have been able to cross the borders, many thousands of them live in Russia under assumed names, and still more thousands live under their own names after serving out their sentences. Their real attitude toward Soviet policy is hidden behind a cloak of reverence and solidarity. But what a flame of just and natural political hate burns under the mask of loyalty!

The real limits of slavery are set by political and moral rather than by purely economic standards. The struggle between humaneness and cruelty, between merciless compulsion and freedom of man, between coercion and individual rights, marks the ups and downs in the history of slavery. Wars, especially great wars, breed cruelty which continues for generations; the effects of such moral degeneration eventually disappear, but very slowly. The resurrection of slavery in the twentieth century has been possible only because of, and as the result of, international conflicts in which millions of men had to kill and maim in order to save their own lives; in which oceans of blood were shed; in which an individual man's life did not count. It was no accident that slavery developed in that country which, in addition to a world war, had felt the firebrand of the greatest civil war in history and in which a warlike tension has not abated for decades.

VI

The Land of White Death

THE FAR EAST

The Kolyma region is a desolate land at the very edge of the world, in the coldest wastes of the Arctic.[1] Its rivers are ice-bound eight to nine months a year, and the continuous polar night covers it for from six to ten weeks in the winter. When a blizzard sweeps over the land, usually lasting for several days, even the hardened inhabitants never go out without first tying themselves to their cabins with a rope. In the blinding gale they might never find their way back and lose their lives within a few steps of their homes. The temperature of the region sometimes drops to —92 or 93° F., so that mercury becomes as malleable as lead, and iron as brittle as glass. The soil of the region is a solid frozen mass; only a thin upper crust thaws out in the short summer. Underneath, reaching down for hundreds and thousands of feet is "geological ice" or permafrost (perennial frost). Scientists view the geological ice with the liveliest interest, regarding it as the guardian of many secrets of the long history of the earth, but to the local population, frozen in not only from above but also from below, it is a curse.

It is easy to understand why until recent times the Kolyma region was practically uninhabited. The census of 1926 showed a population density of 1 to 2 persons per 100 square miles. It is only in the past few years that the Soviet Government has been energetically colonizing the region. The area has been covered with a network of corrective labor camps, whose population must be constantly supplemented by hundreds of thousands of new slave colonists. The majority of

1. The sources of information for this chapter are listed in the last section of the book.

these never come back from this "land of white death." A few lucky ones succeed in returning to Russia, but these are bound to keep silent concerning their observations and experiences under threat of further severe punishment for "disclosing secrets of state."

The secret in this case is one of the most jealously guarded of the Soviet Government—the secret of Soviet gold. The American press has published occasional reports mentioning enormous stocks of gold accumulated in the cellars of the Kremlin treasury.[2] Where have they come from? It is definitely known that they were not there 15 or 20 years ago when the government was obliged to sell the treasures of Russian museums for what they would fetch in order to pay for the machinery it had purchased abroad. The gold has appeared only during the past 12 or 15 years, continuing to flow in even during the war years when the entire nation was straining every nerve to defeat the Germans. Stalin personally is reported to be in charge of this fund, as he also personally supervised the plans for building it up. On his initiative, too, well-organized prospecting for gold has been carried on for a number of years throughout the length and breadth of Russia. At several places the search has proved successful. But the richest find—so rich that it beggars description—was made in the Kolyma region.

GOLD IN THE TAIGA

In comparatively recent times—some 20 years ago—the Kolyma region was considered, as old Russian encyclopedias said, to be "poor in products of the mineral kingdom." It was known to have considerable deposits of mica; big sheets of it were bartered in the town of Sredne-Kolymsk by nomads of the region. The large deposits of iron were used by the local smiths for forging their simple knives and spears. But all this had small commercial value and aroused little interest. To be

2. For example, the *New York Times* (January 9, 1946) reported that the stocks of gold in the Kremlin amounted to something between 2 and 10 billion dollars.

sure, there were vague old tales of gold that was supposed to exist in far-away places. But such tales abounded in Siberia and every Siberian was certain that somewhere in the near-by taiga there was a rich lode, which was known either to his own or to his neighbor's grandfather, who unfortunately died before he could reveal the secret to others.

In 1910 for the first time the possibility of the presence of gold in the Kolyma region began to be seriously considered. That year a fugitive convict brought a small bag of gold out of the taiga on the upper reaches of the Kolyma and sold it to a trader. History has preserved only the first name of the convict, which in its diminutive form, "Boriska," afterward provided the appellation for the first gold field in the region—"Boriskin." News of Boriska's find spread throughout Siberia, but the places of his wanderings were so inaccessible and he himself was so uncommunicative and so jealous of his secret that people began to belittle the importance of his discovery. Actually Boriskin is one of the richest gold fields of the upper Kolyma. Then the first World War occurred, and following it the revolution, and the ex-convict died of starvation on one of his prospecting trips.

The history of Kolyma gold had its real beginning in 1925 when a "white" officer, Nikolayev, who had taken an active part in the military operations against the Bolsheviks in the Far East in 1920–22, decided to take advantage of the amnesty proclaimed by the Soviet Government to come out of the taiga where he had been hiding for more than three years. After assuming Soviet citizenship he proceeded to the branch of the State Bank at Yakutsk (the capital city of northeastern Siberia) and turned over to it a few ounces of platinum, with the explanation that he had panned it in the taiga between the Kolyma and the Indigirka. His story attracted attention. Only two years before, a very rich gold field had been discovered on the River Aldan, and Yakutsk was still in the grip of a "gold rush" fever. It is true that platinum does not arouse as much interest in Siberia as gold, for although higher in price it is found in much smaller deposits. But platinum is seldom encountered alone. Wherever platinum is found one may be almost certain of finding gold too. For this reason the Yakutsk authorities equipped a prospecting party and sent it that same year to the spots indicated by Nikolayev. The next year the Soviet Academy of Science followed suit by sending its own expedition into the region.

One of the unexpected discoveries, possible today perhaps only in northern Siberia, which was made by this expedition headed by a young geologist, Sergei Obruchov, was an unknown mountain range. It rose at some points to 10,000 feet and stretched in a belt from 200 to 250 miles wide for a distance of almost a thousand miles—from the upper Kolyma across the Indigirka valley to about half way down the River Yana. Other ridges, east and northeast of the Kolyma, were discovered by subsequent expeditions, with the result that our knowledge of the geological structure of the entire northeastern part of Siberia has in the past 20 years been completely revolutionized.

The range discovered by Obruchov has been named the Cherski Range, in honor of the self-taught geologist Cherski, who was a pioneer in geological studies of Siberia. An 18-year-old Polish student, Cherski was exiled to Siberia by the tsarist government for participating in the Polish insurrection of 1863. During his exile the young man became interested in the vast unknown continent that was Siberia and turned to its study with great enthusiasm. He undertook several journeys into little-known regions, and his studies, published both in Russia and in other countries, placed him in the front rank of scientific explorers of Siberia. In the famous *Geognosy of Asia* by Ritter, the volume on Siberia was written by Cherski.

Cherski did not break his ties with Siberia or abandon interest in it after his release from exile. He worked out a plan for a geological expedition to the Kolyma, obtained financial backing from the Russian Academy of Science, and in 1892 set out on his journey accompanied by his wife, his loyal companion in his previous travels. The hardships of the expedition broke him, and he died on June 26, 1892, in Sredne-Kolymsk, thwarted in his attempt to reach the mountains which now bear his name. Cherski was not the only one to come to Siberia, a foreigner and exile under escort of soldiers carrying bayonets, and to grow to be an ardent patriot of this "land of banishment" and devote a lifetime to its study. Other political exiles made very important contributions to the vast work of the study of Siberia. Giving one of the most northern mountain ranges in Siberia the name of Cherski was recognition also of the importance of the work done by other Polish exiles. By the bitter irony of fate, the very same mountainsides and defiles which today bear the name of a Polish patriot contain the graves of thousands of his compatriots who were sent there by the Stalin government. They committed no crimes against Russia nor even against the Stalin government. Their sole crime was their struggle against Hitler when he attacked Poland, and for this they were sent to the Cherski Range to mine gold. Stalin's Siberia received the new exiles with far greater cruelty than was meted out to their compatriots who 80 years earlier had risen up in arms against Tsar Alexander II.

With the new knowledge of the geological structure of the Kolyma region came a change in the conceptions of its wealth in minerals. Nobody today will call this region poor. To be sure, for some 15 years now no reports on its exploration have appeared even in the technical journals on geography and geology, for all such materials are regarded as state secrets. But sufficient fragmentary data have somehow found their way into the press to lead us to the conclusion that this land is one of the richest in the world in mineral resources. These include oil, coal, graphite, mica, phosphorites, marble, iron, copper, zinc, tin, lead, wolfram, molybdenum, silver, platinum, several varieties of precious stones, and many other minerals; but most important of all—great quantities of gold.

It appears that blizzards, bitter frost, and the heavy blanket of geological ice which weighs down the soil have been acting since time immemorial as incorruptible guards defending these treasures against that dangerous and rapacious animal, man. Only in our own days has he at last succeeded in penetrating the secret of the existence of this treasure. Since the first expedition under Obruchov not a year passes without several expeditions ranging over the region. Hundreds of young and enterprising geologists are conducting a methodical search of the vast country, reaching into the most inaccessible parts where man has never before ventured, exploring every gorge, every river bank, the tiniest hollows of every stream. Everywhere they measure, register, map; and so inexhaustibly rich is the land that not one of these exploring parties, it is reported, has returned from its wanderings during the brief polar summer without some interesting discoveries.

SOVIET ARGONAUTS

Commercial mining of Kolyma gold began in 1927. At first it was taken up by "free gold-seekers" who worked alone and ventured at their own risk into the gold-bearing upper reaches of the Kolyma River. In 1929, according to official Soviet statements, gold was being panned in three fields, including Boriskin. There were altogether 65 prospectors working in the three fields, and a total of 108 men living in the adjoining settlements.

The Soviet law prescribed delivery to the government trust, Soyuz-Zoloto (Union Gold), of all gold mined. But the nearest branch of the trust, opened in the autumn of 1928, was in the city of Okhotsk, which is more than a thousand miles away from the gold fields. Under the circumstances the trust, hard as it tried to keep its prices for gold on a level with the rising prices of commodities, was unable to maintain the monopoly of gold purchasing which it legally enjoyed. It was outbidden by private traders who managed to maintain a kind of semilegal existence despite the severe government measures enacted to suppress them, and who showed great resourcefulness and initiative. They were the first to cut a direct winter road through the taiga from the mouth of the Ola on the Sea of Okhotsk to the gold fields, and thus bring up mining supplies and foodstuffs. Naturally they sold everything at very high prices. But they were also ready to pay high prices for gold, paying no attention whatever to the fixed government prices. The "black market" dominated the gold fields and absorbed a large part of the gold mined. According to Soviet officials, this privately bought gold actually went to the Japanese, whose fishing boats at that time had free run of the Sea of Okhotsk and were able, in the absence of Russian control, to enter many harbors of this wild and uninhabited coast. It is very probable that there is much truth in all this, for goods sold at the gold fields frequently bore Japanese labels.

Various privileges promised prospectors for loyalty to the trust, as well as the granting to the trust of concessionary rights over a huge territory containing rich deposits of gold (in 1930 this territory covered 6,200 square miles between the rivers Kolyma, Bokhanga, and Buyunduy) failed to improve the situation. Attempts to organize mining under the administration of the trust proved equally unsuccessful. There was increasing and incontrovertible evidence that the Kolyma deposits of gold exceeded the most sanguine expectations. But to obtain it was a difficult matter.

There were two possible solutions. One was to allow unrestricted initiative to pioneer prospectors, who would have obtained the gold in the same way as prospectors in California and Alaska had done before them. The other was to invest a large amount of capital, which was needed not so much to organize the mining itself as to build roads and other means of communication in the region. The policy of the Soviet Government ruled out the first method, since those were the years when private trading and manufacturing of any kind were being relentlessly suppressed throughout the country. As for investing capital, there was none to invest, for the government was passing through a period of acute financial crisis, when it lacked cash to pay for the huge orders of foreign-built machinery under the construction program of the first Five-Year Plan. Credits were not obtainable, and for discounting its short-term bills abroad the Soviet Government was obliged to pay usurer's interest, as much as 36 to 42 per cent or more.

The solution was found in an entirely different direction. While the Soviet Government had no free capital in the old "bourgeois" meaning of the term, it had a plentiful supply of a different kind of capital—human lives.

It was just at that time that Stalin was carrying out "complete collectivization" of farms and banishing to Siberia and other northern districts the peasants who refused to join. These numbered millions, almost all of them good workers, strong and hardy and accustomed to the heavy labor of peasant life. Exiled with them were also hundreds of scientists and engineers who only a short time before had held responsible posts but for one reason or another had come under suspicion of having a critical attitude toward the government. Here, therefore, was a mass of people able to supply both manpower and expert leadership for large projects. Strictly speaking, in the eyes of the government they were all condemned to slow death as "socially hostile elements" who would never reconcile themselves to the Soviet system. The only question was how, by what means, the government could squeeze out of them the remainder of their working power, and how this remainder could best be utilized for the purposes of the government.

Initial experiments in this direction had already been made: large numbers of such "socially hostile elements" had been used in the building of the Baltic–White Sea Canal. Now it was decided to apply the same method in other parts of the country, including the Far East. Operations of this kind were naturally placed in the hands of the GPU, within which, in the winter of 1931–32, a special administrative organ was set up under the name of Dalstroy, which was charged with responsibility for a vast program of work in developing the extreme northeast of Siberia. The central task of Dalstroy was to organize intensive mining of gold in the Kolyma region. The job was regarded as one of the most important in the government program and, accordingly, the government, represented by the GPU, undertook to supply Dalstroy with vast resources of manpower in the form of forced labor. This was the fixed capital with which the Soviet Argonauts of our time set out on the search for the Kolyma Golden Fleece.

To head Dalstroy the GPU appointed one Eduard Berzin, a Latvian Communist who as a boy had been a herdsman in his native village. He took part, at the age of 17, in the uprisings of 1905, was later associated with "the forest brothers," the Latvian Partisans of the time, but was not particularly active and escaped punishment under the repressive measures of the tsarist government. Drafted during World War I, he graduated from a military school and, having been made an officer, joined the newly formed Latvian Rifle Division. This occurred on the eve of the Revolution, and soon after Berzin rose to be Bolshevik leader of the division. Among other things he headed the first armed forces sent to suppress the rebellion on the Don, later fought the Czechs in the Urals, and was made Inspector of the Latvian Red Army in the short-lived Latvian Soviet Republic. He did not reveal any great military talent, and his outstanding achievement, underscored in his service record, was, according to the *Soviet Military Encyclopedia*, his "heroic" fight against the "basmatches," the anti-Bolshevik partisans of the Turkestan region. For these services he received several medals and gold arms.

In 1925–26 he became involved, in some slight way, in the oppositionist flurry that was agitating the Communist party, and, obliged to leave the army, was given an important post in the work of economic reconstruction. When the time came to find an administrative head for Dalstroy, he was selected as a man who combined experience in the military Cheka with work in the economic field, and who as an oppositionist needed to redeem his past faults by an intensified effort in a hard new job. Experience had shown that such Communists were particularly ruthless.

Around Berzin there was assembled a staff of experienced GPU men and "tested" experts: engineers, geologists, construction men. From the outset the project was conducted on

a large and generous scale. The GPU gave Dalstroy priority
rights in picking specialists from among the prisoners, and in
addition a campaign was started to enroll volunteers, who
were offered the inducement of good terms. A Dalstroy advertisement, published mainly in the provincial press, offered
jobs to specialists in 57 lines, from "mining specialists in all
sections" to truck drivers, from soil experts to managers of
provision bases. It goes without saying that the GPU was
also to supply fairly large numbers of its special troops, together with an adequate number of specially trained dogs, the
inseparable companions of all guard troops in the USSR.

In the Far East the campaign was opened in the summer of
1932. After a preliminary survey it was decided to start the
advance on the Kolyma gold from the shore of the Sea of
Okhotsk, in the main following the route cut through by private traders from the estuary of the River Ola. The harbor of
Nagayev, which is situated near that estuary and about 300
miles northeast of the city of Okhotsk, was chosen as the principal base of operations. This harbor is a large one (approximately ten miles long and three wide), deep, and almost completely protected from wind. On the other hand, it had long
been known for one singular feature—the complete absence
of human habitation on its shores. The official *Sailing Directions of the RSFSR*, published in 1923, says: "In Nagayev
Harbor itself there are neither houses nor villages nor native
tents." This fact, of course, can be explained. The shores of
the Sea of Okhotsk have an established reputation for being
extremely inhospitable. But even on these shores Nagayev
Harbor stands out for its dismal harshness. It is excellent as a
ship anchorage but not as a place for human beings. It is surrounded by ridges of rock which overhang the water. The
rocks, sometimes rising a thousand feet or more, protect the
harbor, but on their open sides the winds blow unchecked.
Down below, where the steep cliffs meet the water, there is
no land for human shelter. Up above, one is blown off one's
feet by the force of a wind that is cold, damp, penetrating, and
unequaled in ferocity anywhere in the world.

The stone ridge that hedges in the harbor on its north side is sparsely covered with larch, a feeble tree which barely manages to keep its hold in the stone, and provides neither cover nor protection from the wind. Immediately behind the ridge, overlaying the perennial ice, stretches a swamp of the type familiar in this northeastern region. Beyond begins the withered polar taiga, interspersed with clumps of deadwood, the usual taiga of the areas where trees must keep their roots near the surface to avoid being caught and frozen in "geological ice."

It would have been difficult to find a place less suitable for human beings. But the GPU pioneers were not thinking of human beings. Uppermost in their minds was the fact that Nagayev Harbor could easily accommodate several big ships and—this was the main consideration—that, as the crow flies, it was the harbor nearest to the Kolyma gold fields. The same considerations led to the decision to choose this spot as the future capital of the entire northeast of Siberia, and to build it regardless of the cost that nature might exact. The new capital, even before it was born, was given the name of Magadan.

In the summer of 1932, for the first time in the history of Nagayev Harbor, the steam whistles of ships began to disturb the tranquil air. The ships, which came from Vladivostok, were crammed with Dalstroy cargo: machines, equipment, foodstuffs, and "manpower."

The latter was by far the largest item. The holds of the steamers, which were gifts of the government to Dalstroy, had been made over for permanent service in carrying a live cargo. They contained built-in plank beds mounted one above the other in three or four tiers. These were always so packed with prisoners that walking or even sitting was impossible; one had to lie on the plank bed hardly able to turn over without disturbing a neighbor. Walks on deck were of course out of the question; nobody was allowed to leave the hold during the entire passage and even bucket stools were not always taken out.

Such a tightly packed steamer could carry from 8,000 to 12,000 prisoner passengers. It sailed past Japan with holds covered by tarpaulin, with not a soul on its decks, dark except for signal lights, like the grim ghost ships of the old legends.

Special measures were taken to suppress disobedience or mutiny. Strong iron grilles cut the hold into several completely isolated sections. Armed GPU guards walked constantly along the narrow passages between the grilles. At carefully selected spots there were nests of machine guns which could cover every corner of the hold. In addition there were fire pumps, so arranged that at a moment's notice a powerful jet of cold ocean water could be turned on insubordinate prisoners. Past experience in transport of prisoners was scientifically sifted. These liners of Dalstroy, whose stacks were painted with a bright blue band around them—the color of hope, for it spoke of the great hopes which the Soviet Union pinned on this grand project—were more carefully prepared to meet all unpleasant emergencies than were the ships, a century back, which carried cargoes of black slaves from the Ivory Coast to the American ports of Charleston and New Orleans.

In these crammed and stuffy holds prisoners spent eight or nine days, depending on the roughness of the sea. (And the Sea of Okhotsk is noted for its storms and fierce winds.) Arriving at Nagayev Harbor, haggard and exhausted, they were cast ashore onto a bare land under the open sky. The officials and guards brought tents which were set up on the best sites, those that were comparatively dry and protected as much as possible from the wind. The prisoners were given "freedom" to do the best they could for themselves within the areas of special camps whose only signs of hospitality were the thick rows of barbed wire which fenced them in. The official program was summed up: "Dwellings will be built later. Hardships must be borne for the present. Our first task is to build the port and the town."

The prisoners bore the hardships and built. With bare hands they constructed piers for ocean steamers, setting up caissons weighing many tons under the steep cliffs where the sea was 12 to 15 feet deep at the water's edge. They cut broad roads through the stone, leading down to the piers. They built, in order of importance, several plants: a sawmill, a brickyard, a fish-salting factory, ship repair yards, a power station. They began draining the swamp and clearing the parts of the taiga adjacent to the spot selected for the future town, felling and rooting up trees, pulling up moss by hand, and harrowing the soil over and over to create a semblance of cultivable top soil as a measure of defense against the encroaching geological ice. They built houses for the administrative staff, which included private houses for the officials and their hired servants; for the GPU troops they built "cold-resistant barracks" with double walls filled in with sawdust; they built a special small house for the police dogs which were later to play such an important role in the Kolyma penal camps. There was time and labor for everything except for building barracks for the enslaved workers themselves.

All through the summer and late into the autumn the workers lived in huts made of branches which they put together in their spare time. They gathered the branches in the taiga, brought them to the camp, spread them on the swampy ground for flooring, and set them up on the sides and overhead for walls and ceilings. The branches nearly always were larch, which is practically the only tree that grows in the taiga of the coastal region. It makes valuable tough timber which successfully withstands the damp climate; houses made of larch last for generations. But the branches of this coniferous tree, with their small and widely spaced clumps of soft needles, are poorly suited for protection against inclement weather. The needles quickly fall off, leaving bare, gnarled branches which let through wind and water. On the shore of Nagayev Harbor, it should be noted, there is no land without subsoil water and in the summer no day when it does not rain.

The work on the project itself was hard and strenuous, all the more exhausting for being done under the ever-present threat of punishment. It must be admitted that the methods employed for extracting the maximum effort were not, at that early stage, as "scientifically" developed as they later became. But at that they had enough force behind them. The cause of the worst suffering was the damp. Work had to be carried on regardless of rain. In the swamp men stood in water up to their knees. Those engaged in building the port fared even worse— they were drenched by the spray of the surf and not infrequently forced to wade in icy water. There was no place where one could dry oneself.

In the beginning there were no fixed working hours and prisoners were compelled to work as long as they could stand on their feet; they were required to show "enthusiasm." The food was meager—bread, dried fish, sometimes hot soup, and twice a day a mug of hot water.

The men returned to their camp tired, hungry, and, worst of all, wet through and chilled to the marrow. Campfires, which they had to make themselves, were the only means of drying out and getting warm. At first the fires were kept burning all through the night, but these were given up one by one. Returning exhausted by the day's work, the men in their wet clothes dropped to the sparsely covered ground. It is no wonder that neither clothes nor men could stand it for long. The clothes grew moldy on the men's bodies, and the men fell sick. Epidemics broke out, and mortality rose at a catastrophic rate. The high mortality probably would not in itself have disturbed the authorities. But the epidemics spread to the GPU troops and the hired technical personnel, and this caused great alarm. The defects in the organization of the gold-mining project were revealed—there were far too few doctors and an almost complete lack of necessary medicaments. Prisoners as human beings were still left out of consideration.

Not until late autumn, after a great many lives had been lost, were orders given to build barracks for the workers. These were not like the cold-resistant barracks of the guards. Their walls were of single boards, they had no floors, the plank beds rose one over the other in three tiers, and for heating there were only iron stoves. The prisoners were told that these barracks were only temporary. But they were as tightly packed with men ten years later, and in all likelihood still are today.

INTO THE VALLEY OF DEATH

Every week steamers continued to unload thousands of new prisoners in Nagayev Harbor. These were all long-term exiles picked for their fitness for manual labor, mostly from among Siberian farmers, Don and Kuban Cossacks, and Ukrainian and White Russian peasants. It would have been a waste of money to bring in anybody less capable physically. When the labor needs of the rising city of Magadan were filled, the new arrivals were sent into the taiga to build the long motor highway to the Kolyma gold fields. Compared with the fate of the latter, the life of those who remained at Magadan was a gift from heaven.

The highway was to extend from Magadan to Srednikan, the center of gold mining on the upper Kolyma, and thence to Seimchan, a small settlement on the river below which the stream became navigable. The distance by air from one end of the highway to the other was about 200 miles, and the Moscow authors of the Dalstroy program planned to open the road for motor traffic as early as 1934, provided the necessary manpower was available. But the miles to the Kolyma were not of the usual kind. They led through the taiga, impassable swamps, and wild mountains—an unexplored and untrodden route. The winter road laid out by private gold traders was of little help to the builders of the permanent highway. That road, like all winter roads in Siberia, went over frozen rivers and streams which in summer only presented additional obstacles to the builders. The preliminary survey conducted first by Soyuz-Zoloto, then by Dalstroy, was altogether perfunctory. Problems were solved mainly by means of improvizations contrived during the course of the construction work. It was the prisoners employed on the road who had to pay for all this.

As early as the autumn of 1932 Magadan began, as soon as the swamps and the innumerable taiga streams froze over, to send large parties of workers farther and farther inland, to selected points along the route of the proposed highway. The men were to spend the winter in the taiga and carry out preliminary work for the construction project of the following summer, such as felling trees, stocking beams for laying pathways across the marshy land and building barracks.

Everybody, the authorities as well as the prisoners, feared the coming winter—the first in an unknown and wild region. No clothes were issued to the prisoners by the government, so that they went out in the same clothes, now old and ragged, in which they had been arrested and which were in no way suited for winter, and especially for the Kolyma winter. A winter in the taiga with no better protection than such clothes meant certain death.

Thus was laid the basis for a despair from which all kinds of unrest could appear. The prisoners, in connection with their work, had to be provided with hatchets—in their hands a potentially dangerous weapon. To forestall trouble the authorities took steps to explain to the men how senseless and hopeless it would be to attempt escape or mutiny. And indeed such attempts had no chance of success. No fugitive could run far enough before being caught in the grip of the taiga and suffering death from cold, hunger, or wild beasts. The alternative to this fate was to return and confess guilt. But ruthless punishment awaited those who returned. According to rule, anybody attempting escape was subject to the death penalty. The rule applied not only to the fugitive himself but also to those who knew of his plan and failed to report it. Even harsher was the treatment meted out in cases of mutiny. If a group in any party of prisoners attempted insubordination, especially an armed mutiny, the entire party without exception was subject to "liquidation."

Putting fear into the souls of prisoners was developed into a system. The function of the GPU dogs, which were extensively used, became clearly revealed. Each convoying unit that went into the taiga was invariably accompanied by a number of wolfhounds. The dogs were trained not to attack men in uniform, particularly the GPU guards. They learned and remembered well that it was from these men they received their daily ration, which included a pound of raw meat, milk, and other food—products which the guards themselves, not to mention the prisoners, saw only on rare occasions. The dogs were also taught to show good manners toward civilians wearing good clothes. But the sight of prisoners was enough to make them go utterly mad. For them, anybody wearing ragged clothes was a prisoner, though later, when Dalstroy began to give prisoners clothes of a special cut, they were trained to recognize people so dressed. It was impossible for a fugitive to get away from the dogs in the taiga. Once put on a trail, the dog followed until it caught up with the quarry, no matter where he might hide. With a leap it knocked the man down and tore at him until called off by its GPU master. Sometimes the dog was allowed to kill its man. On other occasions he was saved only to be delivered up to receive the appropriate punishment. The lacerated dead body of a fugitive was, in accordance with the rules, exhibited in the camp from which he had tried to escape. If for some reason the captured fugitive was allowed to live, he was taken, bleeding from his wounds, on a round of the camps so that everyone would know what was in store for them if they followed his example. One of the prisoners composed a harrowing song, which began:

> We fled,
> We were caught
> By the big gray dogs.

It went on to relate how impossible it was for a prisoner to get away or save himself from these dogs. The authorities adopted the song as their own and made the captured fugitives sing it on their exhibition rounds of the camps.

Under these conditions single attempts at escape or mass attempts at mutiny amounted to a special form of suicide.

Everybody was aware of this, and yet there were always attempts at escape. They were particularly numerous that terrible first winter. Mass outbursts of protest occurred and were cruelly suppressed. Nothing could stop the prisoners, since being forced to live in the taiga was a form of murder stretched out over a few weeks or months.

To some extent this was due to the unpreparedness of the administration itself—its ignorance of the conditions under which the prisoners would have to work. But at the bottom of it there lay something else—the deep-rooted contempt for the lives of men who were in any case condemned to destruction.

That first winter of Dalstroy set in exceptionally early and was unusually severe. Blinding snowstorms raged for weeks on end. At times, even in Magadan, walking from one house to another was almost impossible. On several occasions communication with the taiga was completely cut off, and no food could be sent to the inland camps. Since the supplies the prisoners could take with them on leaving Magadan were extremely small, famine would set in in the taiga camps. In addition, in the absence of barracks men had to live in tents or, more often, in brushwood huts, with the temperature at—60°. In spite of the insufferable cold, the prisoners went on with their work. Even under normal taiga conditions prisoners died by the hundreds and thousands, and nearly everybody had frostbitten hands and feet. What went on in some of the winter camps during the weeks of blizzard must have remained a mystery to the authorities, since in some no living beings were left—neither prisoners nor guards, nor even dogs. One of the valleys of the region, the Shaivinski, has since been named "the Valley of Death." It was the place where, says local legend, a party of prisoners numbering several thousand, together with the entire convoy of guards, lost their way in the blizzard and died to a man. It used later to be said in Magadan that of all those who were "thrown" into the taiga in that first "heroic" year of Dalstroy, only one out of 50 to 100 came back.

The preparatory work for the summer building campaign broke down almost completely. The heads of Dalstroy, however, went on with their plans as if nothing had happened. The first steamers from Vladivostok usually reach Magadan at the end of April, while the taiga rivers often remain icebound till late May or the beginning of June. In 1933, as soon as navigation was opened, new parties of prisoners began to be unloaded in Magadan and were sent immediately over the winter route to the taiga to proceed with the building of the highway. Desperate efforts were made to speed up the construction, which was paid for in equally desperate currency— human lives.

From the technical point of view the construction of the highway unquestionably presented exceptional difficulties. There was more involved than the felling and uprooting of trees, construction of numerous large and small bridges, building of dams along the rivers and streams, dynamiting of miles of mountains and boring tunnels, difficult as all this was. The main obstacle was the frost, which during the thaw undermined and "swallowed up" what seemed to be the firmest of construction. It is said that a certain section of the highway, barely a mile long, swallowed up over 80,000 beams— roughly, from 10 to 20 beams for each foot of the road. Even so, this section is far from being firmly set and requires repairs every year.

In this northeastern part of Siberia, summer is no less treacherous than winter. The weather in the summer time is simultaneously sweltering hot and icy cold. For almost 24 hours a day the sun hangs over the horizon casting its slanting rays upon the earth. Under the sun, particularly on the southern slopes of the mountains, the ground becomes heated to almost tropical temperature. But in the swamps between the hillocks the water is freezing cold: the hotter the sun the more stubborn the resistance of the geological ice below, whose upper layer, in that region, frequently comes to within a foot or two of the surface. A man working in such a swamp is mercilessly baked from above and frozen from below. Compelled to work under such conditions for long stretches of time, particularly if not provided with special boots, even the sturdiest man would soon break down. But the Soviet prisoners had to work under such conditions for whole days without a break and, of course, in their usual bast shoes or torn boots, with bad and insufficient food, unable even to dry their clothes. To see that they did not falter in their work there were guards always at their backs speeding up the "tempo" with rifle butts.

Worse than the rifle butts were the insects—scourge of the Siberian taiga, where gnats, midges, and gadflies of various sizes hover in immense swarms, especially over swamps. The taiga of the coastal region of the Sea of Okhotsk, as was noted by the old travelers, is infested with these vicious insects. Among them is a type of large gadfly whose sting can pierce tough deer hide. The pain it causes drives a horse into a frenzy. Native Siberians, who are more or less accustomed to these insects, never go into the taiga unless they are heavily dressed, wear mittens, and have a special netting over their heads. The Dalstroy prisoners, of course, had no protective clothing of any kind, and for them this work was excruciating torture.

The result of all this was that the Dalstroy operations of the summer of 1933 cost more human lives than did the preceding winter. During the subsequent years these human "production costs" grew higher and higher, due, of course, to the parallel growth of the "fixed capital" of slave labor which Dalstroy was investing. Not content with the supply of prisoners flowing to Magadan, Dalstroy organized shipments of labor to the estuary of the Kolyma in the Arctic Ocean, whence the men were sent up the river to build the highway from Seimchan southward, or to mine gold. The shipments to the Kolyma estuary were made either from Vladivostok or from Archangel. The Great North Sea Route, the navigation of which had for three centuries been the dream of explorers and seamen, and the accomplishment of which involved great sacrifices and countless lives, was used "commercially" for the first time by Dalstroy—for shipping slave labor. Slave labor was the cargo of the steamer *Rabochi* (the Worker) which was the first to sail from Archangel to Ambarchik, the new pier at the Kolyma estuary, constructed for its own use by Dalstroy.

One of the early—and the most tragic—of the sailings to the Kolyma estuary was that of the steamer *Dzhurma*. The *Dzhurma*, a large ocean liner especially equipped for shipment of Dalstroy prisoners, sailed from Vladivostok in the summer of 1933 on its maiden voyage to Ambarchik (a distance of over 4,000 miles) carrying a capacity cargo of about 12,000 prisoners. The time of sailing was not carefully calculated, the ship reached the Arctic Ocean too late in the season, and was caught in pack ice in the western part of the Sea of Chukotsk, near Wrangel Island. We are not likely ever to learn what went on in the ship during that terrible Arctic winter, how the doomed prisoners in its holds struggled for life, and how they died. The fully authenticated fact is that the *Dzhurma*, when it finally arrived at Ambarchik, in the summer of 1934, did not land a single prisoner. It is also further reported that on their return to Vladivostok nearly half the crew of the *Dzhurma* had to be treated for mental disorders. However, what mattered for the government was not the loss of prisoners and the sufferings of the crew but the fact that the valuable ship was saved.

In the same winter of 1933–34 and in the eastern part of the same sea, another ship became locked in the ice. That was the famous *Chelyuskin* which had been sent from Leningrad to Vladivostok to prove that the Great Northern Sea route could be navigated without "wintering" in the ocean. Crushed by the ice, the *Chelyuskin* sank on February 13, 1934, but the members of the expedition, numbering 104 persons, set up a camp on the ice. The entire world became concerned for their safety. There was only one way to rescue them—by air—and many persons in the United States were anxious to undertake the task. All such offers of help were declined by the Soviet Union, whose representatives declared that it was a matter of national honor for Russia to organize for the "saving of her sons." She accepted only technical aid, and only Soviet fliers made trips to the Sea of Chukotsk, in spite of the fact that this meant great delay in the salvaging operations. The evidence that has since come through suggests that national honor was merely a screen to hide quite different motives of the Soviet Government. The place where the 104 members of the *Chelyuskin* party were waiting for deliverance was not far (no more than 200 miles) from the wintering place of the *Dzhurma* and its 12,000 prisoners doomed to death from cold and starvation. Moscow feared that in the course of saving the heroes of the *Chelyuskin* American fliers might by accident uncover the terrible secret of the *Dzhurma* martyrs.

REWARD À LA STALIN

The highway from Magadan to Seimchan proved to be much longer and the work of constructing it much slower than was originally anticipated. Instead of 200 miles, the distance by air, it stretched out along the ground for over 400 miles. Planned for completion in 1934, it was not yet finished in the spring of 1937, although by that time the main part of the construction work was done and the road was actually opened to traffic. It was expected that work would be concluded by the autumn of 1937, and preparations were being made for the official celebration of the opening of the highway. Reports from Moscow told of the satisfaction of the government with the work of Dalstroy, despite the delays in the past, and indicated generous awards to the Dalstroy administration on the opening of the highway, similar to those granted earlier to the heads of construction projects such as the Baltic–White Sea Canal, the Moscow–Volga Canal, and others.

Awards were actually made, although not of the kind expected by the administration. Eduard Berzin, the creator and first head of Dalstroy, and his closest associates were arrested, declared to be "foreign spies," and shot.

The event amounted to a revolution in the distant Kolyma region, where the head of Dalstroy was a potentate with unlimited powers over the life and death of those under his rule, that is, the entire population of the region. Apparently Moscow had taken a serious view of the possibility of resistance to the arrest and of other undesirable repercussions in this connection. For this reason exceptional precautions were taken. First a dispatch came to Magadan over direct wire from Moscow which stated that the Presidium of the Central Executive Committee had decided, in connection with the fifth anniversary of the first Dalstroy landing at Nagayev Harbor, to award Berzin the Order of Lenin, the highest honor existing in the USSR at the time, and that he was therefore being invited to come to Moscow to receive the award in person. The airplane that was sent to bring him over also brought an issue of the Moscow *Izvestia* containing the text of the Presidium's decree. Berzin, naturally, did not conceal the glad news of the award from his close associates. There was a farewell party, attended by the highest officials of Dalstroy, and much liquor was consumed. After that, Berzin, accompanied by his closest friends, proceeded to the airfield. There the picture underwent a transformation worthy of a Hollywood thriller.

The plane had brought not only the false issue of *Izvestia* but also a group of NKVD men who had been empowered to assume complete authority in Magadan. While one of the emissaries, the official delegate of the Presidium of the Soviets, was handing Berzin official documents and joining the latter's friends at the party celebrating the occasion, the rest of the NKVD men seized the airfield, preventing everyone working there from revealing the fact to anybody outside, and made preparations to receive Berzin. When the latter and his friends arrived they were met by pointed revolvers and informed that they were all under arrest. The head of the NKVD in Magadan was included among them. All the arrested men were made to sign official orders confirming the transfer of authority to the newly arrived emissaries; then they were sent to Moscow. A general purge began in Magadan which was later extended to the whole Kolyma region.

The charges brought against Berzin were numerous. He was accused of having ties with "capitalist" governments, of selling gold to foreign countries, of surrounding himself with confessed and secret "Trotskyites" as well as other oppositionists, and of planning a coup d'état in the region and seizing all power so that he could secede from the USSR and join the United States or perhaps Japan. As in all the purge trials of 1936–38, the grain of truth in these charges was lost in a mass of falsehood. It is perfectly true that Berzin sold gold to other countries, but he did so with the knowledge of the government and on its authority, in order to obtain *valuta* necessary for paying for Dalstroy's purchases in foreign markets (the machinery for its plants and especially for its gold fields could be bought only in America). Similarly with the knowledge and actual encouragement of the government Dalstroy enrolled in its service a number of persons who had been involved in the activities of various opposition groups inside the Communist party. There were few volunteers ready to go to this dismal land; on the other hand, repentant oppositionists were in many cases openly advised to redeem their transgressions against the party and the Soviet Government by unselfish and trying work in the Kolyma region. Now, however, all this was represented as an attempt at a conspiracy to bring about a secession of the region from the USSR.

Berzin and his closest associates were shot in Moscow. The purge in the Kolyma region, which went on for more than a year, affected not only the hired personnel of Dalstroy and agents of NKVD in the lower and middle grades; the entire population of the camps, especially those being punished for crimes of a political nature, were subjected to thorough investigation. The most ruthless treatment was meted out to persons who had been connected with various groups of the Communist opposition. These were wiped out to a man.

The celebrations which were to accompany the opening of

the Kolyma highway, planned for 1937, never took place. Those were the days of the most feverish purge, and in Magadan they had things other than celebrations to think of. Besides, there was nobody entitled to awards since none of the Dalstroy pioneers was left alive, neither of those who had laid beams over the taiga swamps and who were torn to death by the dogs, nor of those who set the dogs upon them. All of these found their graves in the taiga. Much later, however—in 1940 and 1941—awards and high honors poured from Moscow on the administrative agents of Dalstroy. But it was a new generation that received them—that of the fosterlings of Beria, the new chief of NKVD.

MAGADAN, CAPITAL OF THE SLAVE EMPIRE

In the meanwhile, the capital of the region, Magadan, has become a large and well-ordered city, with a population of about 70,000, made up of MVD officials and hired specialists who volunteered for service under the Dalstroy. There are about 50,000 such specialists throughout the region, of whom about half are settled with their families in Magadan. Another section of the city's population, numbering a few thousands, is represented by exiles, mostly highly qualified experts, whose work in the Dalstroy has earned them the special privilege of living in private houses, though they continue to be under the supervision of the MVD. Outside the city limits there are several big camps for prisoners with a fluctuating population—they are the principal base of manpower reserves for the Dalstroy.

Here and there in Magadan one still comes across taiga stumps. But the central streets are lined with two- and three-story houses. The city gets its lighting from its own power station which also supplies current to the taiga, the lines running from one steel mast to another over the surrounding mountain ridges. There are several plants, a number of technical colleges (mining, fishing industry, and others), a fine "House of Culture" with a theater and movie house connected with it, and an interesting museum of regional scientific exploration, whose holiday visitors number up to 300 a day. The House of Culture, a very handsome building both outside and inside (it was constructed from the plans of a prominent architect exiled to this region), has two companies of good actors who give regular performances in Magadan and also tour the inland centers. The square in front of the House of Culture was until recent times planted with barley and oats, not from any desire for commercial exploitation of every possible bit of land, but simply because these plants are best adapted to the local climate. However, Dalstroy's plant experts have developed some hardy varieties of southern flowers which since 1943–44 have decorated the square, attracting the admiration of visitors.

Problems connected with acclimatization of flowers and useful plants are given much attention in the region. Magadan has a large experimental farm equipped with hothouses. The latter already grow "Kolyma" apples, pears, peaches, and even oranges, not to mention a variety of berries, while all kinds of vegetables are developed in the hotbeds, including cucumber, cabbage, eggplant, muskmelon, and watermelon. The principal enemy of agriculture in this region being the geological ice, the basic problem is to force the upper level of this ice as far down as possible. Repeated deep ploughing of the soil, use of manure in great quantities and similar measures have been used in scientific experiments and have achieved interesting results. Thus, in some places where the ice formerly came up to within a foot and a half or two feet of the surface it has been forced back down to six or eight feet, which has made possible cultivation of cereals.

Magadan has several science institutes, geological, paleontological, gold mining, and others, which have well-equipped laboratories and special museums. Some of them publish their proceedings, but these never reach the outside world and are difficult to obtain even in Moscow.

The large Dalstroy printing press publishes several newspapers, a literary magazine, a magazine of regional studies, and a multitude of books (over 500 titles appeared up to 1944, though they were almost entirely reprints of Moscow editions). All the indigenous literature remains completely unknown outside the region and even the official *Knizhnaya letopis* (Book Index), which is obliged by law to register all publications issued in the territory of the USSR, never so much as mentions the Magadan publications.

While all the scientific and cultural institutions are centered in Magadan, a large number of industrial enterprises have been set up throughout the region in the centers of population that have sprung up in the course of Dalstroy's operations. Among these are the electro-engineering plant in the town of Atka, which manufactures its own electric motors labeled "made in the Kolyma"; a member of fish processing and canning factories scattered over the region, including one as far north as the estuary of the Kolyma River, almost on the 70th parallel; a metallurgical plant at Orotukan, the site of rich deposits of iron, which operates the first open-hearth furnace in the region; and others. The largest number of industrial enterprises is naturally connected with the exploitation of mineral resources discovered at various places. According to *Izvestia*, the total number of new names marked on the map of the region during the Dalstroy era exceeds 10,000 and includes all kinds of mining centers, gold fields, fishing villages, government farms, and so forth.

The sweeping range of Dalstroy's activities has inevitably resulted in a very complex and unusual organization, combining the direction of the economic life of the region with legislative, judicial, administrative, and police functions. In the general structure of governmental authority in the USSR Dalstroy occupies a unique place. It is an organ of the People's Ministry of Internal Affairs, constituting a department of the ministry and subordinate to it; its official name is "Dalstroy MVD." In the organization of MVD Dalstroy comes under the authority of one of the Deputy Ministers; early in 1946 this post was held by Avraami Pavlovich Zavenyagin. But MVD appoints only the head of Dalstroy, leaving to him, under a grant of wide powers, the selection of assistants. During recent years (apparently since 1938) Dalstroy has been headed by Ivan Fyodorovich Nikishov, who has the rank of lieutenant general and has recently been elected to the Soviet of Nationalities (which under the Soviet constitution acts as the Upper Chamber) as a representative of the Autonomous Jewish Republic of Biro-Bidjan. Between Berzin and Nikishov, Dalstroy was headed by one Pavlov, who kept the post for only a short time. A plenipotentiary delegate of the totalitarian state, the head of Dalstroy exercises unlimited power over the entire territory placed under his control. This territory has been rapidly expanding. In the beginning it comprised only the districts of the gold fields on the upper Kolyma and the region traversed by the highway which was being built to connect the gold fields with the coast. Gradually adjacent districts were added, and at present the authority of Dalstroy extends not only over the entire Kolyma region and the part of the Sea of Okhotsk littoral served by the Kolyma highway but also over the regions of the rivers Yana and Indigirka at one end and the whole of the Chukotsk region and Kamchatka at the other. In other words, the jurisdiction of Dalstroy at the present time extends over all northeast Siberia, taking in land east of the river Lena and north of the river Aldan (its exact boundaries have not been made public). This area is approximately six times as large as the territory of metropolitan France.

The constitution of the USSR is not even formally operative in this vast area. The usual authority of regional Soviet agencies does not apply here. There are no local Soviets in the territory. No elections take place there, with the exception of those for the Supreme Soviet. Authority is held and exercised solely by Dalstroy, and everybody representing this authority is appointed by the head of Dalstroy or his assistants acting as his agents. Every inhabited place has a "commandant" who has authority over the territory under his control. Under the Dalstroy rules, such a commandant has the right of inflicting death penalties on all prisoners. A somewhat different status is accorded the small remnants of native tribes, the Chukchas, the Yukagirs, the Evenks, and a few others, which form the so-called "national districts." They enjoy various privileges and are given help by the Soviet Government. But these tribes number only a few thousand and even in their national districts they exercise no real authority.

The population of the region is not accurately known. Before the discovery of gold and the creation of Dalstroy it was extremely small and could hardly have exceeded 25,000 to 30,000. (According to the census of 1926–27, the population of the Kolyma region was 7,580.) It is unlikely that the number of the aborigines has materially increased under the rule of Dalstroy, in spite of the protective policy of the government. During the first period of the Revolution the native population of the region showed a marked tendency to decrease. If, in spite of this, the total population of the Kolyma region during the administration of Dalstroy has risen enormously, the only explanation is the fact of the importation of masses of slave colonists. Their exact number is unknown, since no official data on this subject nor, for that matter, on the population of the region, are ever published. One must turn to other sources for a basis on which to form a reliable judgment on this question.

A first-hand story about Dalstroy has recently appeared in *The Socialist Courier*,[3] a Russian Journal at present published in New York. It was written from the report of a young Soviet seaman until recently a member of the Communist Youth League, who for several years sailed in one of the Dalstroy ships between Vladivostok and Magadan and who is well informed on the situation in those parts. According to his statement, the entire region has been transformed into

a single concentration camp. Into it have been thrown huge masses of the "repressed." How many of them, he cannot say exactly . . . In his opinion it may be calculated with consider-

3. *Sotsialisticheski vestnik,* December 10, 1945.

able accuracy that during the years 1937 to 1940 not less than a
million and a half persons were brought on steamers from Vladivostok to Magadan: during each navigation season from April
to November four Dalstroy steamers (*Felix Dzerzhinski, Dalstroy, Sovlatvia,* and *Dzhurma*) were in operation, each making
from 12 to 15 voyages in the course of the summer and bringing
from 6,000 to 9,000 persons on each voyage.

According to other sources, the number of ships in the
Dalstroy service is higher; and it is positively stated that in
1940–41 five more steamers (*Minsk, Kiev, Igarka, Komsomol,* and *Uritski*) and the icebreaker *Sakhalin* were in operation there, with an aggregate shipping capacity of 35,000
passengers. The steamers carried, of course, in addition to
prisoners, cargo which poured into Magadan and other
Dalstroy ports in enormous quantities. Nevertheless, even
disregarding other shipments over the Arctic Sea route, which
were relatively small, the importation of from 400,000 to
500,000 slave colonists each year appears credible. At any
rate, the total number of prisoners brought into the Kolyma
region during the first ten years of Dalstroy's existence (i.e.,
1932 through 1941) is in the millions.

During the first years of the second World War the importation of prisoners fell off, and certain groups (of nonpolitical prisoners exiled for short terms—from three to five
years) were actually shipped back to be mobilized for service
at the front. But beginning with 1944, as German-occupied
territories were gradually liberated, the shipment of prisoners
to the Kolyma region was resumed with renewed impetus.
Of all these millions of prisoners, however, great numbers
perished. Apart from the convicts, hundreds of thousands of
exiles and forced laborers of various other descriptions have
had to settle in the Dalstroy territory; likewise prisoners must
often stay on in the Far East after serving their sentences. The
total number of all categories of forced labor living in the region at present hardly exceeds one and a half to two million
persons.

THE PRICE OF HUMAN LIFE

Dalstroy's extensive and many-sided economic activities are coördinated in a system of administrative organizations each of which deals with a specific section of the region's economy. The centers of these organizations are in Magadan. The following are known to exist at present: administrations of supplies, fish industry, coal, wood manufacturing industry, road building, agriculture, motor transport, and a few others. Each administration is provided with all the manpower it needs, but is required to carry out its assigned tasks without fail.

Essentially they are given the same single task—they must insure uninterrupted operation of the basic industry of the region—gold mining—and to this end must supply all the necessary materials and products. The ideal pursued by Dalstroy is to buy nothing outside, to be completely self-sufficient, and turn over to the state, as the net profit on its operations, the gold and other valuable metals it obtains. So far, of course, it has not succeeded in carrying out this program, either with regard to machinery, which must still be imported from abroad, or to food supplies. Nevertheless a great deal has been accomplished in this direction. For example, the fishing industry has developed to the point where it is fully able to meet the regional demand for fish and still have a surplus for shipment to Vladivostok. The laboratories of the fishing industry, working on the problem that was specially set for them, have found means of manufacturing margarine out of the fat of sea animals. It is now stated that in the near future the region will be able to fill all its needs for edible oil from its own resources. On the other hand, during the war years the administration of motor transport was able to convert nearly half of Dalstroy's automobiles to the use of methyl gas, thus greatly cutting down the necessary import of gasoline. It may be noted in passing that attempts to extract oil locally have so far been unsuccessful, although the presence of oil deposits in the region has been definitely established. Much has been done in agriculture, as has been previously noted.

Road building made a fresh spurt before the war. In 1939 the administration of road building was split up into two independent organizations, one for the south, the other for the north. By that time the trunk highway from Magadan to Seimchan was being extended in the direction of the new gold fields on the upper Indigirka, and a number of side roads were also constructed to connect the main gold fields on the upper Kolyma with the highway. Altogether there were 901 kilometers (about 600 miles) of paved roads in actual use. But for a region that was developing as rapidly as this one the existing mileage was clearly inadequate. Accordingly a new plan of extensive road building was drawn up in 1939–40 covering new roads in the extreme north, at the Kolyma estuary, and in the south, on the upper Kolyma, in the so-called "old" gold-mining districts. In addition to new tributary roads, work was started in 1939 on the construction of a second motor highway from the Dresva Bay on the Sea of Okhotsk to the gold-mining territory on the upper Kolyma.

Even more far reaching were the plans for road building east of the Kolyma estuary, in the tundra (mossy and marshy plains) of the Arctic coastal region, down to the Bering Strait, where, a short time before, geological exploration had discovered gold fields of exceptional richness, perhaps exceeding those of the upper Kolyma. There have been no exact data concerning these plans. The information coming from the deep interior of the Kolyma region is generally far more meager than that from Magadan. However, at the outset of the war with Germany, all these big plans for road building in the region had to be curtailed. Construction of the Dresva Bay road was stopped in the early stages. In connection with the building of this road, it should be mentioned, the history of the Nagayev Harbor development during the "heroic" winter of 1932–33 was faithfully repeated. The road building around the Kolyma estuary, too, was drastically cut down, if not completely stopped. The cause of this stoppage was the

great falling off in the numbers of prisoners imported during
the early period of the war. In 1939–40 Moscow expected to
have the same unlimited resources of slave labor as in the early
'thirties. The only difference would be that instead of drawing this manpower from Russian, Ukrainian, and other villages it would come mainly from the newly annexed eastern
provinces of Poland, and from the Baltic States, then in the
process of "liquidation." Hitler's attack on Russia eliminated
this possibility and inevitably there was a falling off in the importation of slave labor to the Kolyma region, which affected
primarily the great development projects not directly related
to gold mining. All available forces were concentrated on the
latter.

Gold-mining operations are entirely in the hands of a special gold-mining trust within the Dalstroy organization. In
1939–40 the trust was made up of 7 administrative agencies,
each in charge of its own territory. These were: the Southern
Mining Administration, which exercised authority over 16
gold fields, including the principal old gold fields of Srednikan, Boriskin, and others; the Northern (12 gold fields); the
Western (12); the Southwestern (8); the Northwestern (6);
the Chai-Urinsk (8); and the Tenkino-Detrinsk (4). Altogether these 7 agencies controlled and directed the work of
66 gold fields, some of which spread over such large areas that
they properly should be called groups of adjacent gold fields.
Not included in the above list are the gold fields east of the
Kolyma estuary, which at that time were only beginning to
be worked. We are still ignorant of their administrative organization, but it is known that during the war years their
operations were greatly expanded. The total number of prisoners employed directly in gold mining apparently suffered
no decrease, or at most a very minor one. During those war
years the whole process of gold mining underwent a thorough
mechanization.

The total number of workers engaged in gold mining is
unknown. The fields vary in size, but, according to available

information, there are no small ones among them. Apparently the normal number of workers at each field fluctuates between 5,000 and 10,000. The figure reaches its maximum in May to June of each year: the panning season begins in June, at which time new parties of prisoners just brought to Magadan from Vladivostok arrive at the fields. As the work continues, the mortality among the prisoners grows higher and higher, and by the end of the season great numbers of the workers are dead. This has been confirmed by reports of Polish prisoners who worked in the Kolyma region and who were released. They also speak of conditions in another camp of Dalstroy—that on the Chukotsk Peninsula. Parties of prisoners numbering several thousand were completely wiped out. Such was the fate, according to these witnesses, of a party of 3,000 Poles, consisting largely of army men, who arrived at the lead mines on the Chukotsk Peninsula in August of 1940. In addition to the usual causes of mortality there was a special one in this case—lead poisoning due to the complete absence (at least in 1940–41) of safety measures against it in the Chukotsk lead mines. When the decree releasing Polish prisoners came no action had to be taken because none of the prisoners was alive.

The basic cause of the extraordinarily high death rate is the extreme intensity of work coupled with inadequate food. The working day, which before the war was set at 10 hours, was raised during the war to 12, with no holidays allowed. In the summer time work is done in two shifts in order to utilize every hour of the brief panning season, which lasts a hundred days (from the beginning of June to the middle of September) in the upper Kolyma, and a little more than 70 days (from the end of June to the beginning of September) in the lower reaches of the river. But the official working day is a fiction. What actually happens is that each worker is given a definite "task," and failure to fulfill it means either loss of a part of his meager ration of food or proscription against leaving the place of work. Since work is carried on by groups of workers ("brigades") who are held collectively responsible for each other, each worker is under the constant observation of his comrades. Nevertheless, it frequently happens that at the end of the working day the workers have not completed their task. In such cases the entire brigade stays on for the second shift and on the following day carries on without a rest period, thus remaining on the job for 36 consecutive hours. Those who are punished for failing to make their quota are incarcerated in the special cells which exist in every camp, which are so constructed that they are actually torture chambers.

A highly restrained yet striking description of life in the lower Kolyma gold fields has been given by one of the Polish exiles who was released from there in the summer of 1941. We quote this description in full: [4]

The camp was situated at a distance of a few miles from the working place. The prisoners slept in wooden barracks which were covered with rags; the chinks in the plank walls were filled with moss collected after working hours. The prisoners' garb served both as clothing and blanket. The prisoners were not permitted to sleep fully dressed; they could keep on nothing but underwear. This regulation had to be observed also when they went out of the barracks in the night—it was intended to prevent them from escaping, since some of them were ready to embark upon the desperate attempt. It was depressing to see people with their toes amputated as a result of frostbite go to bed. Others had lost their fingers or had cheeks and noses blackened for the same reason. These were people who had spent one or more winters in the camp. The majority of them had "gone beyond the hill," i.e., toward their grave.

Reveille took place at 4 A.M. At 5, after a breakfast consisting of gruel and bread, the prisoners left for work. The bread ration was 1,000 grams [35 oz.] for the 1st category, 800 grams [28 oz.] for the 2d, 600 grams [21 oz.] for the 3d, and 300 grams [10.5 oz.] was the punitive ration. Before leaving the camp the foreman read in a loud voice the orders for the day, warnings against various offenses during work, and the list of sentences imposed for attempted escape and the theft of gold. All the sentences were identical. Then the brigade was marched off in a file of five and waded

4. Mora and Zwierniak, *La Justice soviétique*, pp. 328–330.

across the river which flowed the whole length of the camp. In the summer, at this early morning hour, mosquitoes were the chief plague. The *nakomarnik*, a black netting covering the face, provided little relief from them.

The brigades waded across all the rivers and brooks on their way. Theoretically, from the moment work started there was to be no interruption. At noon the prisoners received a meal prepared at the working place and consisting only of gruel and peas. There were no fats, meat, or sugar. During the meal the brigades took turns working. Now and then a supervisor, in a moment of good humor, would order a short interruption for smoking. The cigarettes were the strangest possible: rolled in newspaper which each prisoner obtained by his own devices, they contained anything but real or even home-grown tobacco. The latter fetched a very high price: a small package sold for 30 to 100 rubles, and even at this price was very hard to obtain.

A main source of annoyance was the incessant control during work; another was the presence of the shock worker brigades composed chiefly of common criminals. These unfortunates were profoundly discouraged, but for a handful of tobacco were willing to double their effort. In this respect they set an example for us, though even they were not always able to fulfill the norm of output. A brigade which had not fulfilled the norm had to work throughout the night and then continue the following day, without rest or food, so as to deliver the required amount of gold. Prisoners who did not reach the prescribed norm were put, right after work, into a punitive cell. Before entering it, the prisoner had to take off all his clothes except his underwear. He had to spend the night in a wooden barrack, with rain, snow, or frost penetrating through the cracks in the walls. I personally was able to take it because I had wrapped a towel around my chest, underneath my shirt, with which I covered myself and a companion. Toward morning we would hear cries emanating from the cell: "Open the door, chief, I am dying." After emerging the prisoner had to resume his habitual place and work the whole day, along with the others.

Nothing was easier than to get into the punitive cell because of the *zachistka*, i.e., the clearing up of the soil after a gold-bearing stratum had been exploited. This work consisted of sweeping a strip of land of 36 square meters [387 sq. ft.] and brushing it with small brushes so that no traces of gold could be found after jigging. It often happened that the specific rock with tiny grains of gold was deeply embedded in the earth and had to be dug out and carried on wheel-barrows to a designated place. In other instances there were holes filled with water and gravel. After many cubic meters of sewage had been excavated from the hole, examination would still reveal the presence of gold: the soil had not been properly dealt with, and the prisoner usually landed in the dungeon.

From this experience I have learned, at my own expense, that the high price of gold is quite "justified." I began to loathe the confounded metal, and do not wish ever to see again the least particle of it.

The punishment was not always the same. One of my fellow workers, Untenberg, a German from the Volga district, who had not fulfilled his norm of output, was ordered by the guard to undress and to stay naked without budging. The night was clear, . . . and swarms of mosquitoes covered his body. In the morning he was all swollen, he screamed from pain and rolled on the ground despite the order not to move.

The chief of the camp was a man named Kakolin. He must have been a brute judging by the beastly look in his oblique eyes. He was said to be a Tartar. He never spoke, and I wondered whether he possessed a human voice.

THE BALANCE SHEET

We now come to the final question: What are the results of this use of veritable galley-slave labor at the Kolyma? What material benefits have accrued to the Soviet state by this sacrifice of countless human lives?

At the outset we can dismiss all the auxiliary industries of the Kolyma project, which obviously, from the standpoint of state interest, are of no importance whatever. They belong in the same category as the peaches and oranges grown in Magadan, i.e., they are mere evidence of extravagant waste. An American multimillionaire who conceived the crazy idea of growing peaches on the banks of the Yukon in Alaska could certainly bring it to fruition. It would only be a question of the amount of money he was prepared to spend. The Soviet multimillionaires, too, squander huge quantities—but of human lives, not dollars. Even such achievements as the acclimatization of oats and cabbage, interesting as they are from a scientific point of view, bespeak the same callous waste. They have been bought at the cost of the lives of the brilliant men who made them possible—men such as N. I. Vavilov, a scientist known the world over, and member of the Soviet Academy of Science, whose ideas on the mutation of plants failed to agree with the official Soviet interpretation of dialectic materialism, and who died in exile in Magadan from the effects of vicious climate.

The only thing that could justify, even in the eyes of the Soviet Government, the entire experiment in the Kolyma region is *gold*. No official figures on the amount of gold mined on the Kolyma have ever been published. The Soviet Government has gone even further—since the Kolyma slave labor began to play a major role in filling the Soviet treasury, the government has stopped publication of all data bearing on the output of its gold-mining industry. The fact that gold is mined in the Kolyma region is never as much as hinted at in the Soviet literature of the past 10 or 12 years. All mention of it is carefully avoided even when for publicity purposes fairly detailed information is published on the progress of construction projects in the region. The only fairly exact data on this subject come from private sources, mainly from the reports of the Soviet scientists who have cut their ties at home to take refuge in foreign countries. According to these sources, the production of gold in the Kolyma region during the second half of the 'thirties reached about 11 million ounces per year and has since been constantly growing. The war did not check this growth despite the temporary falling off in the number of workers employed. The output was kept at a high level as a result of increasing mechanization of gold mining, for which great quantities of specialized equipment of the latest design were imported from the United States. The latest information gives strong reason to believe that in the postwar period, with the number of forced laborers restored to its prewar level, the production of gold has risen to the record figure of 16 to 18 million ounces per annum.

To grasp the full significance of these figures it may be recalled that on the eve of the opening of the Kolyma gold mines the total annual Soviet output of gold, according to the data for 1929–30 in the *Great Soviet Encyclopedia*, did not exceed 100 metric tons (i.e., 3.6 million oz.), while the total output of the rest of the world on the eve of the second World War, according to the *Encyclopaedia Britannica*, amounted to only 32.6 million ounces. In other words, the Kolyma gold mines have multiplied the Soviet output four to six times,[5] while they have lifted the Soviet share of the total world output to nearly 50 per cent as against 12 to 14 per cent before the opening of the mines.

The figures explain the enormous stocks of Soviet gold reported in the American press. The cost of this gold has been very high. On the basis of the figures given above it appears that every metric ton of Kolyma gold cost the lives of 700 to 1,000 human beings. One human life for every kilogram of gold—such is the price on the slave market of Magadan!

In a speech delivered at the dawn of the Bolshevik Revolution Lenin proudly described the kind of use gold would be put to after the final victory of Communism. "When we achieve victory on a world scale," he said, "we will use gold, I believe, to build public toilets in the streets of the largest cities of the world." The victory of Soviet dictatorship "on a world scale" is still far off. But according to Stalin, Russia has already established Socialism, with the gradual transition to Communism as her next goal—yet gold plays a role different from that predicted by Lenin. The utopian Communists of the early years of the Revolution dreamed of the time when man would cease being the slave of gold and become its master. The "realist" Communists of our days are filling the swamps of the taiga with human bones in order to get as much of this very gold as they can lay their hands on. Much has changed since those early days of the Revolution. Much water has flowed under the bridges. Alas, not only water.

5. Production of gold in other Soviet regions has risen very little, and lately, there is reason to believe, has even been falling off.

PART II

THE ORIGIN AND GROWTH OF FORCED LABOR IN RUSSIA

VII

The First Decade

It was a magnificent experiment, one of the greatest in human history: to abolish not only prisons but crime itself; and to achieve this at a single stroke, in a political upheaval. For generations to come this experiment will be the subject of careful study and analysis. It deserves far greater attention than it has heretofore been accorded.

Lenin prophesied in 1917: "The basic cause of social excess is the exploitation of the masses. The removal of this cause will lead to the withering away of excesses. Simultaneously with their disappearance, the state will die." To abolish crime it is both necessary and sufficient to abolish capitalism, he argued. As soon as the capitalist economy is destroyed, delinquency will begin to diminish and will eventually disappear. A harmonious society is ignorant of crime. In such a society prisons will be done away with or transformed into schools and museums; and the machinery of coercion, which is of the essence of a state, will become superfluous. The state will wither away.

Every crime is a manifestation of antisocial behavior—such was Lenin's conviction. "Crime is a form of social excess." Weakness of social devotion or lack of social conscience lies at the base of crime. And this lack of individual identification with society is rooted in the antagonisms of modern capitalism. The source of crime is to be found in poverty, hunger, voluntary idleness of the rich, and involuntary idleness of the poor; moral degradation is the result of social disharmony.

Lenin was not the originator of this theory. He had inherited it from Marx, and Marx in turn had absorbed it from the currents of nineteenth-century liberalism. The idea that man was simply the product of his environment had been gaining ground steadily since the French Revolution; the great task was to reform not individuals but the environment —society itself. To Marx such a reform of society meant primarily an upheaval in economic relations. Lenin not only adopted this theory but, as he did in other fields, simplified it to the utmost, in order to make it the keystone of a popular movement. The abolition of capitalism was to Lenin and his followers sufficient in itself for the abolition of crime, while all other social factors—the political system of a nation, for example—were disregarded.

Could not the newly created omnipotent state, with its own policy of enforcement, become a new source of criminality? Might not the relationship between the new social classes provide a breeding ground for new delinquencies? These were questions that might have been asked, but doubts were alien to Lenin and his party in this as in other respects. Freedom from doubt was a prerequisite of their great dynamism. They fully expected that after the November Revolution, and certainly soon after the end of the Civil War, crime would begin to vanish. What crime did occur would represent the excesses of the old generation bred in and spoiled by a capitalist milieu.

And as long as there still were offenders, they must be cured rather than punished; they were to be converted by appropriate methods of education into useful members of the new socialist society. Not the punishment but the correction of men was the great task of Soviet justice.

Criminal law and the penal system had to be radically reformed. What had been necessary under capitalism must be done away with in the Soviet state. No stone of the old order of justice and law must remain untouched. The hatred of the old courts and codes, of prisons and katorgas, was still alive. These institutions had to be erased forever!

Peter Stuchka, Eugene Pashukanis, and Nikolai Krylenko, Lenin's ardent supporters, became the reformers of the Rus-

sian system of justice, and Eugene Shirvindt, a jurist and
writer, was eventually put in charge of the network of prisons.
All of them were inspired by the same ideas as Lenin. The
term "guilt" was deleted from the official vocabulary—society alone was guilty when its members perpetrated crimes.
It was even suggested to eliminate from the Criminal Code
prescribed maximum and minimum terms of confinement for
certain offenses. Krylenko wanted to leave it up to the courts
to impose penalties as they saw fit. In the first draft of the new
Criminal Code, the government fixed the maximum penalty at
five years of "deprivation of liberty." In May, 1922, the maximum was raised to ten years, but this still compared favorably
with the prerevolutionary maximum of 20 years. Education
of prisoners was to be fostered. Parole was introduced and
used on a large scale. It was expected with certainty that the
influence of the new Soviet system and the abrogation of
capitalism would swiftly remold every criminal. Years later
Nikolai Krylenko wistfully admitted: "Peculiar motives
guided us when in 1921 we set a five-year limit on prison sentences: it was naïvely assumed that within a period of five
years under the Soviet regime every delinquent would be converted." [1]

In the land of socialism there could be no prisons. Prisons
were remnants of a capitalist civilization, monuments of barbarism and cruelty. So the very term "prison" was abolished,
and the criminal codes mentioned only "places of detention"
or, as was the case in the Soviet Ukraine, "places of deprivation of liberty." Prisons ceased to be mentioned in court sentences and in university courses on criminal law. Scores of
books and articles commented favorably on the great progress
achieved in Russia by the change from the traditional prison
system to one of correction and education of offenders. It
would be vain to look for the word "prison" in Russian official
publications of the time. The *Encyclopedia of State and Law,*
never mentioned the word. *From Prisons to Educational Institutions* was the proud title of a collective work by Soviet

1. *Encyclopedia of State and Law,* III (3 vols., in Russian), 1925–27, 1354.

jurists, published in the 'thirties under the egis of Andrei Vyshinski.

Likewise, the term "punishment" disappeared. It was explained that punishment had meant retribution, and that retribution must be proportionate to the specific crime. Nothing
of this kind was to be permissible under the Soviet system.
Under Soviet conditions the causes of crime ceased to exist.
There were no more criminals in the Soviet land, there could
be only the brother gone astray.

Famous theories of hereditary criminality were emphatically disproved. Cesare Lombroso, the Italian criminologist,
father of the anthropological school, was denounced time and
again in books, articles, and lectures. Only the environment
and society, was the argument, make a criminal out of a man
who is essentially honest. Under Soviet conditions, therefore,
the number of crimes must rapidly diminish; the residuum will
be medical cases requiring treatment like people suffering
from tuberculosis or alcoholism, and these must be cured in
special institutions. One of the first documents the People's
Commissariat of Justice prepared in 1918 promised that
"prisons will be made to serve for correction, not punishment."
The Congress of the Russian Communist party in 1919 stated
in a resolution that "labor is the principal method of correction and re-education"; hence, it demanded "the substitution
of educational institutions for prisons." In the prisons stream-
ers proclaimed: "We are not being punished: we are being
corrected." With the adoption of the Criminal Code of 1924
"punishment" vanished. Now there were only "measures of
social protection." In Soviet "places of detention" there could
be no dungeon cells, solitary confinement, or punishment by
starvation—cruel measures inherited by capitalist prisons
from ancient times. The Soviet law of the 'twenties prohibited
the use of "chains, handcuffs, dungeons, strict solitary confinement, deprivation of food, isolation from visitors by means
of bars." The internal system in "houses of confinement" must
be humane and liberal in the best sense of the word. The sug-

gestion that the Soviet system of detention might be similar
to that in other countries was emphatically denied.

Bourgeois penal policy aims at moral and physical maiming and
destruction, achieved by means of organized torture and violation
of the human dignity of prisoners. . . . The bourgeois prison
not only fails to correct the sentenced individual but on the contrary pushes him to new crimes. . . . [The Soviet] corrective
labor institutions, in contrast to the prisons in capitalist countries,
in carrying out the tasks of obligatory re-education combine in
their activities repression and coercion with the re-education and
adjustment of convicts to life and to work in an organized collective.[2]

Forced labor in prisons, the Soviet leadership insisted and
Soviet penologists and scientists reiterated, is slavery. Their
works abound in descriptions of compulsory labor in the
prisons of the United States, France, Germany, and Britain,
all of which are accused of employing slave labor and of being hypocritical, professing to be free countries fighting
against slavery everywhere in the world while themselves
employing the barbaric system among thousands and thousands of inmates of their own prisons. Nothing of this kind
could happen in Russia. The Chief of "Corrective Institutions" wrote: "The exploitation of prison labor, the system of
squeezing 'golden sweat' from them, the organization of production in places of confinement, which while profitable from
a commercial point of view is fundamentally lacking in corrective significance—these are entirely inadmissible in Soviet
places of confinement." [3]

Of course, work had to be done in Soviet places of detention, but the work performed was considered highly useful
and in the interest of society, and it was done with the aim of
correcting human beings, under the most favorable conditions. Capitalist countries could not afford to institute these
liberal conditions inside their prisons. In Russia, inmates of

2. *Great Soviet Encyclopedia*, XXIX, 600–603.
3. E. Shirvindt, *Nashe Ispravitel'no-trudovoye zakonodatel'stvo*, p. 78.

places of detention were to be considered human beings, entitled not only to a certain degree of freedom but even to some self-government. Even while they were confined in places of detention these people must be educated in self-discipline, and with this aim in view it was desirable to have them serve as their own guards and sometimes even to carry weapons. Newspapers, libraries, and cultural entertainment were mandatory and frequent lectures were to be provided. Publications managed by the prisoners for the prisoners were to be encouraged.

A new mode of punishment was added to the traditional ones, and the framers of Soviet justice were proud of their innovation: obligatory work without confinement, a mild form of "social protection." The convicted person was obliged to do prescribed work among free men, at a somewhat reduced rate of pay. He was not entitled to change his job without permission of the local agents of the Commissariat of Justice.

All these reforms—or rather blueprints of reforms—meant in theory at least a considerable improvement in the penal system; the emphasis on labor was an important step forward; concern for prisoners as human beings was in accord with the ideals that had inspired the Revolution.

THE GREAT TRADITION

Against the background of terrorism that has prevailed in Russia and which has increased in intensity from year to year, an observer might be inclined to consider the ideology that has just been described as outright and systematic deception. It was not a premeditated lie, however, and if it was deception, it was self-deception.

The Communist party came to power as the great heir to an age-old revolutionary movement in which lofty ideals and humanitarian goals were the inspiring stimuli to self-sacrifice and devotion to the political cause. For 90 years thousands of revolutionists, the spiritual fathers and prophets of the Revolution, passed through the prison gates of old Russia, were subjected to the privations and diseases of Russian prison life, the cruelties of the Siberian katorga, and life-long deportation. The Communist leaders themselves had known all the dark sides of the old prison system. Humaneness was an intrinsic element of the expanding revolutionary movement, of which Bolshevism was but one part. In its repudiation of the old criminal law, Bolshevism went even farther than the other parties —it wanted not simply a reform of the law and of the prison system but their complete eradication and replacement by a new system. The old law, it maintained, was inhuman and could not be improved, just as the rest of the old state could not be improved. It had to be smashed and a new one built in its stead!

Practice, however, differed from this theory. The new Soviet regime was one of minority rule; in order to remain in power and function, it had to struggle against the majority of the people. Moreover, the measures taken to accomplish its economic program inevitably antagonized large sections of the population. Out of this constant struggle a spirit of mercilessness grew which was contrary to the conception of humanitarianism and liberal treatment of offenders against law. The "strong arm of justice" supplanted concern for "the brother gone astray." The new system had to fight political opponents in the Civil War, millions of peasants during collectivization, and various other strata of the population at each and every stage of its development. It resorted to terrorism and employed rigorous methods of coercion. The execution of political opponents and common criminals ("bandits") grew into an established system.

In the beginning terrorism could be considered a temporary phenomenon. The right to execute political opponents was abolished by Lenin in 1920. It was soon reintroduced, again abolished, and finally again reintroduced, to become a permanent fixture of Sovietism to this day. At first political offenders, if jailed, were in many cases soon released. But eventually, in this struggle of the two tendencies—humanitarianism and terrorism—the latter was the winner. After the first decade of the Soviet system the new trends were definitely victorious.

The Cheka-GPU was at first regarded as a temporary institution which would soon disappear and leave the whole field to other, more liberal, governmental agencies; capital punishment was likewise part of the new law as a "temporary necessity" against "belligerent counterrevolution." All armed resistance to the new regime ceased in the early 'twenties, but the GPU continued to grow and to expand. It widened its own network of prisons and concentration camps. It made abundant use of its right to pronounce death sentences and to carry out its own verdicts. It soon overshadowed the "liberal" Justice Department, and in this victory of the GPU the prevailing trends and new policies found their clear expression.

This conflict between the lofty ideals and the reality of the postrevolutionary decades marks the ideological evolution of Russian Communism. There is no other domain of political activity in which a retrogressive development—from the highest peak of humanitarian idealism to the lowest methods of coercion—is as clearly discernible as in the field of Russian justice and law, crime and forced labor. It ended, as we shall see, in the restoration of old ideas and terms such as prison, guilt, and punishment in the late 'thirties, and in an unprecedented wave of terrorism. "A prison is a prison," wrote *Soviet Justice* in 1937, why so much shyness? "And punishment is punishment—why be afraid of this word?" "Measures of social protection," it was found, "is a ridiculous term." "We must overcome the sugary liberalism, the compassionate attitude toward the offender."

Concentration camps were the striking innovation created by the Cheka-GPU in Russia.

The two elements which in later years were combined to form the huge system of forced labor—convict labor and concentration camps—were originally independent of each other. Prison labor was considered a humanitarian reform for criminal prisoners; concentration camps were an institution for the severe handling of political opposition. The first was a source of pride to the talkative and evangelical Commissariat of Justice; [4] the second was a hushed-up achievement of the secretive Cheka-GPU. The two potential elements of the corrective labor system were brought into being almost simultaneously.

In January, 1918, a decree was promulgated which was actually the initial step on the long road to forced labor in Soviet Russia. Paragraph I of the decree ordered: "Work details are to be formed from among the prisoners able to work, for the carrying out of tasks necessary for the state, tasks no more strenuous than those of unskilled workers." [5] Soon after the promulgation of this decree the first small farms operated by convicted criminals came into existence.

Concentration camps were erected in different regions of Russia during the Civil War. When, in 1923, a reform of concentration camps took place, 23 of them were found to exist.[6] Most of them were abolished and their inmates transferred in part to prisons [7] and in great numbers to the far north Archangel region, where camps were erected on the mainland and, in particular, on Solovetski Island.

At first the concentration camps in Russia were intended as places for assembling those who during and after the Civil War had participated in the armed struggle against the Soviet regime. The conditions, which were described many times later, were rigorous, and the treatment accorded the inmates was often cruel. There were executions without trial and death sentences were frequently imposed upon innocent peo-

4. In the early years after the Revolution a number of concentration camps and "places of detention" were under the jurisdiction of the Commissariat of the Interior, which at that time had functions entirely different from those it fulfilled, as the NKVD, in later years. In 1922 the Commissariat of the Interior had under its jurisdiction 56 concentration camps with an aggregate capacity of 24,750 prisoners. In 1923 most of the existing prisons were transferred to its jurisdiction. Later on the Administration of Places of Detention was transferred to the Commissariat of Justice and finally, in 1934, to the NKVD.

5. *Gazeta rabochevo i krestyanskovo pravitel'stva* (Government Monitor) (January, 1918), No. 16.

6. M. Isayev, *Osnovy penitentsiarnoi politiki* (Bases of Penal Policy) (Moscow, 1927), p. 101.

7. Despite the official terminology, the term "prison" of course remained in common use.

ple. The severity, however, was often alleviated because of
the general chaos that still reigned throughout the Soviet land.
Isolation of inmates from the outer world was not complete.
Material aid from the outside was a source of great comfort to
the prisoners. There was even a certain amount of political
activity in the concentration camps and prisons. While Lenin
was preaching suppression of political enemies, their conditions were actually incomparably better than they were under Lenin's successor, who professed humaneness and liberty.
Many of the political inmates of the original concentration
camps actually survived and regained their freedom.

THE GREAT DISAPPOINTMENT

Time passed, and by the middle of the 'twenties the facts
began to prove that the great hopes cherished at the outset that
crime would disappear had remained unfulfilled. It was one
of the greatest disappointments ever experienced by the Communist leadership of Russia. The Civil War had ended, the
NEP had been inaugurated, production in industry and agriculture was rising; relations with the outside world seemed to
take a turn for the better; and yet the number of murders,
thefts, burglaries, briberies, and embezzlements was growing
rapidly and far exceeded prerevolutionary levels.

Criminality had reached an all-time high. In 1926 there
were 162 criminal cases per 10,000 population, i.e., roughly
2,365,000 cases. In 1927 the number of cases in which defendants were found guilty reached a million. Besides, about
1,600,000 persons were subjected to fines of a disciplinary
(administrative) nature.[8] The enormous rise in the number of
new cases coming before the courts was the more alarming
since, in Russia, criminality had always, even under the old

8. *Statistical Yearbook of the USSR*, 1927 and 1928; A. A. Gertzenson, *Bor'ba s
prestupnostyu v RSFSR* (The Fight against Crime in the RSFSR) (Moscow,
1928). Corresponding figures, to establish a comparison with the prerevolutionary
period, cannot be given because of a change in statistical methods. The official
Yearbook for 1914 listed as "defendants: 1909, 304,706; 1910, 426,576; 1911,
427,156." Of these, about 40 per cent were found guilty.

regime, rightly been considered a revealing barometer of the moral and social state of the nation. The significant growth of criminality in the last 15 to 20 years before the Revolution had been regarded as a vivid symptom of generally unhealthy political and economic conditions. The mass of criminal offenses—like statistics of suicides—consists of acts of individuals each of whom is impelled by his own motives and interests; but when these individual cases are considered as a whole, the peculiarities and variety of causes disappear and they merge into great social patterns, social waves whose ups and downs are governed by sociological laws.

Under the Ministry of Justice before the Revolution the number of prisoners doubled between 1901 and 1913. The figures were as follows:

1901	84,632
1903	96,005
1908	171,219
1912	183,949
1913	169,367

The rise was only to a small extent due to the growth of revolutionary activity. The overwhelming majority of the convicts were common criminals. New prisons had to be built, and considerable sums of money were spent in old Russia for this purpose. On the eve of the Revolution Russia had about 700 prisons with an aggregate capacity of 201,774 inmates.[9] In the five years before the first World War the number of prisoners fluctuated between 80 and 90 per cent of the maximum capacity of prisons.

Then, in 1917, the number fell to almost zero. In June, 1917, there were only 24,095 persons in prisons.[10] This was due not to any amelioration in the moral or social state of the nation but to the simple fact that in the first months after the Revolution the old prison system had been disrupted; former directors and wardens and many of the guards had been dis-

9. A. Vyshinski, ed., *Tyurma kapitalisticheskikh stran* (Prisons in Capitalist Countries) (Moscow, 1937), p. 54.
10. Utevski, *Sovetskaya ispravitelno-trudovaya politika*, p. 52.

missed or had fled in fear, and the newly created police—the militia—was as yet in no condition to cope with its tasks. Soon, however, the prison population began to grow at a rapid tempo, as evidenced by the following data:

January, 1924:	87,800
January, 1925:	148,000
January, 1926:	155,000
January, 1927:	198,000.

To these numbers the thousands of inmates of the concentration camps and special prisons of the GPU must be added.

In 1927, when the Soviet Government celebrated its tenth anniversary, the prison population had reached unprecedented figures; despite the fact that Russia had lost about 15 per cent of her population in territories ceded to neighbor states, the number of prisoners had risen considerably above the highest prerevolutionary figures. "The statistics of places of confinement in the Russian Soviet Republic reveal an uninterrupted increase [in the prison population]," the Chief of Corrective Institutions reported.[11]

"The number of prisoners in the years 1922 to 1926 has risen at an annual rate of 15 to 20 per cent and has doubled in the course of these five years," another high Soviet justice official wrote. "For every person leaving a place of confinement upon completion of his sentence, three others arrive."[12] And this was the case despite the fact that sentence terms were gradually being reduced. In 1924 the average prison term was 1.25 years; in 1925, .89 years; in 1926, .72 years.

All types of crimes known before the Revolution reappeared in the Soviet courts. Besides, "office delinquencies"— such as embezzlement and bribes—suddenly attained huge proportions: the growth of the new class of state employees brought about a wave of specifically Soviet crimes. During the five years 1922 to 1926 the index of embezzlements rose from 100 to 491; bribes, from 100 to 115; other "office crimes,"

11. Shirvindt in *Sovetskaya yustitsiya* (1927), p. 1063.
12. Gertzenson, *op. cit.*, pp. 20, 89, 105.

from 100 to 228. At the same time, "crimes against property," which had been expected to disappear, were still numerous and their incidence increased. Nor did the incidence of robbery diminish.

A consequence of the rising wave of crime in the 1920's was overcrowding of prisons and the need for new "places of confinement." Of the existing 600 to 700 prisons a number had been destroyed in the revolutionary fighting and during the ensuing Civil War. Other prison buildings were in such poor condition that they could no longer be used, and the central authorities often refused to appropriate the necessary funds for repairs. Only 432 major prisons (including all types of "places of confinement") existed in Russia in 1924.[13] By 1927 there were 177 prisoners for every 100 normally provided for. Congestion was becoming severe. In Saratov prison, for example, the number of prisoners was 100 per cent above the maximum capacity; in Yaroslavl, 170 to 175 per cent above; in Siberia, 300 per cent above normal. Prisoners slept on the floors, never received enough food, and sanitary conditions became a serious menace to the population at large.

To make room for new arrivals in prisons, reform followed reform—reforms which on the surface seem exceedingly liberal. Prisoners were now entitled to petition for parole, and the authorities were generous in granting such requests. Hundreds of thousands thus regained freedom. (Political offenders were of course excluded from such preferential treatment.) Visitors from abroad were delighted to see the wide application in the Soviet Union of this advance in penology.

Actually it served only to relieve the overcrowding somewhat. An official writer cynically remarked: "The institution of parole has become a means of relieving the prison situation." During 1925–26 only 36 per cent of all sentences imposed

13. Vladimir Brunovski, in *The Methods of the OGPU* (Harper & Bros., London, 1931), p. 216, arrives at higher figures for the middle 'twenties: 72 prisons of the GPU, 153 large prisons, and 613 local prisons. To these he adds 4,874 confinement cells in the village Soviets.

were actually carried out.[14] Another means of relieving the congestion was the creation of State Commissions for Individual Amnesty. They, too, handled petitions and pardoned thousands of convicts.

The new penalty of "forced labor without confinement" soon proved a failure, too. This progressive-sounding reform was also meant to relieve the shortage of space. But reports from all parts of Russia were unanimous in stressing the difficulties in finding the necessary jobs and paying for the labor. "The sentenced persons appear three times [before the Commission] only to be told that the government agency organized for this specific purpose is unable to put this sentence into effect." From Orel it was reported that only 10 per cent of those sentenced to labor were actually sent to work. From Amur the prosecutor wrote that "obligatory labor in this region is not organized in view of the prevailing unemployment and the lack of funds to pay for the work." A report from Siberia stated that "in view of the impossibility of getting the convicts to work and in the absence of such work, we must restrict ourselves to simply keeping the convicts on the roster and leaving the sentences unfulfilled." [15]

As a result of this failure the courts more and more refrained from sentencing defendants to this new mode of punishment. In 1922, 38 per cent of the sentences were to obligatory labor; in 1924, only 24 per cent; in 1925, 16.2 per cent; and in 1926, 13.9 per cent.[16] The system of "obligatory labor without confinement" was rapidly losing its importance. Actually it all but disappeared for a long period until it was suddenly revived in the labor legislation of 1940.

The whole system of justice was shaken to its roots because of the utter impossibility of carrying out the decisions of the courts. No matter what the court's sentence was, the paroling and pardoning commissions reduced the sentences and freed criminal convicts long before it was desirable to do so. There

14. *Sovetskaya yustitsiya* (1927), No. 34, and Gertzenson, *op. cit.*, p. 132.
15. *Sovetskaya yustitsiya* (1927), Nos. 16 and 34.
16. Utevski, *op. cit.*, p. 38.

would have been at least 400,000 prison inmates in the prisons
of the Justice Department alone if the normal course of sentencing and carrying out sentences had prevailed. As it was,
even 200,000 prisoners were more than could be provided for.
And then there was also the GPU with its prisoners.

There seemed to be no solution to the problem inasmuch as
the Soviet Government was determined to refuse to appropriate money for construction of new prisons. The matter
was discussed more than once, but the government persisted
in its attitude. New prisons in Soviet Russia!—this would look
like retrogression, an acknowledgment of failure. Had not
the Revolution been fought with the slogan "Down with
prisons!"? Had it not been said time and again that prisons
were necessary only in capitalist countries, and that the Soviet
state would not have to spend its money for this shameful purpose? While millions of workers still lived in slums, how could
a workers' government justify the expenditure of the people's
money for the construction of prisons?

In the summer of 1927 the government again took up the
question. The increase in crimes and the intolerable conditions
in the prisons were emphasized. The need for a radical solution was apparent, yet no immediate measures were taken.
This indecision was the last tribute paid to principles that
had been cherished over a decade of hope; but the principles
had become obsolete and now had to give way to a "new realism"—a realism which soon came to dominate the government's policies in more than one field.

LABOR AS A MEANS OF EDUCATION

The attempted introduction of prison labor in the first
decade of the Soviet regime turned out to be another failure.
Despite great efforts, a multitude of instructions, and the ap-
propriation of necessary funds, only a minority of prisoners
were actually put to work inside the places of confinement.
The reasons for this were manifold; paradoxically enough,
they were the same reasons that prevailed in capitalist coun-

tries. First, there were still thousands of unemployed in Soviet Russia, and prison labor was bound to compete with the free workers. Secondly, the prisons had no room for industrial work, nor did they provide for a sufficient number of instructors or raw materials. So long as the government was not economically interested in forced labor and attributed only corrective and educational functions to it, the utilization of convict labor did not much exceed the level reached before the Revolution or that of the capitalist world abroad.

In an effort to effect some progress in this field, the Commissariat of Justice in several instances experimentally invested funds in the creation of industrial and agricultural enterprises of its own. They were expected to meet all prison expenses through the receipts from their own production, to relieve the state of the financial burden for the prison and thus put the colony on a self-supporting basis.[17]

In 1927, 1,200 "workshops" of miniature size (carpentry, plumbing, blacksmithing, shoemaking, bookbinding, cooperage, and others); 51 "factories" (brickyards, tile factories, sawmills, soap works, leather working, cement, metal pressing, roofing, tobacco, match factories); and 108 miscellaneous establishments (printing, power, wood finishing, baking, dyeing, sausage, knitting, spinning, and others) were in operation; the biggest of these was opened near Moscow in the middle 'twenties. This Lianozovo-Kryukovskaya Industrial Labor Colony comprised 3,000 common prisoners.

Simultaneously agricultural colonies were opened in certain regions. These were the mildest form of punishment and were reserved to those convicted of minor offenses. The agricultural colonies were essentially estates of the state (sovkhozes) run by compulsory labor. The number of these colonies rose steadily in the first decade after the Revolution. There were 2 colonies in 1918, 8 in 1920, 15 in 1923, and in 1925–26, 33 colonies with a total area of 36,942 hectares

17. Isayev, *op. cit.*, p. 159. "Those deprived of liberty must live on their own labor." Shirvindt in *Sovetskaya yustitsiya* (1929), p. 1089.

(about 150,000 acres). Prisoners working in the agricultural colonies were permitted to move freely about the great spaces, and sometimes they were sent out to near-by villages to load grain or to make purchases. The neighboring peasant population often lived in fear of this accumulation of criminal elements who enjoyed freedom. Many a crime—particularly theft—was committed. Besides, the opportunity to escape was tempting and, although this was sometimes denied by the authorities, hundreds of convicts disappeared from the colonies before the expiration of their sentences.

Despite the proud figure of over "1,300 shops and factories" in which prisoners were employed, the actual role of convict labor was very small. In 1925 the value of their aggregate output amounted to 3,800,000 rubles (i.e., .77 ruble's worth a day of production by each prisoner worker). The aggregate payroll of prisoner workers was 1,060,000 rubles, of which only 40 per cent was actually paid out. The amounts rose slightly in the three subsequent years but they never reached sizable proportions from the point of view of the national economy. They accounted for but .01 or .02 per cent of national income of the Soviet Union for the corresponding years.

The principle that prison work must be paid for in accordance with trade-union standards finally broke down, too. According to law, a prisoner was to be paid 70 to 75 per cent of normal wages, the remaining 25 to 30 per cent to be deducted by the state. The majority of prisoners in Russia naturally consisted of peasants who were sent to city prisons to serve their sentences. It turned out that 75 per cent of prevailing workers' wages was often more than they could have earned at home. To them, prison labor meant economic improvement rather than punishment.

Reflecting the general disappointment, *Soviet Justice* wrote, in 1926, that "labor without pay must be permitted, and peasants must be made to work in the country. . . . Obligatory labor has but one highly advertised feature: its cheapness. But the productivity of a man working under compulsion is far lower than that of a freely hired man." [18]

The great failure was acknowledged.

By the end of the first decade of the Soviet state, the disparity between ideology and practice had brought about a state of profound crisis. The expected decline of crime had not materialized; on the contrary, crime had reached new record heights. The abolition of prisons had proved impossible; instead, the congested conditions within the places of confinement called for the erection of new ones. Fair payment for prison labor turned out to be impracticable in most instances. It was general knowledge that thousands and thousands of "counterrevolutionists," political opponents of all shades, were being held in confinement in concentration camps and prisons under severe conditions. Parole, pardon, and other innovations of Soviet justice often resulted in criminals receiving little or no punishment. Compulsory labor without confinement more often than not remained a sentence on paper only. And, finally, the educational, corrective, and ennobling influence of labor on the prisoner was, after a decade, still a nebulous promise.

At the Communist party Congress in December, 1927, a highly respected member of the Supreme Tribunal and of the Central Control Commission, A. A. Solts, launched a sharp attack:

If we were to carry out all the sentences imposed by the courts, we would have to spend millions for prisons. . . . Every sentence begins with the phrase, "Taking into consideration": Give him five years, and then, taking into consideration the convict's proletarian origin, etc., give him two years, with the judge reasoning something like this: he should get half a year, but since they say he'll get out on the amnesty, I'll give him two years, and he'll actually serve half a year.

. . . In general, throughout the Union we have a struggle on our hands between the courts and the executive. The judge is

18. *Sovetskaya yustitsiya* (1926), No. 18.

afraid to impose too lenient a sentence because he reasons like this: if I give him half a year, he won't sit in prison at all; therefore I'd better give him two years. The judge has no serious attitude toward his sentence, he himself does not believe in his judgment. . . .

There are so many cases in court, and there are so many charges for every violation, which should be dealt with by extra-legal means! Everybody is being dragged into court, and in court there is unimaginable red tape, there are an infinite number of instances, controls, appeals, and so on and so forth.[19]

Everyone sensed a great failure, and something had to be done. Either criminality had to be reduced, or else a vast network of prisons and concentration camps had to be erected. The first path would have required a comprehensive liberalization of the political system. It was rejected. Russia took the other road.

19. *Report of the Fifteenth Congress of the Communist Party, 1927* (in Russian), pp. 544–545.

VIII

"The Northern Camps of Special Designation"

The nuclei of the future Russian labor camp network were the Northern Camps of Special Designation (SLON), located in the northernmost region of Russia, on the White Sea islands and in the adjacent regions on the mainland. When they were created, in the early 'twenties, there was no intention of building them up into economic establishments; they merely represented an outgrowth of the Civil War. While other concentration camps, however, were gradually being closed down, the Northern Camps not only survived but developed into an important new institution. Of the component units of the Northern Camps, one was located in Pertominsk, another in Archangel, a third in Kholmogory, and a fourth in Kem—all of them on the mainland. But the core of the Northern Camps was the camps of the Solovetski Islands, called Solovki for short.

THE SOLOVKI

The Solovetski archipelago consists of numerous small islands situated about 250 miles from Archangel and about 40 miles from Kem. The islands are covered with forests interspersed with a great number of lakes. An arm of the Gulf Stream which touches the archipelago mitigates the severe climate, although not sufficiently to make cultivation of grain possible. In the fifteenth century the first monks appeared— Savvati, German, and Zosima—who founded a cloister on the central island, Solovetski, that developed into the Solovetski Monastery and soon became a center of colonization of the Karelo-Murmansk region. All this territory belonged to Great

Novgorod, which, after its conquest by Moscow, came under the rule of the Russian tsars. The monks had built up an efficient economy in the monastery—dairies, fisheries, various shops to meet the needs of monks and pilgrims, a sawmill, and similar enterprises. But life in the Solovetski Monastery, despite its asceticism, was anything but calm. More than once the monastery was assailed by foreign enemies. It was bombarded for the last time during the Crimean War, in 1854, by the British Navy, which made a futile attempt to conquer Solovki.

Under Ivan the Terrible the monastery had become a place of confinement for prominent persons accused of crimes against state or religion. Because of its almost complete isolation (every year from October until June the archipelago is cut off from the mainland by ice floes) the island seemed suitable for this purpose. Short, narrow caves called "stone sacks," devoid of light or fresh air, honeycombed the eastern wall which protected the monastery from enemy assaults, and prisoners condemned to the strictest discipline were put into these caves. Among the inmates of the Solovetski prison were such prominent men of Moscow tsardom as Avraami Palitsyn, high dignitary of the Troitsko-Sergievski Monastery, and Silvester, archpresbyter of the Moscow Blagoveshchenski Cathedral. Members of the Decembrist uprising of 1825 (Prince F. P. Shakhovskoy and V. N. Bantysh-Kamenski) and many others were confined there. The prison was not abolished until 1905.

It was restored in the early 'twenties by the Soviet regime and put under the OGPU.

Escape from Solovki has always been a hopeless undertaking. As a matter of fact, all such attempts have failed, and memoirs about Solovki published in various countries were written by persons who had escaped not from the islands but from the transit camp at Kem, or who had been deported to some other place after having served their terms on the Solovetski Islands and were lucky enough to get across the Soviet frontier.

What happened to the monks during the Revolution is not known. Some of them probably perished, others wandered off, still others were expelled by the local authorities. A few remnants of this once numerous fraternity, having nowhere else to go, continued to work at Solovki as late as the middle 'twenties.

The first groups of prisoners to be brought to these camps were officers of the defeated White armies. They were soon joined by a group of sailors—the participants in the Kronstadt revolt of February, 1921, who had escaped death. During 1921 and 1922 the camps, except for arrant criminals, were filled mainly with rightist opponents of the regime and with the wives and relatives of convicted or liquidated political leaders.

Since 1923 the population of the Northern Camps has been growing, and to the first (rightist) group of prisoners there were soon added Socialists and Anarchists, against whom a wave of persecution was in full swing.

THE JOURNEY TO THE NORTHERN CAMPS [1]

In the spring of 1923 I was sentenced to two years in camp for Social Democratic activities. The "sentence" was one of those peculiar ones passed not by a court but by the political police, in the absence of the defendant. Among the tens of thousands of prisoners held in Solovki there were only a few who had been tried by regular courts. In April I was put in the Taganka prison in Moscow, from whence transports were sent to Archangel.

The oldest in our group of Socialists and Anarchists was 26, the youngest, a girl Anarchist, 17. Included in our group was a peasant woman from the Tambov district with her two-months-old baby, who had been born in jail. She was arrested and sentenced to three years' deportation to the Northern Camps because she was related to a participant in a peasant revolt in the Tambov district. Along with the "politicals," the transport included about a hundred "counterrevolutionists" and criminals. The deported were put into "Stolypin railroad cars," a special type of car for prisoners, in which one of the walls was blind and the other had

1. The following narrative, pp. 170–188, was written by Mr. Boris Sapir, formerly a prisoner in the Northern Camps; he is now in the United States.

iron-barred windows. A wire partition running the whole length of the car left an aisle along the wall that had the windows. In the aisle guards were posted who watched the prisoners through the partition, while the prisoners were put into compartments arranged between the partition and the blind wall. The trip from Moscow took us three days and three nights, during which time the prisoners received nothing but boiled water and bread. (Later the transports were routed from Leningrad by the Murmansk Railroad to the transit center at Kem, and from there by boat to the camp.)

In Archangel we entered a new world, the realm of the "Northern Camps." The transport was taken over by a young man in a uniform overcoat who did not resemble the usual type of Cheka agent. It turned out that he himself was a prisoner and acting commandant on duty in the Archangel Camp. While the other prisoners were left in Archangel, the "politicals"—Socialists and Anarchists—were to proceed to Pertominsk; the commander of the convoy escorting this group was an officer who had somehow clashed with the law and as punishment had been assigned to convoy duty in the Northern Camps. All the members of the camp administration were of this brand, except for a few top-flight officials, and even these were rumored to have received their appointments as a punishment. Such rumors circulated even about the chief of USLON (Administration of the Northern Camps of Special Designation), Nogtev, and his deputy Eikhmans. The administration was recruited from among the prisoners, with preference being given to former GPU agents, especially in appointments to posts which required the carrying of arms.

On our way from Archangel to Pertominsk the feeling of isolation permeated us with mounting sharpness. Our group of 10 to 12 people had to walk the first three or four miles on the frozen Northern Dvina River and then over a road covered with deep snow. It was impossible to walk except along the trail, closely following the sledges in which rode the convoy commander and on which were piled our belongings (the peasant woman with her baby was allowed to perch on one of them). On both sides of the trail the snow lay knee deep. We had to walk for several days. In a day we covered a distance of about 15 miles, resting every two or three hours, thus giving our companion a chance to feed her child. Nights we spent in seashore villages. It was, I think, on the second day that we saw on a crossroad a file of sledges and people on foot exactly like our own. They turned out to be Anarchists being removed from Kholmogory to Pertominsk.[2] We walked together the rest of the way. About noon of the fifth or sixth day we came in sight of walls with guard towers. This was the concentration camp of Pertominsk.

As we approached we saw an inscription on the side of the wall: "Long live the Third International!" In the old monastery church, cold and deserted, there were tables for the nonexistent "educational section"; portraits of Soviet leaders hung beneath the images of saints painted on the walls, and an inscription in bold letters read: "The Soviet Government does not punish; it reforms." This was in a camp where the commandant, Bachulis, personally beat up the inmates and out of sheer deviltry fired his gun at prisoners working in the fields; where in the summer those who incurred the displeasure of the administration were left, with their hands tied, to the mercy of swarms of mosquitoes, and in the winter were thrown for the night into unheated attics, with nothing on but their underwear. Whether Bachulis was in his right mind was questionable.

Bachulis had tried to break the first political prisoners, who arrived in December of 1922, by leaving their barracks without light or heat and occasionally by shooting at their windows. But his strategy seems to have met with no sympathy in Moscow. In the spring of 1923 he was replaced by another commandant, Mikhelson, who was notorious for his active participation in the executions following the liquidation of Wrangel's army in the Crimea. Driven to desperation by Bachulis' measures, and expecting even worse, the Anarchists went on a hunger strike on March 15, 1923, demanding that they be transferred to Archangel. On the seventh day some of them, in a state of frenzy, tried to burn themselves alive. The wooden cots were ablaze in no time, and the corridor was filled with dense smoke. The fire was extinguished with the help of other politicals who had taken no part in the strike. Eleven Anarchists were taken to the hospital and the hunger strike ended in failure on the 16th day. Later, with the approaching warm season, when the roads were clear of snow and navigation was

2. The Anarchists had been brought to the Northern Camps in February of 1922. They were first placed in the Archangel Camp, where they immediately started to struggle for the betterment of the prison regime. By way of punishment they were transferred to the Kholmogory Camp.

resumed, the number of politicals brought to the camp again rapidly increased.

The GPU was evidently dissatisfied with Pertominsk—the monastery was not large enough—and it was decided to use Solovki instead. But the local agents of the GPU feared that the political prisoners would resist the transfer from the mainland to far-off Solovki. On June 23, 1923, two prisoners, Tatyana Romanova and Vladimir Krasovski, recent arrivals in the camp, escaped. The chiefs of administration made use of this incident to break the hesitation in Moscow, and on June 29, Nogtev, chief of USLON, appeared with armed guards and told us to get ready to leave instantly. We strongly suspected that Romanova and Krasovski were themselves agents of the GPU and that their escape had been engineered by the administration to provide the latter with a pretext for the transfer.

We left in July, 1923. Now Solovki absorbed all the other Northern Camps and became the main concentration camp of the GPU. The central administration of the Northern Camps likewise moved from Archangel to Solovki.

THE SOLOVETSKI CAMP AND ITS INHABITANTS

In 1923, when the Solovetski Monastery became the central concentration camp of the GPU, it housed about 4,000 prisoners. The number rapidly increased. When I left the Northern Camps in 1925, there were 7,000 prisoners there. Two or three years later the prisoners totaled well over 20,000. In 1929–30, when the territory of the Solovetski Camps was extended to the mainland and comprised a stretch of land from the Arctic Ocean in the north to the Svir River and Lake Ladoga in the south and to the Finnish border in the west, the number of prisoners exceeded 100,000.

In Moscow two members of the Board of the GPU were responsible for the Northern Camps: Gleb Boki, as chief, and Feldman, as his deputy. The real local masters of Solovki from its foundation until late in the 'twenties were Nogtev, chief of USLON, and his deputy, Eikhmans.

Aside from the Kem transit center on Popov Island, the Solovetski Camp consisted of six divisions: three on the central (Solovetski) island and one on each of the three other islands or island groups—Great and Small Muksolmski, Anzerski, and Kond. The three divisions on Solovetski Island included the Kremlin, the Savvatievski hermitage, and the penal division on Sekirny mountain.

The main division was located in the "kremlin," which also housed the offices of USLON. Kremlin means old fortress walls; they surround the monastery buildings and protect the island against foreign invasion.

The kremlin division was subdivided into 15 "companies" which embraced various groups of prisoners and administrative personnel. There was also a company of women housed in barracks outside the kremlin wall. The lowest among them were the 8th company—the dregs of the criminals; the 12th, comprising those segregated for hard physical labor; and the 13th, a quarantine for new arrivals, who were also put to hard labor. The other companies included various categories of administrative personnel, office employees, technical and other specialists, skilled workers, male nurses, firemen, etc.

There was hardly a nationality of Russia, a creed, a profession, a class, or a trend of thought that was not represented at Solovki. Socialists, Anarchists; so-called "counterrevolutionists," that is, former members of the "white" movement and rightist enemies of the regime; common criminals and prostitutes; former tradesmen and Soviet merchants who had trusted the NEP (New Economic Policy); people sentenced as "spies" (actual spies were shot without ado); clergymen of all denominations, especially the Greek-Orthodox; workers guilty of striking and peasants accused of rioting; Soviet officials who had served their country body and soul and had been charged with wrecking; delinquent GPU agents; at the end of the 'twenties Trotskyites and members of other opposition groups within the ruling party—all were present at Solovki. Very few of them served sentences imposed by regular courts. The function of Solovki consisted not so much in punishing lawbreakers as in terrorizing the population into silence. The political police which passed the deportation sentences did not even pretend to uphold the fiction that punishment was being inflicted for crimes committed. Sentences motivated by reasons such as "married to a princess" or "made propaganda for the war loan in 1914–17" or "merchant" or "industrialist" were not infrequent. One of the prisoners, a Countess Frederiks, had been deported because her brother was Minister of the Imperial Household of the last tsar. A certain Dekhterov was charged with having inquired about the price of a boat ticket to Vera Cruz. Another prisoner, Guriev, was guilty of having been the owner of a tailor shop; a former Moscow dentist, Malivanov, had worked for the American Relief Administration during the famine of 1922–23 and had to atone for this crime.

An important category of prisoners in the Solovetski camp consisted of Greek-Orthodox clergymen. In the middle of the 'twenties—their number reached about 400. Prominent among them were Bishop Illarion (Troitski), who was closely associated with the late Patriarch Tikhon; Bishop Masuil (Lemeshevski), who managed the Leningrad bishopric after the execution of Metropolitan Benjamin; Bishop Peter of Tambov, who died in 1924 in the penal section on Sekirny mountain; the vicar of Saratov (Sokolov); Bishop Serafim of Kolpino; the Father Superior of the Kazan Monastery, Pitirim (Krylov). The confinement of Russian priests at Solovki was an elaborate blasphemy. Detention in a monastery which from time immemorial had attracted numerous pilgrims and had now been converted into a concentration camp must have been felt by the priests as a special insult. The administration, far from sparing their feelings, compelled them to witness the profanation of former churches. Along with other prisoners, the priests were housed in the Troitsky and Preobrazhensky cathedrals. They were subjected to studied humiliation. In the middle 'twenties the commandant of the Kremlin division ordered forced hair cuttings for them.[3] During certain periods, however, the administration tolerated the holding of religious services. The priests would gather on holidays and say prayers. But this was permitted only in off-work hours, although work was done all day long, including Sundays and holidays.

Three groups of prisoners constituted the main population of the camp at that time: (1) common criminals of the type considered incorrigible; (2) "counterrevolutionists," commonly known as "K-R's"; and (3) "politicals." Today this classification is a matter of history, but to the prison inmates of the first decade of the Soviet regime it was a significant and most important classification.

3. A. Klinger, "Solovetskaya katorga" in *Arkhiv Russkoi Revolyutsii*, XIX (1928), 196–197, 220; Anzerova, *Aus dem Lande der Stummen*, p. 160.

The differentiation between counterrevolutionists and politicals had been inherited from the prerevolutionary struggle and from 1917. Adherents and leaders of former rightist parties, supporters of the prerevolutionary regime, the moderate-liberal party of the Constitutional Democrats, commanders of the White armies, and other similar groups were in the sizable category of counterrevolutionists. On the other hand, Social Democrats, all factions of Populists, Social Revolutionaries, Left Social Revolutionaries, and Anarchists were designated as "anti-Soviet" elements and their members in the labor camps were referred to as politicals.

In this first decade the last-named group occupied a privileged position in the prisons, by comparison with the counterrevolutionists and criminals. Their privileges were a vestige of the interparty relationship as it had taken shape in the decades before the Revolution. The leftist parties (Populists, Social Democrats, and Anarchists) had all been persecuted by the old regime and had shared with the Bolsheviks all the hardships and privations of prison and exile. The overthrow of the imperial regime was largely a feat of the political left, in which the Bolsheviks were still a minority. Now, a mere five or six years after 1917, it was as yet impossible to break the ties with the past and condemn members of the leftist parties to the same treatment that was accorded to the supporters of the imperial regime. Only gradually did the old sentiment die out. Moreover, in popular parlance these leftist parties had never been referred to as K-R's, despite the strenuous press campaign that accused them of aiding counterrevolution. In all the prisons and concentration camps the parties of the left were still better off than all the other prisoners.

In the Northern Camps the administration recognized the right of the politicals to self-organization and negotiated with them through their elected representatives. Moreover, the administration accepted their refusal to perform forced labor, and placed at their disposal a special kitchen to which were supplied all food rations allotted to political prisoners; by this device they improved their diet as compared with that of the criminals, whose rations shrank considerably as they passed through the hands of many administration agents.[4]

4. Subsequently, Moscow began to tire of the liberal tradition in Russian jails which accorded a privileged status to political convicts. The GPU resolved to

POLITICAL PRISONERS AT SOLOVKI

I was one of a group of 150 political prisoners brought to So-lovki from Pertominsk on July 1, 1923. We were assigned to the Savvatievski hermitage, about eight miles from the kremlin. There was not a soul around, only here and there an ancient building. The walk would not have been difficult had it not been for the mosquitoes which swarmed in the night air. They entered our mouths and ears and bit ferociously at every unprotected spot. We beat them off as best we could and protected our heads with kerchiefs or paper. After a while fatigue began to overwhelm us.

Finally, we came in sight of a group of buildings fenced in by barbed wire. At several points we saw watchtowers provided with bells. As we approached, the armed sentries on the towers rang the bells to summon the guards and the camp commandant. Once more we went through the routine of being turned over by the convoy to the prison guards. Then, at long last, we were left to ourselves. After our war against the mosquitoes, our three-hour walk from the kremlin, and the sleepless night we had spent on the boat, we did not feel like inspecting our new home. We dispersed to our cells and, without undressing, dropped to sleep wherever we could find places—on benches, cots, or on the bare floor. One thing was immediately apparent: the building was too small to accommodate 150 persons.

The administration took no heed of this overcrowding and continued to bring in new groups from the mainland. We could not possibly protest the admittance of co-prisoners who had been assembled in the courtyard behind the barbed wire, but the over-crowding got on our nerves.

The administration was not in the least interested in establish-ing a peaceful atmosphere; on the contrary, Nogtev tried to pro-voke the political prisoners. For weeks he would withhold letters from relatives who were unable to learn the place to which the

---

extend to political prisoners the general treatment applied to common criminals, and started a campaign against their privileges. In 1923–26 the GPU proceeded systematically against Socialist and Anarchist convicts, and against their en-deavors to safeguard, at the price of great sacrifices, the "rights" which they had won in arduous struggle. Later, after my escape, the attitude toward the different groups in the prisons and camps underwent a radical change. All privileges of the political prisoners were abolished, and after the end of the 'twenties the politicals were even officially treated as inferior to the common criminals.

prisoners had been moved from Pertominsk. At that time only two or three months remained until the end of the navigation season, after which correspondence was no longer possible.

Great indignation was aroused by the treatment of the very rare visitors who came to see a prisoner. The trip required both time and money, and permission for such visits could be obtained only from the GPU office in Moscow, so that people living in the provinces had hardly any chance of getting it at all. Permission for a visit was granted to immediate relatives only: wives, parents, sisters, and brothers. Visits were limited to an hour a day for one week. But when a wife or mother, after endless trouble, sometimes loss of her job, and spending of savings, finally arrived in Solovki, she was put almost on a par with the prisoners: she was supervised by guards, shadowed wherever she went, and charged ridiculous prices for housing and food. Thus the visit turned into a kind of torture for the prisoner, who feared for his "guest" but could not, of course, refuse to see him.

Visitors often brought food for all the prisoners. Meager as the camp's food ration was, there were indications that the administration would not be able to guarantee its distribution throughout the winter. And yet the cost to the visitors of transportation of food in government-owned boats, and of delivery from the port to the Savvatievski hermitage, was so exorbitant that it almost doubled the price of the products. But the administration plagued the prisoners with such seeming trifles, which, in the camp atmosphere, tended to take on giant size.

Soon after our arrival more serious conflicts developed which led to a tragic outcome.

Some of the prisoners in our group were gravely ill on arrival at Solovki. The poorly equipped kremlin hospital, with a poorly qualified doctor, Miss Feldman, in charge, might have served for prisoners who were not seriously ill. Nogtev promised to send our sick to the continent. But time passed, the boats sailed away, winter was approaching, and the sick remained where they were. I remember Mrs. V. V. Trofimova, a middle-aged woman, who had been afflicted in Pertominsk with an acute form of melancholia. At Solovki she never left her cot; she lay there gazing at the wall, without uttering a word for weeks on end. Another patient, an old writer and Social Revolutionary, A. P. Gelfgot, who had knocked about Soviet prisons since 1919, was suffering from a nervous breakdown. He could not tolerate the least noise, was unable to move about in his cell, and moaned helplessly. There was no way of helping such sufferers.

With the coming of winter tragedy began to stalk our hermitage. The trouble began in Kem. A 19-year-old Social Democrat, Jacob Aronovich, committed suicide in one of the barracks. Deportation and life in jail had been too much for him. Taking advantage of a moment when no one was in the barracks, he tied his suspenders into a noose and hanged himself. Two notes were found on him, one addressed to his parents, the other to his friends. Both notes were confiscated.

The feeling aroused by Aronovich's death had hardly subsided when another tragedy occurred, this time at Muksolma. In the dead of night a young Social Revolutionary, Yuzya Sandomir, cut his veins. Next morning the inmates discovered the corpse. This suicide was the reaction of a sensitive youth to the beating, at Nogtev's orders, of a group of politicals, among them Sandomir, during their transfer from the kremlin to Muksolma. As a result of Sandomir's suicide the trade-union leader Mikhail Yegorov-Lyzlov, a metal worker, lost his mind. On the night of the suicide he had been on orderly duty in the barracks, and felt that he was guilty of Sandomir's death because he had failed to watch him properly. He developed a persecution mania, refused to take food, fearing that it was poisoned, and spent sleepless nights, on the alert. Eventually he became raving mad.

But all these events were overshadowed by a further disaster which struck the Savvatievski hermitage like a thunderbolt, taking six young lives.

On the afternoon of December 19, Nogtev came to the hermitage and summoned the representatives of the politicals. Nogtev was being boycotted on account of the Muksolma outrages, and the representatives refused to see him. Shortly afterward, one of them—I think it was the Social Revolutionary, Ivanitski—received a note from the commandant's office, stating that he was "to inform the political prisoners at roll call that from now on fresh air periods would be permitted only until 6 P.M." Roll call usually took place at 8 P.M. It appeared, therefore, that the new order was not applicable to that day. Although nobody took the note very seriously, it produced some uneasiness among the few persons who knew of its existence.

At 5 P.M. about 60 prisoners were taking their customary evening walk in the courtyard when a group of armed soldiers appeared and the prisoners were ordered to go indoors. Even those who knew about the new regulations considered that they had the right to be outside, since the time limit had not yet been reached. The command "fire" was heard, but only after several persons dropped did the prisoners realize that they themselves were the target. When some of them rushed to assist the wounded, a second volley was fired, and a third was aimed at those who were carrying away the wounded. Half an hour later the bodies of five dead and three wounded were lying in the barracks. One of the latter, after three weeks of agonizing pain, died of blood poisoning contracted during the amputation of his arm, which had been shattered by a bullet.[5]

Rumors of this shooting reached Moscow through unknown channels. Relatives besieged the GPU for information. On January 10 the Moscow newspapers reported that the Presidium of the Central Executive Committee had appointed a commission "to investigate the events in the Solovki Camps," and in February *Izvestia* published the names of the victims. Nothing else happened; no investigation was conducted and none of the culprits was ever punished.

The winter of 1923–24 was hard. Illness spread, food rations became more and more meager. Tuberculosis and scurvy caused by lack of vegetables was rampant among the prisoners. Only with great difficulty was it possible to provide the scorbutic with a few onions a week.

The administration continued its policy of baiting the politicals. A reaction to this policy was the hunger strike of Anarchists and Social Revolutionaries, which lasted from October 3 to 14, 1924, and ended in failure. On the eve of the hunger strike a GPU commission consisting of Boki, Katanian, and Krasikov arrived in Solovki. It was informed of the forthcoming strike but did nothing to meet the prisoners' demands. It simply ignored the complaints. Later, Krasikov concocted in the name of the commis-

5. The following persons were killed on December 19th: Elizaveta Kotova, 25; Natalia Bauer-Tsetlin, 32; Gavriil Bilima-Pasternak, 27; Meier Gorelik, 26; and Georgi Kocharovski, 26. Vsevolod Popov, 28, died following the amputation of his arm. Leonid Lebedev, 24, and Emmanuil Shik, 32, later recovered from their wounds. All but the anarchist, Lebedev, were Social Revolutionaries.

sion a report on the life of the politicals at Solovki, which slandered the prisoners and extolled the humaneness of Soviet penal methods.

On the assumption that it would be easier to degrade the politicals to the status of criminals if they were split into small groups isolated from one another, the GPU decided to stop deporting them to Solovki. In 1925 all politicals were shipped from Solovki to the continent and confined in remote prisons.

HARD LABOR

Up to the middle 'twenties the prisoners were put to work solely to meet the needs of the camp, and their tasks were accordingly limited. Later, however, the camp began to work "for the market," i.e., for Soviet trusts and enterprises, and on special assignments. The expansion of hard labor in Solovki and its development into a widespread system are connected with the names of two prisoners, N. A. Frenkel and Ivan Seletski.

Frenkel, supposedly an important Hungarian manufacturer, was sentenced by the GPU to hard labor for alleged espionage. This was the era of the NEP, when considerable numbers of Russian and foreign businessmen tried their luck in capitalist economy under a Communist government. One rumor had it that Frenkel had been caught in a forbidden foreign exchange deal; others said that he was suspected of espionage on behalf of Turkey. At any rate, he was sentenced to ten years of exile and hard labor. His chance of surviving was slight, especially since Moscow had ordered him "kept on the hardest labor and in a punitive company." Frenkel, an astute, enterprising, and ruthless man, submitted to the authorities a plan to organize local production on a grand scale. The camp officials, in dire need of efficient organizers, liked his ideas and entrusted him with a number of projects. The results were brilliant. He effectively reorganized forest work; he supervised the construction of a brickyard; he had a new building erected for the Central Administration of the Northern Camps at Kem. Later, long after my escape, Frenkel was appointed Chief of Supply of the GPU forces. He continued to rise rapidly, soon becoming one of the GPU chieftains at the Belomor Canal. During the war, in September, 1943, he was awarded the Order of

Lenin for his role in the building of the Pechora Railroad with prison labor.[6]

Ivan Seletski, the other founding father of the labor camps, had been, before the Revolution, a prison warden in Siberia. He likewise offered to organize production in prisons and camps, and was entrusted with important tasks in the Vishera Camp. His career, however, was soon ended; he was reported shot by the GPU.

Now that the camps had to perform work for the state's economic agencies and thus try to make up for their costs, every additional brick, every additional piece of timber produced by the prisoners increased the revenue of USLON. The drive for more intensive work became the supreme purpose for which the system introduced in Solovki was shaped. Mass labor was applied to lumbering, production of peat, sawmills, quarries, brickyards, timber floating, loading and unloading of ships. The norm of output was set high, despite the shortage of tools, the poor physical condition of the workers, and their inability to withstand the severe climate. In the north, hard physical exertion requires special training and adequate clothing and nourishment. Yet most prisoners lacked clothing and were kept on a semistarvation diet. At first some British canned meat, seized by the Red Army after the liquidation of the northern front, was thrown into the general cauldron, but later the food which the prisoners received twice a day consisted of nothing but soup and a small portion of porridge without butter. In addition, they received one to one and a half pounds of bread and a tiny bit of sugar. There were no fats, no meat, no tobacco, no tea and—what was of special importance in the north—no vegetables. Because of lack of vitamins scurvy was prevalent among the prisoners. The miserable housing provided no rest for the weary after a day's work.

In the former cathedrals of the Solovetski Monastery assigned to the worker "companies," plank beds covered the whole floor space. The number of inches allotted each prisoner was some-

6. An official Soviet source once commented on this extraordinary career: "Beginning as a prisoner, an ordinary lumberman in Solovki, Frenkel went up the entire ladder of camp life and was given a post with *tens of thousands of people under him*. An organiser and administrator to the core, . . . he owed all his success to the organisation in which he found himself. . . .

"When Frenkel got into this organisation he had either to submit to it, or to be damned as an organiser. He chose submission. . . . [The organisation] educated him, and . . . some good hard pushes were needed." *Belomor* (Eng. ed., Smith and Haas, 1935) p. 229. Italics ours.

times so small that it was impossible to lie on one's back. Over-crowding, disgusting sanitary conditions, lack of opportunity for washing, and lack of soap played havoc with the prisoners' health. The unsuitable buildings afforded little protection against the cold. To demand strenuous labor from men living under these conditions meant to jeopardize their health and lives. But this was precisely what the administration aimed at. There is no other explanation for the elaborate punishments resorted to by the ad-ministration to force these hapless people to work beyond their strength.

The punishments often were a product of the ingenuity of the foreman, himself a prisoner, who tried by hook or crook to keep his privileged position. They also depended on the instructions given to the armed guards. In some cases the prisoners were beaten up or hanged from trees; in others they were compelled to stand in the freezing cold for hours without moving. And, upon the report of guards, they could be sent to Sekirny mountain or could be executed.

About half way on the road from the kremlin to the Savvati-evski hermitage, not far from the seashore, there was a hill, called Sekirny mountain, the highest spot in the Solovetski archipelago. There USLON established, in 1923, a special penal institution (Sekirka) within the Solovetski Camp. Before that the adminis-tration used to throw delinquent prisoners into the so-called "stone sacks" which once served as punitive cells and were later used by the monks for food storage. When Sekirka was estab-lished there was no longer any need for the "stone sacks." In the winter season a small iron stove made the air in Sekirka lukewarm for a few hours during the day. Prisoners were not allowed to wear anything except underwear. They had to sit on their cots without talking or moving, and their food rations were inferior even to the general Solovki rations. Commandant Antipov super-vised the strict observance of the Sekirka regulations.

USLON was vested with the right to execute prisoners—not only under the pretext of "an attempt to escape" but also for simple "stubborn refusal to comply with work instructions." I well remember an order of the day read at a roll call at the Kem transit center, which contained a list of prisoners executed for vio-lation of labor discipline. On the other hand, the administration could free a prisoner from "general work" and use him as an office employee or farm hand, positions which implied improved living conditions and thus provided a chance of surviving imprisonment at Solovki.

But even those who had been lucky enough to escape "general work" had no assurance that their good luck would not one day come to an end, and that they would not be returned to share the common lot. No wonder that, however slight the chances of success, foolhardy plans of escape constantly haunted the minds of the most active prisoners. It seems that all attempts to break jail ended in failure. It was a firmly established rule that escape from Solovki was punished by execution. I remember the case of two prisoners who escaped in 1925 from the transit center in Kem. They were seized two hours after their flight. One of them was killed on the spot, the other was brought to the commandant's office, beaten unconscious, put into a penal cell, and a few days later was executed upon orders received from USLON.

The prisoners sometimes wondered whether the central government was aware of what was going on in Solovki. As if to uphold the pious legend of Moscow's innocence as regards the club-law rule in Solovki, a commission of two or three inspectors visited the camp from time to time. The commission conducted an inspection, questioned the prisoners—and departed. Now and then a prison official was dismissed, but no such measure was ever taken against a high-ranking officer of USLON. After the departure of the commission everything continued as of old. The Northern Camps were under the direct control of GPU; nothing happened there without GPU sanction.

Prisoners confined to Solovki lost even the negligible rights which they had enjoyed in jails on the mainland. Whether or not they would survive their hard life depended on the good will of their superiors, who were themselves prisoners and whose well-being depended, in turn, on the good will of their bosses. This was true all the way from the bottom to the peak of the pyramid formed by the population of Solovki. The nearer to the peak a prisoner was, the better was his chance to survive and avoid a prolongation of his sentence. The danger of this prolongation was quite definite and became a reality by a stroke of the pen in the office of USLON. Hence the atmosphere of moral deterioration in the camps. Eavesdropping, denunciation, and attempts to profit at the expense of fellow prisoners were everyday occurrences. Especially tragic was the lot of women. They were faced with a choice between hard labor, privations, the risk of remaining in the camp forever, and an easier life at the price of their honor. Few of them had the stamina to pass this test. Men were faced with a similar dilemma, only the price was different.

The system prevailing in the camps tended to destroy the personality of the inmates. This purpose was achieved at Solovki by strict militarization of the camp. The division into companies was more than a symbol. Within the companies there was military discipline, drill, and goose-stepping. Men and women, regardless of age or occupation, were subjected to rigid training, though without the benefits accorded soldiers. Upon their arrival at the transit center, Kem, and later at Solovki, prisoners were drilled in military formation and were taught to greet their superiors in a smart, military manner. Civilians through and through, they were trained for hours to shout in unison, "Good day." Whenever administrative officials appeared they had to line up and sometimes wait in the courtyard in the rain and cold. They stood in line in the morning during roll call, which lasted for 40 minutes. When the commandant walked along in front of them, they had to stand at attention with eyes trained on him. A punch in the jaw or a whack with a rifle butt were the favorite methods of enforcing proper military bearing.

KEM

At the end of the autumn of 1924 all prisoners whose terms were to expire in the spring or winter (when there was no navigation) were transferred to the Kem transit center of the Northern Camps of Special Designation, situated on Popov Island,[7] near the Murmansk littoral, about 40 miles from Solovki.

Unlike Solovki, where we had been isolated in our hermitage, Kem displayed all its facilities before our eyes. The politicals were kept in a separate barracks fenced in by wire. The camp was so small that nothing could be hidden from us. The Kem transit center was organized in the worst pattern of military jails. The camp was regarded as a regiment, and each barrack as a company. At

7. The Bolsheviks renamed Popov (meaning priest) Island the Island of the Revolution, but the new name did not stick.

the head of the regiment was a "regiment commander," and at
the head of each company a "company commander," appointed
by the camp commandant from among the prisoners. The prisoners were drilled like soldiers. Whenever the commandant appeared the inmates of the barracks had to line up, stand at attention, and answer his greetings by yelling in unison: "Good day,
comrade commander." Woe to the barrack which did not learn
this nicety to perfection. The assistant camp commandant, Popov,
would place the inmates of such barracks under a punitive regime.

What got on our nerves more than anything else were the roll
calls, which lasted up to an hour. In the winter they were conducted inside the barracks, but in early spring and late autumn
the prisoners had to line up in "Main Street," in front of the barracks, at the prescribed time and wait in cold or rain for the arrival of the bosses, and then stand with their eyes glued on them.
Discipline was enforced by means of the dungeon and the knout.
The camp commandant, Kirillovski, his assistant, Popov, and the
so-called "regiment commander," Telnov, carried heavy clubs of
which they made liberal use.

A small structure on the shore was converted into a dungeon.
It was divided by a partition running along its whole length; on
one side of the partition was a narrow corridor for the sentry, and
on the other, six or eight cages for the offenders. Aside from a
small iron stove in the corridor, there was no heat, so that the temperature in the cells differed little from that outside. Men and
women, often stripped to their underclothes, were thrown into
this dungeon for periods of several days. In reality the punishment consisted of torture by cold. A few instances may indicate
the kind of offenses for which the prisoners were put into the
dungeons. A prisoner, Ivanov, relayed a letter that had passed
through the camp censorship and had been mistakenly handed to
him in the office, to the addressee, a woman who lived in the "political" barracks. Allegedly, it was Ivanov's duty to turn the letter
over to the office. In another instance the assistant commandant
put into the dungeon a woman charged with having greeted him
with insufficient courtesy. He punished another prisoner for using
foul language. (Administration officials hardly ever spoke to the
prisoners without peppering their words with choice profanities.)
Ironically, prisoners were incarcerated for uncleanliness despite
the overcrowding and lack of soap and even water.

The second part of the barracks in which "regiment commander" Telnov lived with his retinue, was called the "ladies barracks," not to be confused with the "women's barracks" at the other end of the camp. Female prisoners, upon their arrival in the camp, were divided into two groups—"ladies" and "women." The first category consisted of better-educated and "clean" persons. I never observed any of these doing hard work. As a rule "women" and not "ladies" were assigned to laundry and kitchen work, floor scrubbing, etc. The inhabitants of the "ladies" barracks had duties to the camp officials. The "women's" barracks were not spared in this respect, either, although the higher officialdom held them in contempt. Sometimes the solicitations of the officials met determined resistance, but high courage was needed to withstand the temptation of more endurable conditions of life.

In general conditions in Kem were disgusting. Housing space was apparently considered unlimited; whatever the number of prisoners shipped from Leningrad, they had to be accommodated. Plank beds filling the whole barrack did not provide sufficient sleeping room for all the inmates. A prisoner at best had at his disposal only 14 inches of space, so that he had to sleep on his side. Bedclothes were nonexistent. Filth, vermin, and foul air filled the barracks. An outsider entering them became dizzy. Reading or writing was out of the question because of the constant shouting and because the single lamp shed but a dim light. In the daytime everybody was driven out to work. Sowing, cleaning the courtyard, and fetching wood from the forest constituted the main occupations. But sometimes the prisoners were put to absolutely senseless work. I remember the camp commandant, Kirillovski, in 1925, making up his mind to have spring before May Day. Snow lay deep and the cold was bitter, but, conforming to orders, the camp ushered in the spring. Everybody was busy chopping ice and removing snow. As if to spite Kirillovski, fresh snow fell right in the midst of our work. But he was unperturbed and urged the prisoners to increase their efforts.

We were brought from Solovki to Kem because our terms had nearly expired. On their expiration, however, none of us was set free—the Kem administration had no right to liberate a "political" without special orders from Moscow. These orders usually arrived after a delay of one to three months, and usually provided for a new sentence. My term expired in April of 1925. Six or eight weeks later I was summoned to the camp office and told to sign a paper, which appeared to be an excerpt from the minutes of the Board of the GPU. According to these minutes the Board had reviewed my case and decided that after serving my term of imprisonment I was to be deported for three years to western Siberia.

In June of 1925 I was included in a transport of prisoners. After a six-weeks' trip I reached my destination—the town of Kurgan. In the autumn of the same year I escaped from Kurgan, and early in 1926 I crossed the Latvian frontier.

RAPID EXPANSION

On June 19, 1925, the Council of People's Commissars issued the following decree signed by Premier Rykov:

On the proposal of the OGPU, the Council of People's Commissars has resolved:

1. To cease the detention at the Solovetski Concentration Camp of Special Designation of members of anti-Soviet parties (Right Social Revolutionaries, Left Social Revolutionaries, Mensheviks, and Anarchists) condemned for political offenses.

2. Members of the anti-Soviet parties listed in par. 1 of this decree and confined in the above-named camp are to be transferred by August 1, 1925, to places of detention within the jurisdiction of the OGPU on the continent.

3. Henceforth prisoners listed in par. 1 sentenced to concentration camps are to serve their terms in places of detention within the jurisdiction of the OGPU on the continent.

Nevertheless, from time to time political prisoners were shipped off to Solovki from other camps as a special reprisal. They were subjected to the regime established for criminals detained there.

In 1929 a group of prisoners resolved to attempt a desperate coup. They plotted to disarm the guards, seize all the arms stored on the island as well as USLON's steamers, and sail abroad. Whether one of the conspirators unwittingly divulged the plan or betrayed the others is not known. The plot was discovered in the autumn of 1929, and 53 prisoners paid with their lives for it. Later 140 more were shot for participation in the affair.[8]

Rumors about the terrible conditions on Solovki continued to spread. In 1929 Maxim Gorky was invited to visit the labor camps in order to silence the protests at home and abroad. Gorky actually did visit Solovki on June 20–22, 1929. For a whole month before his arrival barracks were scrubbed and cleaned; regulations and orders informing the prisoners of punishments and of sentences of their fellow inmates were removed from the walls; cozy rooms with books and newspapers (so-called *krasnyi ugolok*—literally "red corners") were arranged, and an afternoon recess introduced. Gorky walked through the camps, inspected a few barracks, talked to prisoners in the presence of guards. The prisoners, assembled to greet him, sang:

> Deported as we are for our deeds,
> We still enjoy many a right.
> We publish newspapers which everybody reads,
> We stage performances—a lovely sight!
> We write, and our songs we sing.
> Abroad they've never dreamt of such a thing!

As soon as Gorky left, the old order returned.

The following winter, 1929–30, was the most dreadful in the annals of the Solovetski Camps. The deportation of peasants was getting under way, and despite the overcrowded conditions in the barracks, another 20,000 men arrived. An epidemic of typhus spread among the prisoners, who were in no condition to resist disease; many thousands died.

Finally, in 1930, a new commission dispatched from Moscow discovered flagrant abuse, crime, and monstrous cruelty on the part of the camps' administration. At last a purge of camp officials took place. In the camp of Kem the notorious foreman Kurilko was executed. In the Solovki three local

8. Nikonov-Smorodin, *Krasnaya katorga*, pp. 25–26; and *Red Gaols*, p. 45.

chiefs were shot. A few other officials were sentenced to deportation by the GPU.

Living conditions did not, however, improve noticeably because, from 1931 to 1933 the food situation throughout Russia deteriorated considerably. The prisons and labor camps were naturally the first to suffer the consequences of the growing famine.

By the middle of 1930 the Camps had a population of about 662,000. Work was being performed at 873 different places.[9] Among the prisoners only 3,000 were common criminals; the great majority were peasants, NEP men, and other "socially dangerous elements." A few other interesting groups of camp inmates were also listed: 4,550 émigrés who had returned from abroad; thousands of priests; 1,250 Ukrainian separatists; 18,956 "murderers of Voikov" (men and women exiled to the Northern Camps in reprisal for the murder of Soviet Ambassador Voikov in Warsaw in 1928); 875 Chinese deported during the short war with China in 1929; about 9,000 members of the Red Army; and at least 800 members of "anti-Soviet" parties.

In the meantime, the Northern Camps of Special Designation had expanded far into the interior. From punitive establishments they had changed into important economic institutions. The camps were considered a success, but while continuing their existence as labor camps they soon receded to a place of lesser significance, becoming but one—nor by any means the most important—component part of the vast new web of camps throughout Soviet Russia.

9. These figures were supplied by Kiseliov-Gromov, a GPU official in the administration of the Northern Camps, in his *Lageri smerti v SSSR*. His statistics must be considered with some reservation; they are evidently only approximations and estimates.

IX

The Great Upheaval (1928-1934)

Everything changed, once the Soviet Government embarked on the First Five-Year Plan and proceeded to fulfill its program of complete collectivization of agriculture within a few years. The years between 1928 and 1934 marked an impressive upheaval in internal politics and economy—one of the greatest in Russian history and probably one of the greatest in the history of mankind. The living conditions of the people were more deeply affected than they had been during the initial years of the Soviet Revolution; no sector of human endeavor remained untouched. It was during those years that an entirely unexpected way was found out of the impasse reached in the penal system and the prisons and concentration camps at the end of the first Soviet decade. And it was in this period that the system of corrective labor camps was established and developed.

Stalin termed these years "the Great Turning Point." The objective was rapid development of the Russian economy as a highly centralized state enterprise and without foreign investments, which had played such an important role in the prerevolutionary growth of Russia's industry. Realization of this objective was possible only if the general standard of living of workers as well as peasants was systematically held at a low level, so that the surplus of national income would constitute a great fund in the hands of the government. Low wages and substantial deliveries of agricultural produce were the prerequisites of a successful Five-Year Plan. In order to achieve these goals all the police power of the state had to be exerted, and extreme coercion resorted to. Under these conditions the "Socialist offensive" announced by the government meant a colossal increase in repressions.

In order to achieve the transformation of the peasants' private economy into a system of centrally directed collective farms, force had to be used. The peasantry's resistance was chaotic, sporadic, and futile and was frequently expressed with the energy of despair, but it attained considerable proportions. The government reacted by mercilessly annihilating entire villages and carrying out mass executions and deportations. The government issued new decrees which were ruthlessly applied against the perpetrators of "damages to state and collective property." Thousands of peasants, with their wives and children, were deported for slaughtering their livestock rather than turning it over to the new collectives; children were deported for destroying ears of corn in the fields. As a result famine descended upon many regions, especially the Ukraine, in 1932–33 and the death toll was variously estimated as between 5 and 8 million.

All reserves of manpower seemed to have been absorbed during the first two years of the Five-Year Plan. Unemployment disappeared, and the labor shortage became a serious problem. Under other conditions the situation would have been favorable to labor, and independent trade unions would have been able to obtain considerable wage increases for their members. This, however, was contrary to the aims of the industrialization program, since wage increases diminished the available surplus, i.e., the investment fund. It was, therefore, made the trade unions' task to hold the line and prevent strikes and other collective labor action. By keeping wages low the government and the trade unions were able to achieve another success, namely, to force wives and daughters of workers into jobs. The lower the income of the principal wage earner of a family, the more necessary it becomes for other members of the family to seek employment. Female and child labor increased rapidly after 1928.

THE TURNING POINT

During the first 12 years of the Soviet regime the individual citizen was still allowed considerable liberty insofar as his economic activity was concerned. A worker, in spite of the fact that he was employed in the service of the state, was nevertheless free to accept or reject a job, change from one profession to another, and even not work for a certain time if he so desired and could afford to do so. He was free to quit his position and to travel over the country, and he needed no permission to accept employment elsewhere. Workers often abandoned industrial work and returned to their peasant families. According to the Labor Code, "The transfer of a hired person from one enterprise to another or his shipment from one locality to another, even when the enterprise or institution moves, can take place only with the consent of the worker or employee concerned."

The so-called intelligentsia was no less free in the choice of professions. Men with technical or engineering backgrounds for one reason or another often preferred to work in other professions. Physicians often derived their main income from private consultation. In the nonpolitical fields the intellectuals were relatively free.

Much economic freedom was left to the peasantry, too. The land was privately owned by peasant families and, except that he was prohibited from selling the land, each farmer was free to conduct his affairs as he pleased. He had the right to divide his land among his sons, to sow whatever crops he chose, and to sell the produce on the free market.

The only important institution in which compulsion prevailed was the army. Conscription had been retained from prerevolutionary times, but in Russia, as in most European countries, compulsory military service was considered a democratic achievement, and no objections were raised to it in principle. In contrast to the rest of the population, the army was the only organism that could be transferred rapidly from one region to another, made to work or fight whenever necessary, and to carry out all orders unswervingly.

These attributes of military discipline were soon to be extended to the other classes of the population. Since 1929 there has been a gradual conversion of the labor force of Russia into a streamlined, controlled, and regimented working mass. New measures marked the beginning of a thorough transformation which was to continue for more than a decade; its essence was the creation of a society more totalitarian in character than any in history. The civilian labor force assumed the characteristics of the military forces: arbitrary assignment of tasks; rigid discipline; transfer of manpower by governmental order; prescribed wages and standards. This conversion, which is still under way, was the necessary and inevitable consequence of the rapid industrialization and collectivization of the country. An integral part of this general transformation, which began in 1928–30, was the creation of an army of millions of forced laborers.

The People's Commissariat for Labor, which was created in 1917 for the purpose of developing labor legislation and for the protection of wage earners, was now assigned the task of supplying labor for industry. Central and local agencies had to figure out where and how many workers could be *mobilized* to meet the needs of the state economy, particularly in seasonal employment. Each agency had to control the "export and import" of labor in its area of jurisdiction.

In February, 1930, a decree was published concerning the means of securing the required labor force for industrial work. The decree ordered an increase in the number of working women and the attraction of fresh labor from the villages. In September, 1930, all Soviet industrial enterprises and institutions were forbidden to hire workers who had left their previous positions without permission. In October the Commissariat of Labor decreed that "in view of the great shortage of labor in all branches, insurance bureaus are requested to discontinue payment of unemployment benefits."

In December, 1930, a decree prescribed sharp measures against "deserters" and "jumpers," [1] ordering the training of 1,300,000 new workers in the shortest possible time. It also contained a vast, utopian scheme of immediate mobilization of all labor. In March, 1931, the Labor Department again ordered a census of potential labor reserves, reiterated its instructions concerning the wider employment of women and against unauthorized quitting of employment, and recommended the introduction of a system of "voluntary bondage" —*samozakrepleniye*.

So-called "specialists" were forbidden to advertise for employment in the press. Students of universities and technical schools were assigned to their future positions a year before graduation and were compelled to serve for five years in the job assigned to them by the government agency. Government agencies were also empowered to transfer trained workers and specialists from one job to another wherever, in the opinion of the authorities, the workers in question were not being used in their optimum fields.

By a series of decrees the worker's freedom to leave his job was being systematically restricted, and a press campaign was initiated which advised workers to enter into long-term contracts. Since these measures did not prove fully successful, the government, in December, 1932, proceeded to introduce obligatory passports: now no one could move about in Russia without one. In every job, the management had to mark the dates of service in the passport. Thus increasing control over the workers was becoming possible. Another decree issued in 1932 ordered that workers dismissed for repeated failure to report for work were to be evicted from their apartments. The effect was considerable; an apartment was and is the main treasure of a worker's family. The Soviet press of the time was full of strange notices about engineers and technicians who had "deserted" their jobs; thus all other agencies were

1. "Jumpers" are workers and employees accused of frequently changing jobs in search of better conditions.

warned not to hire "deserters" who were looking for jobs with other state enterprises. Under the new conditions this was considered an unwarranted right.

"The Northern Caucasus *Sel'stroy* and the regional labor office declare engineers N. A. Timoshevski and A. N. Krashennikov to be malicious deserters from work and ask that they not be hired," one such advertisement read. Another stated: "During the compilation of the yearly report, the accountant-instructor, E. N. Shcherbakov, deserted and fled from Dubenski plant." Or: "Construction engineer Nicholas R. Bleze, chief architect of the Tashkent Project Office, not having returned from leave, is hereby declared to be a deserter." A fourth notice read: "Engineer Ivan N. Zhukov, student at the Leningrad Institute of Civil Engineering, had been under contract with *Lesbel* . . . He worked there only three weeks and fled." [2] These announcements were reminiscent of the times when Russian landlords pursued their fugitive serfs.

The Labor Department was now streamlined and working as a recruiting agency for industry. In this activity it had to draw on peasant labor, transferring huge numbers of workers from the land to the cities. The newly established collective farms were obliged to take part in these operations.

The kolkhozes are usually considered purely agricultural units. It is well known that by converting 20 million individual peasants into some 250,000 greater economic units the government tried to achieve regularity in the supply of agricultural produce for the cities and the army. It is less well known that the kolkhozes have had another task, too: that of recruiting manpower for industry. This was done by compulsion, by creating contingents of forced labor from them.

In 1931 the government ordered the punishment of agents of the People's Commissariat of Labor if they failed to fulfill their recruiting assignments. The larger kolkhozes were instructed to appoint special representatives for the recruitment of workers. The kolkhoz administration was made to sign con-

2. *Za Industrializatsiyu*, January 26, February 8 and 11, March 28, 1931.

tracts by the terms of which it was obligated to supply a designated number of men to the agents of the Labor Department. In February, 1930, the Central Executive Committee decreed that members of collectives could be sentenced to up to two years of "deprivation of liberty" for nonfulfillment of required work. The Chairman of the Council of People's Commissars of the Russian Soviet Republic reported, in October, 1930, that the GPU would "assist in the recruitment of labor for certain industrial needs." Likewise, the Council of People's Commissars of the Karelian Autonomous Republic decreed, in January, 1930, that force could be used to "compel obedience from peasants who did not report for forest work." Another Karelian agency instructed officials to "deny food supply to all able-bodied persons who refused to cut trees."

IN SEARCH OF LABOR

In a few branches of the economy the labor problem was a source of great concern, as, for example, in the building industries, which needed enormous labor forces when the industrialization program began, and the lumber industry, which had to supply material for both domestic construction and export.

In order to fulfill the economic plans, certain purchases had to be made abroad, especially of machines and equipment, without which the initial phase of industrialization was impossible. To pay for imports an increase in exports was necessary. Lumber and lumber products constituted the major item of Soviet export. Foreign loans were being granted on a small scale, and for short terms only; prompt payment was necessary since Soviet credit abroad had been shaken by the Russian repudiation of foreign loans in 1917 and had never been restored. Payment was possible only in goods, of which England and Germany were the main buyers. For this reason the government was exacting, as far as the lumber industry and forestry in the Russian north were concerned; a default in meeting contractual obligations might lead to financial catastrophe. But the supply of labor for Russia's lumber industry was insufficient; wages were too low to attract workers from other parts of Russia, and living conditions in the forests were miserable in the extreme.

Here again the government tried to achieve its goals by force. In February, 1930, a decree provided that local authorities could "sell the property of persons fined for failure to report for forest work."

A few weeks later a new order of the Department of Labor regulated the compulsory mobilization of labor for loading and unloading operations. "A refusal by the unemployed worker to undertake loading and unloading operations without valid reasons is to be considered as a refusal to perform work of any kind, with the consequences arising therefrom (removal of his name from the register, withdrawal of relief, etc.)." The GPU was ordered to help mobilize labor; peasants and collective farmers were "induced" to sign contracts for a season and obligate themselves not to leave their work before its completion; individual peasants and collective farmers often had to bring their horses with them. But despite all these strenuous efforts, the results were in many respects unsatisfactory. In 1930 serious failure appeared imminent and the situation became alarming. The northern lumber industry needed an additional 1,700,000 workers from other provinces and of these the kolkhozes were to provide 900,000. The government ordered that a plan for drafting manpower be prepared within 24 hours and that the prospective labor force reach its place of employment within a week. A few weeks later special commissions were appointed to screen industrial plant personnel and dispatch immediately to timber work all those whose political sympathies were questioned.[3]

Of the 900,000 men called for, no more than 50,000 were immediately recruited, and of this number only a part actually went to work in the forests.[4] The Commissariat of Agriculture ordered the utilization for forestry work of all per-

3. *Za Industrializatsiyu,* September 17, 1930, and *Trud,* December 6, 1930.
4. *Pravda,* January 10, 1931.

sons sentenced to the mild punishment of "forced labor without deprivation of liberty." This measure had almost no effect, since all of this group were needed at the jobs they were holding. On the whole, facts showed that the program of recruiting a labor supply remained unfulfilled.

In March, 1931, the Commissariat of Labor ordered the compulsory registration of all forestry specialists, who were then drafted to work in this capacity wherever ordered by the government.

The Central Committee of the Communist party had adopted a resolution on October 22, 1930, reprimanding the Commissariat of Labor for its "rightist deviations." Stalin saw criminal manifestations in the Commissariat's reluctance to introduce compulsory measures against all categories of labor, in its payment of relief benefits to the unemployed, and in its facilitation of changing employment. "The People's Commissariat for Labor has kept on the dole hundreds of thousands of unemployed to whom they have paid out tens of millions of rubles, failing to combat the fliers [workers frequently and systematically changing their employment] and malingerers. . . . The Central Committee of the All-Union Communist party regards these facts as an obvious manifestation of 'rightist opportunism.' "

This reprimand was not wholly deserved. The Labor Department had already begun the mobilization of labor, although not with the diabolic energy which Stalin demanded.

These were the circumstances in which the expansion of the system of convict and other forms of forced labor took place, the labor force involved being much better suited to the needs of the Five-Year Plans than were free workers. The great network of labor camps emerged as a function of industrialization and the Five-Year Plans.

The total labor force required in the northern lumber industry was 2 million at the season's peak.[5] After the most

5. According to the director of the Soviet Wood Agency, Gorski. Allan Pim and Edward Bateson, *Report on Russian Timber Camps*, p. 54.

strenuous efforts it attained about 1,300,000, but not until various groups of forced labor had been put to work.

The labor force consisted of four main groups:

1. Free workers and employees;
2. Peasants recruited forcibly, with the prospect of returning home at the end of the season;
3. Exiled peasants, deported to the northern regions, but living outside of prisons;
4. Inmates of corrective labor camps and prisons.

Only the first group was really voluntary labor; it was a small minority. But all the groups, though differing from one another in legal status, were paradoxically enough condemned to live at a common standard that was almost identical for all of them: the lowest possible level, a marginal minimum for all groups of forced labor.

"The food rations of free lumberjacks are worse than those of the prisoners," *Izvestia* wrote on February 25, 1930. Likewise their homes were sometimes worse than even the barracks of the prisoners, who were working alongside them. The huts of the free workers were so low that one could not walk upright inside. When at home, workers had to lie on straw and branches. A Soviet newspaper reported that these barracks "looked like animal lairs." [6]

An engineer who had left the Kholmogory lumbering project stated that "this is worse than anything man can imagine. This is worse than Uncle Tom's Cabin. On the Negro plantations, at least it was warm, the slaves did not suffer from frost, there was no such transformation of men into cattle, no such cruel hardship." [7] In the Archangel region, he reported, 950 men died within three days. There was one medical assistant for every 500 workers, one physician for every 5,000 workers. "No one (except a few experts at sorting wood) was paid anything," a fugitive reported. "My own impression is that the real reason for my arrest and for people of my type

6. *Ekonomicheskaya zhizn'* (Economic Life), July 29, 1928.
7. *Posledniya novosti* (The Latest News) (Paris), March 6, 1931.

having been arrested was that more labor was required for the purpose of pushing the Five-Year Plan."

"In Penuga, where the weaker were sent, conditions were very bad," another one revealed. "They were housed in a locomotive works, in which there were three tiers of bunks, all full up, and men died there every day. . . . The peasants who were mobilized were also living under very bad conditions, and were very little better off than the prisoners."

The camp prisoners, the investigators add, "included a proportion of men who, by reason of their antecedents or lack of stamina, were wholly unsuited for this type of labour. How many such men there may have been in 1930 we cannot say, but for them the conditions were inhuman and oppressive, though there is no evidence of organized brutality." [8]

RIGHTIST AND LEFTIST DEVIATIONS

On the political side, this experiment in accelerated industrialization, collectivization, and the introduction of a widespread system of forced labor was pressed as an issue against the Communist "rightist faction" which was opposed to the radical agrarian reforms and in general to the terrible strain on the people which the program entailed. The rightist opposition was the only Communist group that could have veered Russian policy to the path of gradual evolution of the Soviet regime toward democracy; this was precisely the reason why it was liquidated in the early 'thirties. Many former leaders were out of place now. They were now accused of too much liberalism in their teachings and writings, of reflecting a pro-bourgeois state of mind. Rykov, the Premier, had to resign and make way for Vyacheslav Molotov; Mikhail Tomski, the trade-union leader, was dismissed and replaced by Nikolai Shvernik, the present President of the Soviet Union. And Nikolai Bukharin, ideologist and leader of the Comintern,

8. Pim and Bateson, *Report on Russian Timber Camps* (London, 1931), pp. 80, 93, 132.

was relieved of all important jobs. The opposition of these men to the new trends was vigorous but of no avail, and it was actually for this opposition that they were later brought to trial and convicted. One of the offenses of the rightist faction was proclaimed to be their concern for "class enemies," kulaks, and others; as far as internal policies are concerned, these men were later accused of leniency toward enemies of Communism. Under the old Penal Code of 1924, for which they were made responsible, every prisoner, whether kulak, "wrecker," capitalist, Menshevik, or any other kind of "class enemy," was entitled to improving treatment in prison as the years of his sentence went by (this is the so-called "progressive treatment of prisoners"). The very hope of the "liberals" of converting a "class enemy" into a useful member of Soviet society was now declared to be anti-Communist.

This was not a purely academic discussion. As has so often been the case in Communist disputes, seemingly theoretical theses had a tremendous practical significance. Millions of "class enemies" were being exiled at the time, and their fate— wholesale starvation and probably death—was the issue. If a "class enemy" was able to develop into a loyal Soviet citizen, the cruel treatment of the deported masses of humanity was a crime. If, on the other hand, there was no hope for them, if they would forever remain carriers of counterrevolution, no pity was permissible, and they must be considered outcasts of society. At best they could be used for a short while as labor.

Shirvindt, one of the authors of the Penal Code of 1924, was "unmasked" and accused of rightist deviations. He tried publicly to oppose the trend toward what he called "rolling back to the old prisons." He aimed his arrows at Nikolai Krylenko, Commissar of Justice, who was adhering strictly to Stalin's party line and who now demanded the introduction of greater severity in the prisons. Shortly afterward it was stated that the Penal Code of 1924 "rolled down the tracks of bourgeois-liberal penal theory. . . . It unquestioningly took over the so-called progressive system from bourgeois penology and on its basis frequently equalized all those deprived of liberty, regardless of their class affiliation." In accordance with the "general line" laid down by the Politbureau, Krylenko's Commissariat of Justice reprimanded its prison administration (not the GPU, of course) for too much leniency for "class enemies." In a resolution dated May 13, 1933, it instructed "the Administration of Corrective Labor Institutions to effect a cardinal change in the work of corrective labor institutions so as to straighten out existing deviations of corrective labor policy and the class aspect in particular." [9]

The large volume edited by Andrei Vyshinski (*Ot Tyurem k vospitatel'nym uchrezhdeniyam* [From Prisons to Educational Institutions], [Moscow, 1934], p. 43) proclaimed Shirvindt a "rightist opportunist" because he had believed in the possibility of "correcting all men" and had "smuggled" this idea "into the code of 1924." Shirvindt himself managed to escape punishment but lost all his influence. He was made responsible for a trend that had actually been dominant in Communist ideology in Lenin's days and in the first years after Lenin's death.

To balance the drive against this "rightist deviation," the party authorities and the press often spoke of a "leftist trend" in regard to the "suppression of class enemies." Actually the leftist trend was a fiction. Moscow's insistent instructions to labor camps and prisons called for severe treatment of inmates, especially of so-called class enemies, among whom the kulaks constituted the major group. Local authorities were often over-anxious in their endeavor to carry out the instructions and to earn commendation from superiors. Soon reports began to reach Moscow of such atrocities in certain northern camps that even the heads of the GPU were shocked. Cruelty became a system. The death rate among prisoners reached unprecedented levels. In some instances, prisoners guilty of insubordination were stripped of their clothing, then guards poured water on them, and they were left standing in the cold for hours; unheated dungeons for the punishment of prisoners

9. Utevski, *Sovetskaya ispravitelno-trudovaya politika*, p. 35, and *Sovetskaya yustitsiya* (1933), No. 10.

in the winter time were deadly in their effect. Commissions went out from Moscow to the distant camps to investigate such reports and, despite the generally lenient attitude toward the commanding personnel of the camps, many camp commanders were removed and a few even executed.

Obviously these were instances of bestiality without any special political, anti-Stalinist, background. But they were made use of in the internal party struggle. They were proclaimed to be instances of "leftist deviation." Excessive cruelty toward "class enemies" in the camps was presented as the fruits of Trotskyism. The Council of People's Commissars, stated, on July 11, 1929:

Along with manifestations of rightist opportunism, "leftist" deviations have been observed, expressed in an oversimplified understanding of the class approach . . . in exaggerated production requirements for class-enemy elements, etc.

The permanent eradication of these deviations constitutes one of the fundamental tasks of corrective labor institutions, especially since the distortion of the class policy has in practice been fostered by rightist-opportunist trends in the theory of corrective labor.[10]

Of course, no connection whatsoever existed between Trotsky's faction and barbarism in the labor camps. Even after the removal and punishment of certain camp officials little change occurred in the treatment of prisoners and in the living conditions in the penal labor camps. The persecutions and the encitement to "severity" continued unabated until 1934.

THE SOCIAL LADDER

In these years a new class society emerged out of the revolutionary upheaval. It is no longer a capitalist society but it is just as far from the pattern of a classless community.

The division of society into classes is an abstract scheme, which necessarily disregards the fact that in reality each of the classes consists of most heterogeneous elements; hundreds of

10. Quoted in *Sovetskaya yustitsiya* (1932), No. 3.

thousands, even millions of men occupy intermediate positions between the well-defined boundaries of social classes. Actually social strata are not separated by solid walls of demarcation; on the contrary, they merge into one another imperceptibly.

This general maxim also applies to the two elements that make up the working class of Russia: free workers and forced labor. The scope of their economic rights is not uniform for all the free workers; certain jobs and industries afford considerable leeway, while laborers in other branches of the economy are greatly restricted and rather closely bound to the places of their employment—with all the consequences this entails.

The same differences, in turn, apply to the unfree labor force. It does not constitute a homogeneous social stratum. Conditions in the agricultural penal colonies would seem like paradise to the prison workers in coal mines and lumber camps. But even the latter are an unattainable hope for the thousands who must toil in the gold mines and certain other enterprises of the Far East or European north.

The social scale of the Russian working class reads, in descending order:

1. Workers free to change or relinquish their employment (at present a dwindling minority);

2. Workers obliged to stay at their jobs on terms prescribed by the authorities;

3. Workers recruited (mostly from the collective farms) and shipped away to perform certain tasks under conditions set by the authorities;

4. Exiles, special migrants, settlers, and similar groups;

5. Criminal offenders in corrective labor colonies and camps;

6. Political prisoners of corrective labor camps;

7. Prisoners of the punitive corrective labor camps.

X

Forced Labor and the Five-Year Plans

When the first Five-Year Plan became law, in 1928, it was considered natural and necessary that prison labor should be placed at the service of general industrialization. It was not anticipated, however, that it would attain any significant proportions in the over-all planning.

The first decree prescribing "a greater use of penal labor" appeared on March 26, 1928. The intention was "to bring about the realization of a series of economic projects with great savings in expenditures . . . by means of widespread use of labor of individuals sentenced to measures of social protection." [1] In July of the same year the Commissariat of Justice ordered the introduction of compulsory prison work for *all* able-bodied prisoners.[2] In January, 1929, the government let it be known that all persons and institutions failing to comply with these instructions would be punished.

The government took an unusual step when it ordered the reopening of a multitude of cases which had resulted in prison sentences of less than three years. It ordered "an appeal [by the prosecutors] of verdicts on the ground of excessive clemency wherever a class-alien element has been convicted for socially dangerous offenses." [3] At the same time a measure was adopted which has remained in force ever since: persons sentenced to more than three years must serve their terms in corrective labor camps. This decree, dated April 7, 1930, in

1. Official circular of the Central Executive Committee of the USSR, May 21, 1928.
2. An exception was made in the case of members of anti-Soviet parties and Communist factionists.
3. *Sovetskaya yustitsiya* (1930), No. 1, pp. 23–24.

its first paragraph specified two groups that were to be sent to these camps:

1. "Persons sentenced by a court to deprivation of liberty for not less than three years," and
2. "Persons sentenced by special decision of the OGPU." At the same time the authorities ceased publishing figures concerning the number of trials and convictions. After 1929 only percentages were published: those sentenced to forced labor constituted 14.3 per cent of convictions in 1926; 21.2 per cent in 1927; 48.1 per cent in 1929; 56 per cent in 1931; and 58 per cent in 1932.[4] On the other hand, sentences to prison terms dropped from 31 per cent in the first half of 1928 to 11 per cent in January–June, 1929.

This was the way the prison problem was to be solved. Most of the prison inmates were sent off to labor camps. It was no longer necessary to release prisoners prematurely because of overcrowding or to grant wholesale pardons. Parole commissions and the central Amnesty Commission ran out of work. The labor camps became "the basic and the numerically prevalent type of place of confinement. Special-purpose 'isolators' and transitional houses of corrective labor are being liquidated. Similarly the small places of confinement are being liquidated."[5]

The collectivization of farms was now in full swing. Thousands of kulaks were shipped to the northern and eastern labor camps, where the population increased rapidly. The number of the camps, too, increased and it soon became evident that they could well play a much more important role in the grand "socialist offensive" than had been anticipated. The number of peasants deported to labor camps and of members of their families shipped to remote villages was never announced. It was merely reported that "the kulaks have been liquidated as a class." The official statistics had listed 5,859,000 kulaks in 1928.

4. *Sovetskaya yustitsiya* (1930), No. 13; (1934), No. 2.
5. Shirvindt in *Sovetskaya yustitsiya* (1929), pp. 1087–1089.

In the fall of 1929 prison labor became a subject of economic planning. At a conference of higher prison officials in October of that year it was declared that

The Five-Year Plan . . . requires tasks involving a great demand for unskilled labor. Local conditions sometimes present serious obstacles to the recruitment of labor. It is here that the places of confinement, having at their disposal excess labor in great quantities and engaged in production near the places of confinement, can come to the assistance of those economic enterprises which experience a labor shortage.

The resolution adopted by the conference stated:

The Chiefs of the Administrative Districts of the Ural region, the Northern region, and the NKVD of Karelia must at an early date provide for the organization of timber collecting colonies, furnishing them with quarters, tools, clothing, etc.[6]

Not until 1930 did the planning agencies receive instructions to "incorporate the work performed by those deprived of liberty into the planned economy of the country and into the Five-Year Plan." From then on forced labor was a factor of growing importance in the over-all economic blueprints. Neither the authorities nor public opinion realized at the time how significant and how symptomatic was this action, which made forced labor a permanent and important branch of the "socialist economy" of the Soviet Union.

The GPU established a new department, the GULAG (Chief Administration of Camps), which has had a brilliant development and is still in existence as the central agency of the vast network of labor camps. Observing more discretion than the Commissariat of Justice and the other agencies, the GPU has never made public any data or reports concerning its economic activities and the personnel it employs. Gleb Boki, who administered the camps of the GPU in the late 'twenties, was succeeded by M. D. Berman as the Chief of the GULAG, and Semion Firin became Deputy Chief.

During the first Five-Year Plan the work performed in

6. *Sovetskaya yustitsiya* (1929), pp. 1087–1089.

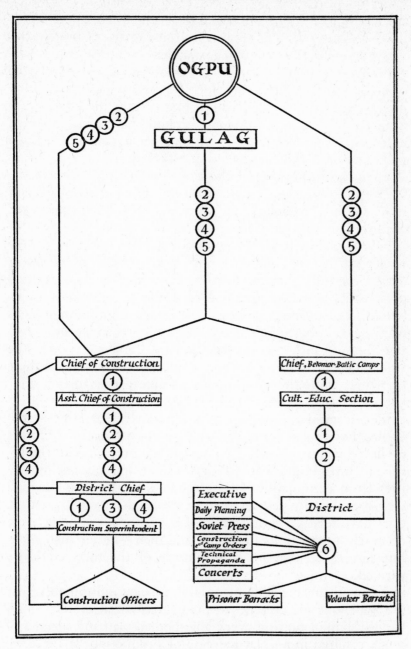

Organizational Structure of the GULAG.
(*After* Baltiisko-Belomorski Kanal, *Moscow, p. 118.*)

these camps did not always appear under either GPU or GULAG in the official reports. In these early years the GPU was often considered merely a provider of labor to Soviet economic enterprises. Usually contracts were between the economic agencies and the camp (or prison) administration. They were of a purely business-like nature: the labor camp was to deliver certain amounts of goods (or men) at fixed dates, and was to be paid in the manner agreed upon. Such contracts provided for "economic discipline" and served to assist in the fulfillment of the Five-Year Plans. Nor did the GPU proper engage in the sale of raw materials abroad; it remained in the background, formally fulfilling "contracts" with the government's economic agencies.

Side by side with men supplied by the prison camps, free men were at work. From reports and statistics it has never been clear just what proportion of the total was performed by free men and what part by forced labor. Hundreds of thousands of kulaks and "wreckers" were turned into lumberjacks by the GPU, but official production reports spoke simply of the "lumber industry and trusts" and "Soviet export," the value in rubles, and the number of persons employed in these branches, while the specific issue of free versus forced labor was passed over in silence.

The Commissariat of Justice was not as secretive as the GPU, though it too was reluctant to publish detailed reports on living conditions in its prisons and colonies and on the results of introducing compulsory labor. Some interesting figures from compilations of its agencies were released. Such data were usually restricted to "concealed statistics"; that is, they gave relative figures only—for example, the percentage of yearly fluctuations in output and men—rather than absolute figures, so that no clear picture of the facts could be formed.

From all the available material it appears indisputably that in the prisons and colonies of the Commissariat of Justice the rigid system of putting every able-bodied man and woman to work resulted in a great increase of production. If the contribution of prison labor to the Five-Year Plans is reckoned at 100 in 1930, its growth in the succeeding years may be put as follows:

1931	220
1932	335
1933	552 (as planned) [7]

Only once, in 1932, did the official organ of the Commissariat of Justice of the Russian Soviet Republic publish production figures for the first Five-Year Plan for forced labor institutions. The value of the work, in millions of rubles, was reported as follows:

	Industry	Agriculture	Mass Projects	Total
1930	50	3	9	62
1931	109	10	33	152
1932 (as planned)	193	19	93	305

To bring out the significance of these amounts, it may be worth mentioning that the aggregate value of the entire motor vehicle industry of the Soviet Union amounted to 92 million rubles in 1930 and 180 million in 1931. In the peat industry, another important branch of economy, the total output was valued at 83 million in 1930 and 135 million in 1931.

The above figures refer to the Russian Soviet Republic only. As for the Ukraine, the second largest republic of the Union, it was anticipated that the forced labor output would increase from the 1929 base of 100 to 176 in 1930 and 298 in 1931.

THE LABOR CAMPS IN THE FIRST FIVE-YEAR PLAN

The actual development of the network of labor camps started in 1930 with the reorganization of the Northern Camps of Special Designation. From the Solovetski Islands they spread back to the mainland and, in the course of a few years, expanded far to the east and south, infecting, like a growing cancer, new towns, provinces, and regions. In trac-

7. *Sovetskaya yustitsiya* (1932), No. 33; (1934) No. 2.

ing their history, we are using, in addition to the firsthand reports of inmates, almost exclusively official Soviet sources, which contain such an abundance of information that the picture of the expansion of the forced labor system during its first five-year period becomes clear.

At the same time that the agriculture, fisheries, and brickyards of the Solovki labor camps were being expanded, oil drilling and coal mining were begun in the Ukhta region with the aid of the near-by labor camps. At Khibinsk, phosphate was mined, and in Vorkuta, coal; on the island of Vaigach, lead and zinc; at the Yugor Strait, fluorite; and in Novaya Zemlya, lead. In his report of March, 1931, Molotov stated that prison labor was being employed in the construction of highways: Kem-Ukhta, Parandovo-Kikshozero, Syktyvkar-Ukhta, and Syktyvkar-Pinyug.

A new stage in the use of forced labor was marked by the construction of the great canal from the White Sea to the Baltic—the so-called "Belomor Canal named after Stalin."

The decision to build this canal had been taken in 1930. At the outset Stalin was the spur behind it. The strategic purpose was to connect the Arctic and Baltic Seas in order to enable the Baltic navy to reach the White Sea directly through Russian waterways. In case of war the Russian Navy in the Baltic would be sealed in by Germany, Denmark, and Sweden, or by England, but would be free to reach the oceans from the White Sea. For the first time, a project of this magnitude was entrusted not to an economic agency but to the GPU, and in particular to Henrikh Yagoda. At that time Yagoda was still "Deputy Chairman of the OGPU," but he was actually already in charge of the agency. Stalin had gained faith in the abilities of Yagoda and in the effectiveness of forced labor in 1929–30, when the GPU had demonstrated its efficiency in the lumber economy of the north.

In April, 1931, the GPU began to prepare blueprints for the canal, and in November construction was begun. The number of working prisoners, including engineers, reached almost 300,000 at its peak. On August 2, 1933, in the initial phase of the second Five-Year Plan, less than two years after the work was started, the canal was proclaimed completed and given the name of Stalin. Throughout the Soviet Union the opening was celebrated as a tremendous achievement. Seventy-two thousand prisoners were amnestied.

The majority, however, of those who had worked on the Belomor Canal were transferred, as soon as it was completed, either to the Baikal–Amur Railroad construction project in the Far East, or to the Moscow–Volga Canal. This was a great disappointment to the prisoners, who had expected, on the basis of promises made to them, actual liberation as a reward for their good work. The disappointment caused a good deal of trouble, scores of prisoners mutilated themselves; others tried to resist transfer. But resistance was obviously futile.

Next to Stalin himself, it was Henrikh Yagoda who was most loudly acclaimed in the Soviet press. The preface to a volume describing the new canal was written by Maxim Gorky, who stated that the only shortcoming of the book consisted in the insufficient attention devoted to the merits of Yagoda. Two years later Gorky was dead, and two years after that Yagoda was tried and found guilty of having poisoned him!

Yagoda's subordinates and psalmodists praised their chief fanatically. The tendency to servile flattery had already affected many among Soviet personnel and "independent" writers, and Stalin was not the only object of it. Under Soviet conditions, one who has power over life and death arouses vociferous, if sometimes hypocritical, adoration. The paeans described Yagoda's inexhaustible energy, his selfless devotion, his incessant care for the well-being of the inmates of the Belomor labor camps, his interest in every detail of the work and his daily reminders "to be attentive to the human being."

The Belomor Canal was in operation until the war with Germany broke out. It was damaged by the German air force during the war, and was not repaired and put back into opera-

tion until 1946. It has never been of great strategic significance.

Other large projects were begun at the same time, with the
aid of forced labor, in the Karaganda (Uzbekistan) region in
a newly developed coal center where, in addition to mining,
the construction of buildings for housing and offices was being pushed. In the Leningrad region work on waterways at
the River Svir was begun which took years to complete. In
the same region troops of prison laborers were made to store
firewood in the forests for use in the city of Leningrad. New
railroads were started—from Soroka to Kotlas in the north,
and the Syzran–Kungur line on the Volga; the eastern link of
the Turkestan–Siberian Railroad was completed. The construction of the great city of Magnitogorsk, the new center
of the iron and steel industry beyond the Urals, was initiated.
The project took several years, and forced labor played a
prominent part, particularly in the early stages. In and around
Stalingrad the prisoners were busy building major plants, such
as "Red October" and "The Barricade."

In addition to these huge projects, a multitude of minor
works was carried out by prison labor, according to official
sources. Only a small part of them can be listed here. In
Kamenskaya, in the Donbas, a blast furnace and an open-
hearth were built by forced labor. The prison in Atkarsk sent
its "brigades" to speed harvesting. In the Mozhaisk area grain
deliveries to the state's collecting centers had stopped because
of a fallen bridge. Prisoners were immediately dispatched, and
soon "the kolkhozes' red trains of carts were crossing the
bridge." Similar "brigades" worked at Berezniki, Balakhna,
Kosogor, Stalinogorsk, Bobriki, and other points. "One could
cite *thousands* [8] of similar examples," the official publication
of the Commissariat of Justice reported.

These enterprises and construction projects account for
only a part of the forced labor used during the first Five-Year

8. Italics ours.

Plan. The most important assignment of this labor, rating higher than any of the listed projects, was lumbering, which was not confined to any limited area but extended over the whole north and east of Russia. This is described in a subsequent chapter. At the start of the second Five-Year Plan millions of men were busy in lumbering.

THE LABOR CAMPS IN THE SECOND FIVE-YEAR PLAN

At the Seventeenth Congress of the Communist party, Molotov and Kuibyshev had reported that great waterway projects were included in the new plan: the 80-mile Moscow–Volga Canal; the 63-mile Volga–Don Canal; reconstruction of the Mariinsk Canal system and of the Moskva River system; the creation of through-navigation on the Dnieper; damming of the Sozh River; improvement of the middle course of the Volga; and, last but not least, the completion of the Belomor Canal. Of these waterworks the Moscow–Volga Canal received the most publicity. Construction lasted from 1932 to 1937, and it was not until July 4, 1937, that the Soviet of People's Commissars announced that it was finished, expressing "gratitude to the NKVD and the builders of the canal." The freeing of 55,000 prisoners before the expiration of their terms was announced.

At Magnitogorsk construction continued. In Kuznetsk, coal mining was growing in importance; enormous labor camps of the Siblag, in which living conditions were exceptionally bad, surrounded the region.[9] In Millerovo (Donbas) large-scale chalk and stone quarries were operated by prison labor. "Hundreds of thousands of cubic meters of construction materials have already been taken from there. At the foot of one mountain, five huge furnaces have raised their 11-meter chimneys into the sky. Production expands and engulfs more

9. "When we arrived," Feldheim reports in his memoirs, "the barracks veterans met us and encouragingly informed us that no one would stand it for more than three to four months, and if he managed to survive, he would be sent away for a 'rest.'" *Sovremennyye zapiski* (Paris, 1939), LXVIII, 413.

and more territory. Like mushrooms after the rain, units, houses, mess halls, services spring up." [10] Peat was cut around Moscow. Hydroelectric works which had been begun on the Svir River and at Shatury were continued. Potash was produced at Bereznikov.

A great new span across the Volga was built at Gorky (formerly Nizhni-Novgorod), where "the best prisoner brigades worked relentlessly under hard winter conditions, in a number of instances outdoing the shock-troop brigades of free workers." Chemical plants were built by prison labor on the Berezina and at Vishera.

While work in the forests of the north continued as before, two large new projects were begun: the laying of a new track on the Trans-Siberian Railroad, and the start of a new northern Baikal–Amur line in the Far East (where the international situation was menacing); as many as 400,000 laborers were reported busy on these great projects.

In 1933 gold mining was begun at the recently discovered mines along the Kolyma River. Within a few years the mines developed into an important industry, extending over a wide territory in Siberia. The number of labor camps in the Kolyma region was constantly growing. Hundreds of thousands of men were shipped to these new districts, and soon, with the use of the ports, ships, and aviation of the NKVD, the area of the Dalstroy, with its capital at Magadan, developed into an enterprise of prime importance to Soviet domestic and international policy.

10. *Sovetskaya yustitsiya* (1934), No. 2.

XI

World-Wide Resentment and Soviet Reply

The fact that the first great labor camps were situated in the far north and on the White Sea seemed to afford assurance that news of them would not spread and that complete secrecy about conditions of forced labor could be observed. The authorities were preoccupied with endless problems—collectivization, the growing famine, the factional struggle within the party—and nothing was done to prepare public opinion in Russia or abroad for the innovation which the GPU had in store. The so-called "foreign observers"—diplomats and journalists—although aware of all the decrees and pronouncements concerning recruitment of labor and extension of prison labor, had failed to realize the full scope of the reforms and their fateful significance.

What the authorities had not foreseen were the numerous escapes from the labor camps during the first years of their existence. True, escape entailed the greatest dangers, and the chances of success and survival were slight. The prisoners were closely guarded and shot if caught in an attempt to get away. The neighboring peasants were promised rewards in the form of grain for every fugitive captured (five poods [1] of grain, for instance, if he were caught alive, three poods if dead)—and in those years of famine, grain was life. All passengers on railroads had to present identifying documents to the police. Finally, the very appearance of the prisoners was bound to arouse suspicion as soon as they reached a town.

Still more difficult—next to impossible—was escape abroad. The only possibilities were by land to Finland or by ship from

1. A pood is about 36 pounds.

the White Sea. The northern way to Finland led through almost impassable and uninhabited forests. Neither carts nor horses nor railways went in this direction. There were no roads in the north, food was unobtainable, and it took weeks of strenuous walking, with all the dangers involved, to cross the hundreds of miles that separated the camps from the Finnish border. The foreign ships loading at Archangel and other ports on the White Sea were closely watched, their captains were instructed to beware of conflict with Soviet authorities, and many a prisoner who was caught hiding among the logs and lumber aboard a ship was turned over to the GPU.

In spite of the obstacles, attempts to escape occurred repeatedly, and a number of prisoners actually escaped. Living conditions in the camps were such that no risk was enough to stop the stream of desperate flights. It was generally recognized that a man sentenced to five, eight, or ten years had small chance of surviving, and that an attempt at escape was worth while. How many men actually did get away and regain their freedom inside Russia or abroad will never be known. Many are certainly living under assumed names, carrying false documents, never betraying their past to their friends and families. These constitute, however, but a small minority of those who tried, the great majority of whom were doomed to perish.

Only a few succeeded in reaching foreign shores. When the first stowaways got to England and Scandinavia in 1930 and told of their lives and their escapes, their tales created a certain stir. But the world was not prepared to believe that the Soviet Government was capable of resorting to an institution diametrically opposed to its professed principles. At that time the gulf between Russia and the West was not so deep as it is today. The reports of the fugitives seemed incredible at first.

But their numbers multiplied, and their testimony, given independently, led to a serious change of attitude outside of Russia. In the summer of 1930 slave labor in Russia became, and remained for a couple of years, a subject of heated discussion in legislatures, in the press, and in public debate abroad.

The *Stockholm Tidningen* reported in April, 1930, that 15,000 peasants from near-by Ingermanland in Soviet Karelia had been sent to work in the forests of northern Russia. In July, 1930, British Foreign Secretary Arthur Henderson stated in the House of Commons that Soviet laws empowered the authorities to employ compulsory labor. Numerous reports of fugitives were published in the English press and one book after another appeared offering the public authentic testimony and firsthand reports.

The Anti-Slavery Society in England instituted an inquiry, and the fact that such an organization felt impelled to investigate Soviet conditions was a severe blow to Russia's prestige. Allan Pim and Edward Bateson conducted the investigation in a careful and objective manner. They not only quoted statements of refugees but evaluated these statements critically. They reached the conclusion that in the lumber camps of northern Russia six different kinds of labor were being employed, ranging from completely free workers to "those convicted by the GPU" and "prisoners sentenced to terms of more than three years." Commander Carlyon Bellairs, M.P., published sworn statements of escaped prisoners concerning overcrowded conditions in the camps, the situation of children, daily deaths from exposure and freezing, about 19,000 deaths from typhus on Solovetski Island within one year.

In France the *Revue Hebdomadaire* printed an article by Senator Frédéric Eccard, who quoted the testimony of priests and officers, refugees from Russia's north, and mentioned the slavery investigation of the League of Nations in Liberia. This was another degrading comparison of Russian conditions with those of the most backward parts of the world.

In the United States the first reports on forced labor in Russian lumber camps coincided with the arrival of Russian lumber and manganese and matches. The deep impression created by the news led not only to a vigorous debate in the press but also to government action. Section 1307 of the new Tariff Act of 1930, which was essentially taken over from the Tariff Act of 1922, prescribed that

All goods . . . mined, produced, or manufactured . . . by convict labor or / and forced labor . . . shall not be entitled to entry at any of the ports of the United States . . .

"Forced labor" . . . shall mean all work or service which is exacted from any person under the menace of any penalty for its nonperformance and for which the worker does not offer himself voluntarily.

On the basis of this act the United States Treasury Department imposed an embargo on Soviet pulpwood and matches. The reports on which the Treasury founded its action were published in part in the press; they were mostly collected from Soviet refugees and from Scandinavian sailors whose ships had visited the White Sea. For example:

The vessel was loaded by convicts and political prisoners, who were marched down under guard to the steamer every day. The loading pier was within an area enclosed by high wire fences. . . . The chances of escape were very remote. . . . The prisoners were poorly clothed, mainly in rags, evidently the clothing they had at the time of their arrest. They used canvas on their hands and feet. The meals served to the prisoners consisted of black bread and warm water. Women were not employed in loading ships, but they were employed in unloading carloads of pulpwood in the yard. Three prisoners caught stealing bread from another steamer were immediately shot without trial.[2]

In February, 1931, conditions in Russia were discussed before the Ways and Means Committee of the House of Representatives. A number of statements were made on forced labor by American engineers who had returned from Russia, as well as by members of Congress. Among the testimonies presented was a detailed report by Dr. Arthur Kopman, who had spent eight years in Russia, three of them in prisons and labor camps. He described living and working conditions in the Vishera lumber camp, where he had cut wood for nine

2. *New York Times*, July 26, 1930.

months before becoming prison doctor in a hospital organized by himself.[3]

The American Wage Earners' Conference, led by Matthew Woll, of the American Federation of Labor, began a nation-wide campaign in favor of stern measures against Soviet imports into the United States. While Woll's group, as well as some other organizations, were moved by purely humanitarian considerations, certain commercial interests complicated this movement by injecting private pecuniary and trade interests. This was the case both in the United States and Britain. Asbestos companies, manganese firms, certain boards of trade, raised their voices in favor of a complete embargo on Soviet imports, while at the other end certain paper companies and mills interested in Soviet goods opposed the embargo movement. Shipping interests demanded free trade and opposed all forms of embargo. Senator Burton K. Wheeler likewise demanded abolition of impediments to Soviet-American trade. In London, the MacDonald government, although adverse to an embargo on Soviet imports, had to listen to insistent Canadian demands; to Canada Soviet lumber exports represented a vital threat of competition.

This injection of economic and profit motives into a worldwide campaign in which the driving force was the resentment of free men against slavery poisoned the movement and doomed it to failure. Commercial interests rivaled one another, and it was easy for the Soviet Government and its agencies abroad to present the whole "antidumping" campaign as a tool in the hands of certain capitalist circles. It was this consideration that made it impossible for the British Labour party to take a definite stand, while the Conservatives—at that time strongly anti-Russian—called for stern and immediate meas-

3. "One of the members of the Committee," Dr. Kopman concluded his statement, "wanted to know as to who was paying my expenses to come here and to testify before the Committee. I want to assure you, gentlemen, that if you held your hearings in San Francisco and I had to walk there to testify I would certainly not hesitate to do so. I was waiting for over a year for the opportunity to come before the American people and to tell them of what I have seen in Soviet Russia."

ures against free trade with Russia. Winston Churchill urged
a ban on Soviet products, while Prime Minister MacDonald
and Foreign Secretary Henderson were reluctant, and the
Labour press opposed all concrete measures. On April 28,
1931, the House of Commons rejected a proposal for the ex-
clusion of products of forced labor from Britain.

The embargo placed by the United States Treasury on July
25, 1930, on Soviet goods that arrived at that time was not sup-
ported by the State Department, and, after a week of delibera-
tions, it was lifted, never to be reintroduced.

This campaign in favor of an embargo on Soviet products
was the first in a series of similar failures to intervene in the
affairs of a strong dictatorial government by means of international trade. A few years later the League of Nations tried
to stop Mussolini's war against Ethiopia by an appeal to all its
members to prevent the shipment of oil to Italy. This had no
effect on Italian policy. Some time later, many groups in many
countries urged a boycott of German and Japanese goods.
They did not succeed, either.

MOLOTOV, THE YOUNG PREMIER

Just as this international movement was hitting its peak,
Aleksei Rykov, Premier of the Soviet Union, was "purged"
and Vyacheslav M. Molotov, unknown abroad and little
known within Russia, was appointed to succeed him. One of
his first tasks was to counteract the campaign and calm the
rising wave of indignation abroad.

Molotov was not the highest leader of Russia; he shone by
reflected light. But it was, of course, his—not Stalin's—task
to make speeches and issue instructions to fight the embargo
movement which for a while seemed seriously to endanger
Soviet foreign trade. In dealing with the problem of forced
labor, the young Premier developed certain abilities which
were eventually to make him a statesman of world-wide fame.
He never liked to use a petty lie which would convince no one
and leave everyone doubting; if a false statement had to be

made, let it be huge and impressive. Only a stupendous lie can
be effective—so Hitler later taught his pupils. Molotov knew
it before Hitler. His detailed statement on Soviet labor camps
was based on an assertion that belongs on the gravestone of
the present Foreign Minister of the Soviet Union: "Many an
unemployed worker of the capitalist countries will envy the
living and working conditions of the prisoners in our northern
regions." [4] He proceeded to paint an idyll of human life in the
prison camps: "Sufficient supplies," "an eight-hour working
day," "guaranteed rations," and even "from 20 to 30 rubles
cash each month." Magazines and books were at the disposal of
the inmates. A labor camp, Molotov alleged, was just a settlement where the workers move about freely. And, he added
slyly, please compare these excellent living conditions with the
real slavery that exists in capitalist society. The wage system
abroad is slavery, while the political power in Russia is in the
hands of the working class.

Molotov did not deny that great projects employing slave
labor were under way:

The labor of those deprived of liberty who are healthy and capable of working is being used by us on certain communal and
highway tasks. We did this before, we are doing it now, and we
shall continue to do so. This is profitable for society. This is beneficial for the culprits, for it teaches them how to work and makes
them useful members of society. . . .

These mass projects employing those deprived of liberty are
organized for a variety of different objectives: for highway construction, in particular on railroads, in the construction industry,
in peat exploitation, in charcoal burning for metallurgical plants,
in wood-storing works, in phosphorite mining, stone quarries,
gravel and stone crushing, on transportation projects, etc.

So far as export goods were concerned, Molotov said, with
an eye on international trade, that nothing produced by prison
labor was being exported:

4. Speech of March 8, 1931, at the Sixth Congress of Soviets.

1,134,000 men are working on forest work this season; they all work under conditions usual for free labor, and the labor of prisoners has no connection whatsoever with wood storing.

He proceeded to describe the wide scope of projects carried out by prisoners, omitting, however, lumberjacks and stevedores. The list was in itself quite impressive. He mentioned the Kem-Ukhta Highway (208 km.), the Parandovo-Kikshozero Highway (190 km.), the Syktyvkar-Ukhta Highway (313 km.), the Syktyvkar-Pinyug Highway (305 km.), and the White Sea–Baltic Sea Canal (914 km.).

Molotov concluded his statement with an invitation to foreign correspondents to ascertain that "work on *export goods* has no connection with the work of prisoners." He also invited foreign workers to send delegations to Russia in order to ascertain the true state of affairs in the Northern Camps.

This proposal was in line with the general trend of those days to have as many delegations as possible visit the Soviet Union for a short time, a practice which in a number of instances yielded favorable results since the foreign delegates were even less able to investigate and comprehend the situation than were the famous foreign correspondents of later years. These "workers' and trade-union delegations" were guided around and granted interviews by the highest Soviet officials; a few pro-Soviet members could be found in every delegation. Thus any attempt at a critical study of Soviet conditions was made impossible both from within the delegation and from without.

Molotov's statement was obviously the result of careful deliberation and painstaking preparation on the highest party levels. There was a risk, even a probability, that some trade-union group would take up his offer and that a few weeks later foreign commissions would be traveling about the northern forests. Immediate measures were therefore taken to erase most traces of prison work. A few weeks before Molotov's speech, frantic activity began in the administrative offices of the labor camps, as rumors spread that "an American commission will arrive" or "Maxim Gorky is on his way," or "George Bernard Shaw and some Britishers will visit" the Russian camps.

These developments were later reported by various escaped prisoners, writing independently and without knowledge of each others' reports. They gave similar descriptions of what went on in a number of camps. Professor Tchernavin, for example, relates that from 1930 on measures were taken to conceal the nature of the work performed in the forests. "Sometimes we were driven out to load logs on small hand cars," but "other men moved them down to the wharf and stowed the lumber aboard foreign ships. This procedure had been in effect since the beginning of the campaign abroad against the use of convict labor in the lumber business. The prisoners were kept out of sight of foreigners . . ." And then, suddenly, lumber camp workers were hurriedly withdrawn in anticipation of the

arrival of an "American" Commission which was going to investigate whether forced labor camps actually existed.

In preparation for this visit all lumber camps were liquidated in a few days, the prisoners' barracks leveled to the ground and the prisoners themselves herded back to the distribution points. . . . A special messenger on horseback came riding swiftly to distant camps in the midst of the wild forest, delivered his message to the chief and galloped away to the next camp. Orders followed to stop work, to pull down the barracks, to tear down everything which could be destroyed. Special attention was given to the wrecking of punitive cells, guard towers, and barbed-wire fences. In barracks built of logs, which were hard to destroy at short notice, all inscriptions made by prisoners, all notices, orders and placards were scraped off or removed. Everything that could be burned was set on fire. A special agent of the GPU made a tour of inspection to ascertain that no sign was left which might indicate that prisoners, and not free lumbermen, had been at work there. Then, whether day or night, prisoners were driven out of the woods to the railroad. The rush and panic was such that many believed war had been declared and that all were being removed further from the border.

If a train appeared in the distance while the large crowds of prisoners were being driven along the railroad tracks, they were made to lie down in the swamp, in the snow, and remain hidden until the train had passed; the GPU was afraid that somebody might see them from the car windows.

After this retreat the prisoners were dispersed among the various distributing points, where they languished on meager rations.[5]

Another author, Nikonov-Smorodin, reported that in February, 1931, "the camps began to be cleared of prisoners in the most urgent manner." Within 21 hours all guard towers were removed: G. B. Shaw was expected.[6]

The most vivid picture of the tragic consequences of Molotov's offer is given by George Kitchin, a Finnish citizen who returned to his country after spending many years in Soviet labor camps. He worked as a clerk in the office of a camp in which he was "detained," and hence was aware of all the happenings. One day, he writes, the officials of camp were called to an extraordinary meeting, at which it was suggested by the chief that a resolution be adopted stating that "the prisoners were satisfied with living conditions, liked their food, were well treated, and were eager to give all their strength to their country so that it might successfully complete the Five-Year Plan." The resolution was of course unanimously adopted.

A week after the meeting had taken place . . . a secret code telegram was received from the head-office in Moscow instructing us to liquidate our camp completely in three days, and to do it in such a manner that not a trace should remain. . . .

A veritable panic ensued. The usual Bolshevik methods were employed for the liquidation. After a short conference in Sienkevicz's office, telegrams were sent to all work posts to stop operations within twenty-four hours, to gather the prisoners at evacuation centers, to efface all external marks of the penal camps, such as barbed-wire enclosures, watch-turrets and signboards; for all officials to dress in civilian clothes, to disarm the guards, and to wait for further instructions.

In reply to these instructions, many telegrams were received stating that it was impossible to execute the orders in so short a

5. Tchernavin, *I Speak for the Silent*, pp. 251–253.
6. Nikonov-Smorodin, *Krasnaya katorga*, p. 274.

time, that there were not enough horses to effect the evacuation, that the sick would have to be left in the forest, etc. Sienkevicz answered that whoever failed to execute his orders within the stipulated time would be shot.

Pandemonium broke loose. At the Kotlas Transfer Station the double barbed-wire enclosure was speedily removed, the shop equipment was packed. The crowded barracks were filled to overflowing by the influx of prisoners evacuated from the Uftug forests. At Solvychegodsk Karjalainen, the Finnish carpenter who had recently been appointed commander there, exhibited wild energy, the result of a triple ration of alcohol. He ran into the toy-making shop, which was manned by invalids, remonstrating at the slowness of packing there, shooting at the ceiling and yelling so loud that the scared invalids took to their heels and ran out of the building.

"I'll kill you," yelled Karjalainen at the superintendent of the shop, waving his revolver. "I'll kill you if you don't have everything packed in an hour."

From all sides the forest-workers were marching in groups to Solvychegodsk. They carried government equipment in addition to their own belongings. Those seriously ill were crowded on teamsters' sleds, the sick who could still walk followed in the rear. Some of the sick died en route and were buried in the forest.

The situation at Archangel was even worse. The evacuation of the thirty thousand prisoners working there required eight hundred railway cars. None was available and the prisoners were loaded on old discarded freight and flat cars. Trains picked up groups of prisoners at the stations to which they had been forced to march from their remote outposts. While waiting for the trains, they spent several nights in the forest, hungry and freezing. Prisoners suffering from fever, scurvy, or tuberculosis formed no exception, and endured the same privations. Many men died during the mad rush of the evacuation. There were also many attempts to escape, but the cordon of guards had not yet been lifted and most of the fugitives were caught.

In order to show his zeal and to merit praise by his superiors, Okunev, the commander of the Archangel camp, peremptorily ordered all prisoners to leave the barracks, removed the barbed-wire enclosure, reversed the signboards and painted new names on them, calling the old penal camp buildings schools, clubs, restrooms, etc. His ingenious plan cost the lives of many prisoners. They spent many days in the open waiting for cars near the railway station and suffered great privations.

At the end of the year, it was learned that the evacuation of Archangel and Uftug cost thirteen hundred and seventy lives.[7]

The well-organized deception was completed a short time before Molotov made public his offer to workers abroad. Idyllic, peaceful work seemed to reign where only a week before a katorga had stood.

The Kotlas Transfer Station was transfigured. The harsh-looking barbed-wire fence had disappeared, the old sign over the gates was replaced by a new one, telling the visitor that he is approaching the dormitories of "Severoles" [state lumber agency] workers. The new sign on the warehouses designated them as "Warehouses of the Penug-Syktyvkar Railroad under Construction"; to all telephone calls the Transfer Station's office responded: "Railroad construction office talking."

A telegram was received from Archangel stating that the evacuation had been completed on time as ordered and that no outward sign of a penal camp remained. The transformation was thorough and complete both at Kotlas and at Archangel. A commission of foreign investigators could now be freely admitted. In exactly the same manner the evacuation was carried out at the Solovetsky camp, both on the islands and on the mainland. . . .

During the evacuation of the Kotlas hospital, three of the typhus patients who had recently had fresh charges of anti-Soviet agitation in the penal camps brought against them, were dragged out into the nearby forests and there Nazarov, chief of the secret intelligence department, personally shot them. They were immediately buried in a pit which was dug at the place of execution.

The way was now ready for Molotov's statement about the enviable life of Soviet prisoners.

THE BATTLE OF THE PRESS

The efforts of the Soviet Government to refute the facts which had become known abroad were not made solely in

7. G. Kitchin, *Prisoner of the OGPU*, pp. 267-270. Italics ours.

connection with the northern labor camps. A group of Americans working in Russia were induced to sign a statement, published in the *Moscow News* (an English-language paper), asserting that there was no forced labor in the Soviet Union. It was presented under the caption, "Unsolicited Statement from American Specialists." How this statement was concocted was later revealed by Mrs. Eve G. Grady, wife of an American engineer who worked for some time in Kharkov. American consultants of Soviet coal trusts

received an invitation . . . in February of 1931, to sign a statement which had been prepared for their signature to the effect that "there is no forced labor in Soviet Russia!" . . .

To the best of my belief, to a man, the American mining fraternity brusquely refused to sign, saying that their presence in Russia was for business reasons only and they did not care to become involved in the country's politics. . . .

Of course it is common knowledge on the part of all of the Americans who are employed by the Soviet Coal Trusts that for the past two years this very type of subversive prison labor has been going on. Russian engineers who work side by side with Americans day after day, mysteriously disappear, one by one.[8]

In the meantime the battle abroad was proceeding on both the diplomatic and public opinion levels. Danishevski, president of the Soviet lumber export agency, sent a message, similar in content to Molotov's, that "not one unit of timber exported from the Soviet Union is produced by forced labor." The vice-president of the Archangel Soviet imitated Molotov, picturing the attitude toward deported kulaks in the rosiest colors: "The State is aiding them to build homes and create villages, where they can hunt, fish, farm or do whatever they please. The government is giving them land, lumber and building material . . . food . . . clothing . . . postal services."[9] He did not deny that the stevedores working in Archangel—some 23,000 men—were "imported" from the Volga region. But Trofim Karnashov, vice-president of the

8. E. G. Grady, *Seeing Red* (Brady, Warren & Putnam, 1931), pp. 51, 53-54.
9. *New York Times*, March 29, 1931.

Soviet timber trust, Severoles, was more honest than his colleagues. He plainly stated: "The exile system is as old as Russia." [10]

Maxim Litvinov, the Foreign Commissar, invited the British Ambassador to call on him and, no doubt on instructions from the Kremlin, informed him that "neither prison labor nor labor of sentenced persons in general is employed in the branches of the timber industry which produce for export, including the work at ports." In Britain it was immediately noted that while it was impossible for the outer world to differentiate between lumber production for domestic needs and for export, "work at ports," i.e., loading, was continually being performed by prisoners, and hundreds of British and Scandinavian sailors bore witness that Litvinov's statement was contrary to fact.

The *British-Russian Gazette*, an organ favorable to the Soviet Government, published a little book containing statements by Soviet officials and pro-Soviet engineers and trade-union representatives. By a strange misunderstanding, a detailed report by J. F. Stuart, consulting forest engineer, describing his extensive travels in Russia on behalf of British lumber companies, was included. Brushing aside many false reports, he stated that "no outsider has been permitted into these camps except myself." There is no bedding, he reported; "conditions are appalling in the lumber camps; food is scarce; thousands are dying from hunger, hard work, and exposure."

The net result of the controversy, which lasted for almost two years, was twofold: as far as trade was concerned, the Soviet Government won, and all attempts to impose an embargo on forced labor products ended in failure. As far as public opinion was concerned, the fact was nevertheless established for honest students of Soviet Russia that forced labor was being employed there on a large scale, and that this institution added a new feature to the enigmatic physiognomy of the Soviet Union.

10. *New York Times, ibid.*

XII

Forced Labor in Operation

The combination of obsolete liberal ideas and a harsh domestic policy created a strange amalgam rich in hypocrisy and cant. Until 1935 the exaltation of labor as the great corrective of human vice was still in evidence, and the system of forced labor was officially hailed as an outstanding achievement of Soviet society, a source of pride when compared with the capitalist world, its prisons and its cruelty. At the same time, however, Soviet prisons, and especially the newly established corrective labor camps and settlements, were swallowing up millions of human beings and subjecting them to living conditions which verged on bare subsistence or even less. As we have seen, the government did not aim in reality to ameliorate the fate of "class enemies"—kulaks, bourgeois, and intellectuals—in its places of detention; courts were prodded into sentencing defendants to labor camps instead of to milder forms of punishment. The official ideology, however, remained the same—humanitarian and liberal.

"Workers' delegations" were invited to visit Russia, individual students came and went, prominent persons, Russian and foreign alike, dealt with the burning question of Russian prisons. Among these Maxim Gorky exerted the greatest influence, and his utterances were everywhere listened to attentively. In Germany, Hitler came to power during this period, and the concentration camps he created were both the object of Soviet anti-Nazi propaganda and one more reason for picturing a Soviet regime in the most liberal colors. "Concentration camps," wrote the *Great Soviet Encyclopedia*, "are special places of confinement, created by the Fascist governments in Germany, Poland, Austria, and other countries. Fascism, a regime of barbarism and popular enslavement, continually increases the mass of prisoners, which it is unable to crowd into the usual prisons." Likewise the *Political Dictionary* (Moscow, 1940) asserted that "concentration camps exist in many capitalist countries."

While these official sources asserted that only in "Fascist countries" do concentration camps exist, the *Small Soviet Encyclopedia* frankly stated that the former Solovetski Monastery, which under the tsars had "served as a place of ecclesiastic and political deportation, is today a [Soviet] concentration camp." It was also hypocritical to say that "in the capitalist prisons with their compulsory labor the inmates became disenfranchised slaves." And People's Commissar Nikolai Krylenko still insisted—although certainly no longer believing his own words—that "the fulfillment of court sentences must assure the re-education of the laborers." [1]

"Re-education" of the prisoners was a far cry from the truth, since every responsible writer and speaker was well aware of the real state of affairs in the prison camps. Only 12 to 15 per cent of the inmates were common criminals sentenced for burglary, theft, murder, and other misdeeds recognized as crimes throughout the world. The great majority— at least 85 per cent—now comprised essentially honest men, sometimes men of outstanding moral integrity. What the labor camps often did achieve was not the moral improvement of the criminals but a striking degradation of the moral character of thousands of others, forced into close association and collaboration with the scum of the criminal world. Not moral regeneration but a new potential of criminality was the real consequence of the operation of this new institution.

Actually the one and only aim that inspired the authorities was maximum production. With the start of the Five-Year Plans everything was forgotten except economic goals. Corrective labor camps were not institutions to improve men but to increase output. What the "re-education" that the authorities spoke of actually implied was later admitted quite

1. *Sovetskaya yustitsiya* (1933), No. 7.

frankly: "In the 'twenties it had meant culture and enlightenment. In the 'thirties it meant labor." [2]

Whether or not the human character of the prisoners improved no longer mattered. It was only for the benefit of the
credulous that the propaganda machine still insisted on the
miraculous "regeneration of man." A few Soviet writers, invited to eulogize the forced labor system, produced immortal
specimens of hypocrisy. I. L. Averbakh, for example, found
that as early as a few months after the prisoners' delivery to
the camps, "You could not recognize the men. . . . A fever
of industrial activity; they begin to operate and manage thrift-
ily; they go in for cultural achievements."

"To reforge" and "reforging" became the most widely used
terms for this hypocritical front of "re-education." In the
yards of the labor camps which the tired prisoners in their
ragged clothes had to pass on their way back from work, huge
posters hailed the "reforging": "Work Without Beauty and
Art Is Barbarism." From their less than meager earnings the
prisoners had to subscribe "voluntarily" to the state loans for
the fulfillment of the Five-Year Plans. In other cases they "ordered" airplanes for the Red Army, which were then incorporated into the air force, and bore the name of the particular
corrective labor institution. Since aircraft production was
operating at maximum capacity anyhow, the real effect of the
prisoners' "enthusiasm" was not an increase in the Soviet Air
Force but merely a financial operation of the NKVD at the
expense of the prisoners.

MUSIC, POETRY, AND HARD LABOR

How little the real moral condition of the criminals was
affected by forced labor and "enlightenment" is obvious from
a story told by A. Shestakova. In Soviet prisons common
criminals often have an unwritten code which bans stealing
from one another; and their leaders may punish them with the
utmost severity for such thefts. Shestakova reports that at a

2. Vyshinski, *Ot Tyurem.*

trial conducted by *ooroks* (common criminals), in which one of them was the defendant, the sentence read: "Stealing is permitted on the fourth floor only. This sentence is not subject to appeal." [3] The fourth floor was inhabited, of course, by political prisoners.

Every healthy prisoner is of course compelled to work in order to get food. For a certain time an attempt was made to punish various misdemeanors in the camps by forbidding the culprits to go to work and thus earn their food. The prisoners have been pictured as being so devoted to their tasks that not being permitted to work saddened them. "The prohibition against working is a means of exerting a *moral* influence." [4]

All methods of increasing labor efficiency and productivity introduced in the early 'thirties for the free labor force of Russia and offered to the world as the product of their enthusiastic devotion to the Soviet land were immediately aped in the labor camps. Nobody dared to ask how it came about that murderers and burglars were inspired by just as fervent "enthusiasm." "Shock troopers" were organized from one end of the forced labor universe to the other; they were to serve as models for the others. When work was particularly urgent and deadlines had to be met, criminal leaders "by their own initiative and volition" suggested the prolongation of the working day to 12 and even 15 hours and the cancellation of the days of leave. Sometimes a band provided music in order to increase the workers' output—another alleged feature of cultural enlightenment. A "red banner"—a trophy for the unit showing the highest achievements in camp—passed from one shock troop to another. Everything—except of course normal living conditions—was provided in order to encourage the exertion of the highest possible physical effort; this was called "re-education" and "reforging."

"Collectives" were organized, which worked as units. Each collective, consisting of 7, 10, or 20 members, was given a specific task to be performed in the shortest possible time.

3. *Ot Tyurem*, p. 276.
4. *Ibid.*, p. 114.

"Collective" had an attractive sound, but in reality the collective was just another means of increasing production by compelling its members to watch over one another and to denounce to the administration all those who were unable or unwilling to exert an all-out effort. "The collectives," a Soviet writer reports, are often considered "organizations for spying and denunciation." [5]

A large network of prison press organs developed, assisted and financed by the authorities. The Central Organ of Labor Camps and Prisons has the characteristic title, *Toward a Working Community*. The central publication for the Ukraine is called *To Work!* More than a score of newspapers are published in labor camps and prisons, and hundreds of so-called wall papers, most of them written in longhand, are posted in conspicuous places. The Soviet press has stressed the fact that the titles of these publications have undergone a significant change. At the beginning of the Revolution the titles included, for example, *A Ray amid Gloom, Prisoner's Thoughts, Behind Iron Bars*. In the 'thirties, on the other hand, titles were borrowed from the Five-Year Plans: *For Faster Work, Shock Trooper, Collective Labor, The Excavator*, etc. The most widely used title was *Reforging*. In the 'twenties it had stood for moral improvement but in the 'thirties it referred to fulfillment of economic tasks.

"At the top of the sheet," a former prisoner writes,

were two inscriptions: "Not for circulation outside the camp" and "Work in the U.S.S.R. is honor, glory, valor and heroism!"

In the text, the same talk about phalanxes, shock workers, storm columns, enthusiasts, vanguard of storm positions, socialistic achievements, fronts of proletarian victories, and so on—all this enhanced by an immoderate use of exclamation marks and titles in the imperative, such as "Stop!"—"Accomplish!"—"Liquidate!"—"Develop!"—"Break!"—"Strike!" . . . Articles, written by prisoners of the editorial staff, sing praises of the authorities or demand the disclosure and punishment of those guilty of various "breaches in the front." [6]

5. Averbakh, *Ot Prestupleniya k trudu*, p. 184.
6. Tchernavin, *I Speak for the Silent*, p. 291.

The political prisoners are not allowed to take part in the editing of newspapers. This is a privilege reserved to former Soviet officials, of whom thousands and thousands have been sentenced to labor camps for bribery, speculation, and other offenses in line of duty—or for no good reason at all. Sometimes a few common criminals are permitted to do newspaper work. All of them compete in saying the nicest things about the camp administration and the economic plans and in praising the Soviet Government to high heaven. Poems written by prisoners hail happiness and freedom in Russia more than does any other poetry. Every "campaign" initiated by the Soviet leadership has been immediately adopted by the labor camps, whether a threat against the Pope of Rome or British Tories, or a campaign against Soviet slackers or the world bourgeoisie.

> To hell with the Koran, the Talmud, the Torah,
> To hell with religion!
> Let's shift our motors and engines instead
> And drive on direct current ahead! [7]

In another poem a shrewd prisoner "takes leave" of his sharp knife and tells of his new passion for books and the Soviet land:

> My book is my friend.
> It entices me. . . .
> Now let's play, guitars,
> A new song of a joyous era. . . .
> There is nothing better in the world
> Than to serve the Soviet land.

Whoever stands at the helm of the NKVD is hailed as an eminent leader. Henry Yagoda, an outstanding rascal, was lauded in every labor camp and colony of the NKVD. A colony in Bolshevo was named after him and a poster inside read:

7. *Ot Tyurem*, p. 287.

And if some day the enemy's ring
Cruelly tightens around us,
We shall rise like an army of daring men
And follow Yagoda to battle! [8]

An official author figured out what kind of literary material is being printed in the press of the labor camps. He found that 48.3 per cent of the individual items deal with work and the economic tasks of the camps, 5 per cent with exposing "class enemies" in the camp, and 6.2 per cent with Soviet policy, domestic and foreign.[9]

The peak of hypocrisy is reached in the fulfillment of the famous slogan of "self-guarding" of the inmates. This slogan, invented in the early 'twenties and sounding most democratic, now means in practice that former GPU-NKVD men sentenced for the basest of crimes have been entrusted with watching over their fellow prisoners. Many of these criminals are even considered worthy of carrying arms, of being relieved of excruciating physical labor, and of playing the role of intermediaries between the camp administration and the mass of inmates. They occupy the highest, and often highly privileged, positions in the rigid hierarchy of the forced labor institution.

Next to these GPU criminals come the common criminals. It is emphasized, reiterated, and impressed upon everyone in the camps that the common prisoners are no enemies of Communism, while the rest of the camp population have been incorrigible and unworthy of concessions. This is another piece of official hypocrisy. Theft—so the old theory runs—is the consequence of poverty and unemployment. Thieves are therefore victims rather than enemies of society. It is intentionally overlooked that among the criminals a great majority are not petty thieves but capital offenders, embezzlers, and bribe-taking Soviet officials.

Only grave offenders have been kept in the corrective labor camps, since a sentence of less than three years is served in a

8. Maxim Gorky, ed., *Bolshevtsy* (Moscow, 1936), p. 7.
9. *Ot Tyurem*, p. 260.

"colony." The great majority of the criminals in the corrective labor camps are the "thirty-fivers," sentenced under Paragraph 35 of the Criminal Code as old offenders or "back-sliders." They have had their leaders in the camps—invariably notorious bandits, guilty of some bloody crime which they proudly relate to the *shpana,* the lower rank of criminals: "We stained our hands in blood in the struggle against capital."

And Semion Firin, high NKVD official, insists:

We say to you, the common criminals: We consciously do not consider you as enemies, because in your midst there are no sons of landowners and manufacturers. We know that your wretched past and criminal life have stung you severely. We don't even condemn you for having stolen at some time once in your life, for we know that sometimes a man starts stealing because he has nothing to eat, because he is hungry.[10]

The Soviet writer Averbakh explains why she sympathizes with these criminal elements: They were thieves, but their crime was less than that of the kulaks, who by their very activity were stealing from the poor peasants. The "thirty-fivers," she says, look with contempt on the class enemies, and "among this part of the prisoners the personnel can easily be recruited for the posts of junior commanders in the field of economy and cultural enlightenment." [11] The system of putting the scum of the criminal world (the "thirty-fivers") in posts of command is still in force.

INTELLECTUALS IN THE CAMP

The overwhelming majority of the camp inmates was and is composed of national and social elements which in the usual sense of the word would never be considered offenders: engineers, technicians, doctors imprisoned for alleged wrecking activities; bookkeepers and industrial managers held respon-

10. Firin, S., *Itogi Belomorstroya* (The Balance Sheet of the Belomor) (Moscow, 1934), p. 48.
11. Averbakh, *op. cit.,* pp. 193–195.

sible for defects of which they had no knowledge; a great many peasants labeled kulaks; members of national minorities suspected of insufficient loyalty to the Soviet state; and an endless array of groups accused of actual or fantastic, specifically Soviet, crimes. At a moment when the great tide of arrests and deportations had subsided, and the responsibility for the committed outrages had to be shifted to the various local officials, Andrei Vyshinski, the rising star of Soviet justice, told how the NKVD and the courts had sentenced the accused:

How are people convicted? What are people convicted for? Here are a few examples. A woman cook failed to salt the dinner. She was prosecuted under Par. 111 [Par. 111 deals with "failure to perform official duties" and with exceeding one's authority]. A kolkhoz worker took a horse and went about his business; the horse was stolen; the kolkhoz worker was prosecuted under Par. 111, although it would have been much fairer and simpler to have him make up for the value of the horse. A one-eyed foal was born in a kolkhoz; it was killed and eaten. The chairman of the kolkhoz was prosecuted for "failure to protect" the young horse. A kolkhoz worker was prosecuted for reducing the sowing norm, even though the harvest turned out to be good; he was tried and convicted. The manager of a farm had pity on two calves and brought them indoors out of the frost. The calves' ears froze up, and the man was tried and convicted under Par. 111. In January, 1935, the People's Court sentenced a certain Pankratov under Pars. 109 and 111 of the Criminal Code for inflicting damages totaling 69 rubles on his kolkhoz. The accused had been sent into town by the kolkhoz to sell rye; instead of selling it at 26 or 27 rubles, he sold it at 23 rubles. He was arrested and convicted for poor salesmanship. . . .[12]

Among the millions of these "criminals" and "wreckers" the non-Communist intellectuals in the camps have occupied a separate place. Basically, they have belonged to the "class enemies" and therefore had to be treated with far greater severity than the common criminals. Besides, they have always been subject to suspicion of instigating fellow prisoners

12. Vyshinski in *Sovetskaya yustitsiya* (1935), No. 18.

to protests and sabotage. The central authorities send instruction after instruction to the camps directing them to differentiate in their treatment between "class enemies" and other inmates. The local camp administration carries out these instructions to the letter, in order not to be accused of "rightist deviations." A commission of the Commissariat of Justice, after making an inspection tour of prisons in 1933, reported that "class-alien elements are being kept under strict observation, are sent exclusively to hard labor tasks." [13]

Hard physical work under such conditions has been murderous for the intellectual elements of the camp population, and their only hope has lain in the great shortage of "specialists" in the local camp offices as well as in the central administration in Moscow.[14] The huge economic enterprise of the GPU-NKVD needs advice and expert leadership, just as would any other Soviet or non-Soviet industrial or agricultural enterprise. The available force of engineers, teachers, and agronomists has always been insufficient in Soviet Russia, and so the NKVD and its agencies have often been compelled to give the intellectuals jobs according to their qualifications, although this was contrary to the principle of severe punishment of "class enemies."

The intellectuals are lucky to find occupation in the camp offices, as technicians or as engineers supervising construction or other work. All try to escape the hard physical labor, for which most of them are unfitted. Those who are fortunate enough to remain at such a sought-after job have a chance of surviving. But in order not to be returned to the harder forms

13. *Sovetskaya yustitsiya* (1933), No. 23.

14. For a few of the older intellectuals, kitchen work sometimes meant temporary salvation. A professor, having seen it done or done it himself, gives an eloquent picture: ". . . huddled together on narrow wooden benches, with thin, sharpened-down dinner knives in hand sit professors and other educated and cultured men. In front of them are bags with dirty, rotten potatoes which in 'capitalistic' countries would not be used even to feed pigs; and here these men sit diligently, seriously and clumsily peeling such potatoes for the prison soup. . . .

"Highly qualified engineers competed for the right to do plumbing jobs, repair locks, electric lighting and telephones. Learned professors claimed the jobs of polishing floors and cleaning stairs. One clergyman, until his execution, was for a long time in charge of the boiler." Tchernavin, *op. cit.*, p. 134.

of work, they sometimes have to humiliate themselves or perform acts against their own consciences.

The status of physicians, for example, has been particularly degrading. The administration of every labor camp tries to fight malingerers who attempted to stay away from work. The doctors are therefore instructed to be extremely severe and not send a person to the hospital unless his condition is very grave. Sometimes the administration prescribes a maximum quota of permissible illness—say, 5 or 10 per cent—and the physicians are obliged to send to work all except this small quota. The memoirs of former prisoners abound in descriptions of the misery of honest and conscientious doctors who are compelled to send their fellow prisoners to hard labor when they know it is tantamount to a death sentence. The doctors can of course decline to carry out these inhumane instructions—and be reasonably certain of being assigned to cutting and trailing trees or moving rocks, and of themselves falling sick after a short while.[15]

For a while it was usual to "sell specialists." A labor camp possessing among its inmates professors, engineers, able lecturers, and similar people would conclude contracts with other Soviet institutions by which these "specialists" were placed at the disposal of the institution for a specified period of time and for an agreed payment. The contracts, very similar to those of sale or lease of livestock, contained, for example, such clauses as the following:

15. In his book on the GPU Kitchin tells of a discussion between the administrators of the camp and a prisoner, Dr. Movsh: " '. . . you forget the instructions . . .' " said the commander of the camp: " ' "to fulfill the plan, no matter at what cost." And I shall fulfill it. Tomorrow all those will go out to work whom I shall order to do so . . .' "

"He slammed the door and left the room."

"The doctor jumped up excitedly and started pacing the room . . ."

Another of the chiefs said to the doctor, " 'We do not build the revolution with kid gloves. There must be sacrifices and if so, rather let the enemies of the revolution be sacrificed. . . .

" 'You had better not quarrel with us, doctor. . . . You know our slogan—"he who is not with us is against us." What is your term, for instance? Three years? There, you see how it is. . . . If you do not reform, we shall add another five, and after that we might give you some three years of exile. Be level-headed and consider whether it pays to quarrel with us.' " (Pp. 139-140.)

The administration of Camp N places at the disposal of governmental agency Y two professors, the prisoners K—— and Ch——, who have had considerable pedagogic experience, for the purpose of delivering a series of courses [list follows] . . .

The administration of N reserves the right to recall either of the above-mentioned prisoners at any moment and without any notice, but is bound to replace them by other prisoners of similar qualifications. . . . Y agrees to pay five rubles for every lecture hour.

Of the sum paid by the "buying" institution to the "owner," the prisoner was to receive 10 per cent. Actually this payment was rarely made.

Later this cynical form of "sale" transaction was forbidden. It was unnecessary to write documents on slave trades for posterity to read!

HYPOCRISY AT ITS PEAK

A monumental hypocrisy, humiliating to Soviet writers, was perpetrated in 1933 when, at the urgent call of the Central Committee of the Communist party, a group of 120 persons which included Maxim Gorky, made a trip to the site of the Belomor Canal (White Sea–Baltic Sea), then under construction by the GPU. The trip lasted a few days, after which 35 of the writers sat down to prepare a book, which they completed within a few months and published within another four weeks. It was a beautiful volume called *The Stalin Canal*, which was immediately translated into English. It is full of praise for the agents of the GPU and the miracles performed with the prisoners in a short span of time. No doubt, only a few of the authors believed what they wrote; as for the rest, they were merely carrying out orders, earning the blessing of the GPU and besmirching the high calling of the independent writer.

Maxim Gorky belonged to the first group. He was a strange mixture of great literary talent and childish naïveté. Almost until his death, he wanted to believe that the avowedly terroristic Soviet regime was in the process of establishing a community of human brotherhood. The world-famous name of Gorky was used by the NKVD to cover up many a crime and monstrous cruelty. At the invitation of the government— probably of Stalin personally—Gorky visited the Solovetski Island Camp in 1929 and the Belomor in 1933, as well as several other camps. He invariably brought back favorable reports. Before his arrival—as we have seen—the camps were cleaned and tidied, sick prisoners were removed, and a noon recess of a few hours instituted, after which the honored guest was guided about by the administrators, who anticipated commendation and rewards for their exemplary achievements.

Another well-known Russian writer, Nikolai Pogodin, in 1935 published a play entitled *The Aristocrats*, which will remain a model of literary subservience to the powers that be. The play depicts the prisoners of a camp assigned to building a canal. They are bandits, thieves, wreckers, priests, engineers, women of all sorts, etc. At the outset all swear that they will never work. The bandit declares, "Anyway, I'm going to steal, beat, and wreck, and little I care about any canals." One engineer wrecker says to another: "Remain an engineer, but don't become a slave!" A card shark and thief says, "I was and I will be a criminal. I won't work."

But the NKVD chief, Gromov—a very clever man, of course—finds ways of drawing them in.

A few days pass and the card shark has become an enthusiastic worker who proclaims, "There is no fortress that could frighten us!" He has been "reforged." Sofia, the thief, suggests that the card shark compete with her in productivity; she wins the banner. She, too, has been reformed. A bandit organizes a "productive commune." Engineer Sadovski, a base anti-Soviet wrecker, regenerated, too, in the course of a few days, asks the administration to let his old mother visit him in the camp, and Gromov, the humane chief, gives permission. The mother arrives and is delighted by her son's healthy physical appearance. The chief of the camp even places his car at her disposal.

Then one of the thieves returns a gold cigarette case which he had stolen from an engineer in the camp, and says, "Take it, it is the last thing I shall ever steal." A burglar proclaims: "From a thief, I have become the chairman of a commune. Now I am an outstanding shock trooper, the builder of a world edifice. How beautifully you have re-educated me!"

Finally the last of the thieves, Aliosha, sings:

> The past is a dream,
> A terrible thing;
> I am reborn,
> I want to live and sing!

THE ADMINISTRATIVE PERSONNEL

The administration of labor camps is a complex matter. A large labor camp is in many ways like a city. Its inhabitants must be fed and clothed; its economic efficiency must be maintained on a high level; it must have its own courts and prisons. Because of the huge scope of the forced labor projects, the GPU in Moscow has always suffered from lack of qualified and reliable personnel capable of carrying out its policy among thousands of prisoners off in the remotest corners of Russia.

Special courses and schools for training supervisors and administrators of labor camps and prisons were established in the 'thirties and have continued in operation. Such importance was attributed to membership in the Communist party that after the early 'thirties no important position in the labor camps and prisons could be occupied by a non-Communist. Among the prison officials of the Commissariat of Justice members of the Communist party constituted 14.2 per cent in 1925, 16.6 in 1928, and 50.2 in 1932. This ratio of Communists continued to grow in the 'thirties, when the official goal was to raise the number of party members among the administrative personnel of the camps to 70 per cent and that of members of the Communist Youth League to 20 per cent.[16]

16. *Ot Tyurem*, p. 426.

The small group of non-Communists now embraces only the lower classification of employees with no responsible functions in the system.

The remuneration of prison officials was, and still is, inadequate. This is one cause of the widespread abuse of the prisoners' property by camp authorities. Rations are misappropriated in the camp kitchen—for the benefit of the higher-ups; clothing and shoes sent by relatives are lost somewhere in the camp offices. Very often members of the administration cover up for each other. Graft reaches outrageous proportions, and many a prisoner has been able to save his life by offering gifts to his superiors. The system of bribery and gifts has become so prevalent that Moscow has actually ceased fighting it. As a matter of fact, precious gifts are sometimes sent by the administrators of far-off camps to the heads of the GULAG and in this way the poison of corruption has infected the entire institution from the bottom to the very top and become one of the outstanding characteristics of the "moral improvement" in the "corrective" institutions.

Among the departments of the camp administration, two are of particular interest—the VOKhRA and the internal NKVD, or ISO.

The VOKhRA is the armed guard of the camp, invested with extensive prerogatives. Commanders of the VOKhRA are employees of the NKVD; they are assisted, as mentioned above, by a multitude of convicted NKVD officials, who in their attempt to reingratiate themselves and regain freedom try to exceed their superiors in severity. Members of the VOKhRA have orders to shoot on sight all prisoners who attempt to escape. They are seldom held responsible for cruelty, and their immunity adds further to the hardships of the prisoners.

Then there is an NKVD inside the NKVD labor camp. Every camp is a mass of humanity, and all possible types of real and alleged crimes are perpetrated behind the barbed-wire fences. The local agency of the NKVD works according to precedents and principles established by the central NKVD. It recruits stool pigeons from among the prisoners; it has its secret agents in the barracks; it has its "correspondents" working for the "cultural section"; and there are always many "volunteers" who attempt to derive benefits and alleviate their conditions by close collaboration with the NKVD. All furnish information to this agency about morale, suspicious persons, and sabotage, as well as about officials of the camp and even members of the NKVD itself. Most important are tips as to preparations for escape. Information furnished by these voluntary and involuntary agents may doom their closest friends.

Dungeon cells and all forms of solitary confinement are at the disposal of the camp NKVD. Sentence to such punishment, especially in winter time, frequently leads to illness and death. In other instances the culprits are tried and sentenced to prisons or to deportation to camps in the far north or east. On November 28, 1933, the OGPU issued a circular ordering deportation to the Northern Camps of "all incorrigibly lazy inmates." [17]

Attempts at self-mutilation, made in order to avoid hard labor, were frequent in the old Russian katorgas, but in those days the deed was not considered criminal. In the labor camps of the Soviet period, self-mutilation is regarded as an attempt to prevent the fulfillment of the Five-Year Plans, and therefore prisoners who chop off their fingers, toes, or hands, are subject to punishment with or without trial. "Self-choppers," as they are called throughout the camps, are often denied admittance to hospitals. So-called show trials are organized. Sentences run up to one year to be served in the severest type of prison.

Liberation from labor camps upon the expiration of a sentence is not automatic by any means. A special order must be issued in Moscow before any prisoner may be released. If the order is overlooked or forgotten, or is lost in the mails, the prisoner spends additional time in camp before the mistake is

17. Averbakh, *op. cit.*, p. 174.

corrected; the intimidated prisoners often do not dare to protest, and no one knows how many have died in confinement after their terms have expired.

The Central Administration in Moscow usually extends the terms of political prisoners when they near expiration, whether these prisoners are held in prisons or in the corrective labor camps.

As to the mass of physical laborers—mostly recruited from among the peasantry—the NKVD has prescribed that two months before their liberation they are to obtain assignments indicating where they are to go and what kind of employment they are to accept.[18] Once the decision is made, they are not free to change jobs. Sometimes prisoners have been pardoned after spending a certain time in the labor camps as a reward for good work. Amnesty, however, did not bring freedom for them. They have had to sign up to go to work on similar projects elsewhere for a considerable length of time.

Sometimes commissions dispatched from Moscow would visit individual labor camps to ascertain whether the complaints of prisoners or their relatives were justified and whether the local authorities were successful in coping with their tasks. Such an inspection seldom led to fundamental reforms. The terrorized prisoners rarely dared bring complaints before the "guests from the Center" in the presence of the local bosses, knowing that they would have to suffer the consequences. There are many descriptions by former prisoners of how these Muscovite emissaries were dined and wined by their local subordinates, and by what means they were frequently induced to overlook the mismanagement, graft, and bribery reigning in the camps, as well as the miserable food and living conditions. For the officials the journey from Moscow to these God-forsaken holes far from civilization was an annoying assignment, and they tried to cut it as short as possible. Usually they would return to Moscow after a few days, rarely bringing changes for the better in their wake.

Occasionally, however, their reports did contain some criti-

18. Circular of the NKVD (1935), No. 143.

cism, and sometimes these criticisms even reached the press. One such report read:

We often scorn and disregard such "details" as tidiness of rooms, washing of floors, walls, disinfecting of rooms, etc. We do not always supply [the prisons] with closets, tables, lockers, dishes, spoons, spittoons; we do not care about the condition of toilets; we fail to install ventilation, etc.; baths, fumigating chambers and barbershops do not by any means work as they should. . . . There is a soulless, bureaucratic approach to work.[19]

On another occasion it was stated that

despite a series of very definite instructions and despite a number of criminal prosecutions for rude treatment of prisoners by the administration and the guard, in some instances it has still not been eradicated. A number of cases of entirely inadmissible treatment of prisoners have been established, demanding the sternest prosecution.[20]

The result of such criticisms is practically nil. Under the conditions prevalent in the 'thirties and 'forties, the NKVD has been virtually immune from criticism from without.

19. *Sovetskaya yustitsiya* (1933), No. 12.
20. Utevski, in *Sovetskaya yustitsiya* (1933), No. 23.

XIII

The Swings of the Pendulum

ANDREI VYSHINSKI, HENRY YAGODA, AND THE GREAT PURGE

By 1934 a certain relaxation had set in after the severe strain of the preceding years.

The collectivization of agriculture had been virtually completed, and work in the collectives began to improve. The long resistance of the peasantry, with its accompanying violence and bloodshed, had been smashed. In this struggle, which had often resembled civil warfare, the government had won a decisive and complete victory. The great famine, in which millions of Ukrainian peasants had perished, was past, and the food situation began to improve. Domestic affairs likewise took a turn for the better: Communist factions opposing Stalin had been defeated, and their leaders had publicly repented and acclaimed the wisdom of the Leader. In fact, no opposition of noteworthy proportions any longer existed.

The Soviet Government considered it possible now to make some political and economic concessions which brought about a certain release from the strain of years of terrorism and constant pressure under the Second Revolution. Reforms were introduced and others planned but never carried out; there was an expectation of improvement, which was consciously reinforced by the government.

On July 10, 1934, the old OGPU was abolished and its functions transferred to the newly established People's Commissariat for Internal Affairs—the NKVD. This measure was intended to symbolize liberalization of political conditions and an easing of the grip of the police. It was significant that the new decree ordered the GPU to "turn over all investigated cases to the organs of justice," meaning the regular courts, and that the harsh Judiciary Collegium of the GPU—the caricature of a court—was abolished. (Only in its last paragraph did the decree mention a mysterious new "Special Council" with far-reaching powers.) The official press hailed the transition from GPU to NKVD as a step toward greater guarantees for the individual. "The Soviet State," *Izvestia* commented, "is changing its methods of struggle. . . . The role of the courts is growing more important." *Pravda* added that "now that the enemies are smashed and the dictatorship is firm," the government is going to operate a "unified system of Soviet justice." Henry Yagoda was appointed People's Commissar for Internal Affairs. Then, by a decree of October 27, 1934, all Soviet "places of detention," including those under the Commissariat of Justice, were transferred to the NKVD.

A few months later the Special Council of the NKVD was organized. While its prerogatives were vast—it was authorized to impose sentences of up to five years in corrective labor camps, deportation, and expulsion from the Soviet Union—a guarantee was provided against unlawful practices by the Special Council: the Prosecutor of the Soviet Union (a position created in 1933 to exercise "supervision over the legality and correctness of the activities of the OGPU," among other purposes) was made a member of the Council, and no action could be carried out against his veto. There was thus created an agency whose striking role in subsequent years could not have been foreseen at the time. At its helm were two men, Henry Yagoda, the People's Commissar, and Andrei Vyshinski, the Prosecutor.[1] Collaboration and then life-and-death struggle between these two men belongs to the dramatic history of the following years.

As far as the peasants were concerned, the government made an important concession in permitting members of the

1. In 1934 Vyshinski was still Deputy Prosecutor; actually, however, he was already in charge of the department.

kolkhoz to own individual small plots of land; more than that, every peasant family was entitled to possess one cow, and more than one sheep or hog. The produce of the plots and the cattle were of tremendous importance to the peasants as a source of subsistence, since the collectives were obliged to deliver a large share of their produce to the state.

In March and May, 1934, government orders eased the punishment of obstinate peasants and—sensationally enough— of some exiled kulaks. Members of kolkhozes sentenced to corrective labor for terms not exceeding six months were now to serve their sentences in their own collectives.

Kulaks were to regain their civil rights after five years of exile; those among them who had worked in the gold and platinum mines were to be rehabilitated after three years. This half-hearted amnesty of course applied to exiles only and did not affect the inmates of corrective labor camps; it was applicable only to those individual kulaks whose reinstatement was approved by the local GPU. The local administration was instructed to apply these new regulations above all to the younger "migrants" who could boast of good production records. On the whole, the people of Russia looked forward to a series of reforms, not only of an economic nature but also relating to individual freedom and the over-all political system. During this period the first discussion of a new and "democratic" Soviet constitution was initiated by the government. It was even expected that an amnesty for all or most of the émigrés would soon be announced.

It did not take long to realize that a liberal swing of the Soviet pendulum would have to be a short one and rapidly give way to a swing in the opposite direction. The social system of Russia had already been radically remolded in the brief course of a few years. The new concessions to the peasantry were to be limited in scope lest the very meaning of the previous upheaval be lost. Reforms could not reach very far without shaking the whole structure. The improvement of food conditions, likewise, was limited to bread and vegetables; the

shortage of meat and fats could not be overcome in the brief
span of a few years. Housing conditions continued critical.
The industrialization and expansion of war industries consumed enormous quantities of labor and material, and the balance of goods available for general consumption remained
meager. It proved impossible to proceed on a road which in
the eyes of the people was to lead to a significant increase in
personal liberty and in the standard of living.

Nor was it possible to abolish or curtail the use of forced
labor. The system had already become deeply rooted in the
Soviet economy; it had become an organic element of the
new Soviet entity; any attempt to reduce its ramifications necessarily would have led to unforeseen complications. Lumber
was still the major item of Soviet export and in order to make
possible the importation of essential industrial equipment lumber exports had to be stepped up. Large quantities of gold had
to be mined in the Far East if sufficient funds were to be accumulated for the needs of foreign trade and—what seemed
more important—of a looming world war. Highways and railroads had to be built. New industrial buildings had to be
erected, new canals constructed, and so on.

For the bulk of these projects the Soviet Government
would not have been able to recruit voluntary workers in
sufficient numbers. Unless a sizable wage increase were put
into effect, gold, lumber, coal, and a score of other commodities could not have been produced in the necessary amounts,
and the proud Five-Year Plans would have ended in a fiasco.

Forced labor could not be eradicated as long as other elements of the Soviet system remained unaltered. Either a great
transformation, extending far beyond prison walls and barbed-
wire fences, would build a new Russia on a new foundation,
or the system of forced labor had to be maintained, strength-
ened, and further expanded.

The government chose the latter alternative. It took advantage of the first pretext to put an end to the brief political
spring of 1934. In December, 1934, Sergei Kirov, a member
of the Politbureau, was killed by an assassin who had acted out

of strictly personal motives. The government decided to use this incident as an excuse for gradually reverting to the policy of "mercilessness" and the mailed fist.

NO MERCY FOR THE ENEMIES

From then on, up almost to the outbreak of the European war, a wave of increasing repression and terrorism engulfed the country.

In the beginning the new offensive developed rather slowly; in 1935 and the first half of 1936 it was still in its initial phases. Although they had already reached large dimensions, the persecutions were still on a considerably lower scale than during the terrible years of 1930–33.[2] The wave of arrests reached a new peak at the time of the great Moscow trials of 1936–38, which, however, included only a very small fraction of those executed, deported, dismissed from office, or sent to forced labor camps.

In the second half of the nineteen thirties the iron curtain fell upon forced labor and the labor camps. In contrast with the strenuous propaganda of the early 'thirties, the press and the public spokesmen were now silent concerning Soviet penal policies. There was no more talk in public about the exemplary

2. Avoiding concrete data, Vyshinski stated in November, 1936, that the number of people sentenced in the Russian Republic in the first half of 1936 was 48 per cent less than in the corresponding period of 1933. *Pravda,* November 11, 1936.

Later he tried to revive the legend of diminishing and vanishing criminality in the Soviet Union (*Sovetskoye gosudarstvo i pravo,* 1939, No. 3). Employing the usual device of slanted selective statistics, never giving the absolute numbers of arrests, trials, and convictions, he compares criminal offenses in 1934–37 with those in 1933 and comes to the conclusion that in 1937 the number of crimes had diminished by 52 per cent as compared with 1933. It is nowhere explained, however, how criminality had developed until 1933 and why that year was selected as a base for his computations; nor is any comparison given between criminal offenses in the 'twenties and 'thirties.

Actually 1933 represented the all-time peak of "criminality" in the Soviet Union (before the second World War). Despite a certain relaxation in governmental policy between 1933 and 1936, the prosecutions still considerably outnumbered those in the preceding decade. The disappearance of crime in Russia as implied by Vyshinski is a deliberate untruth, as contrasted with the early 'twenties, when it was a sincere delusion.

correction of criminals in the Soviet land, about humane treatment and the therapeutic effects of labor; no more invitations were extended to "workers' delegations" abroad to visit these peculiar Russian institutions. Complete secrecy prevailed.

The international situation as well as domestic affairs made this change imperative. The Soviet press was "exposing" German Fascism and harping on its manifestations. The Soviet Union signed an alliance with France; promised help to democratic Czechoslovakia; and its participation in common action of the "democratic" states now seemed possible. It was obviously necessary to keep the subject of Soviet forced labor and labor camps from becoming a focus of international discussions and to shut off all publicity.

A second reason why forced labor had to be removed from the public eye was connected with internal affairs. In the new purge which was getting under way thousands of former administrators and Communist officials were sent to camps and prisons. It was impossible to continue the old sugary propaganda about the exemplary treatment and the beneficial influence of the labor camps. Too many of the elite of Soviet society had been thrown into "places of detention," too many families of Soviet "high society" were aware of the problem, to permit the old line of propaganda.

Stalin reacted to the murder of Kirov in his habitual way. Not only was the actual assassin executed but, in order to prevent new outbreaks against other Soviet leaders and to terrorize every actual and potential enemy of the regime into obedience, thousands of men all over Russia who had never even heard the name of Kirov were arrested; a great many of them were executed without trial. The philosophy underlying this upsurge of terrorism had been established following the attempt on Lenin's life in 1918: the argument was that only among the survivors of the old capitalist classes can the idea of such crimes and the determination to commit them take root; hence these classes and their intellectual leaders bear the real guilt for the death of a Soviet leader; punishment must therefore be meted out to great sections of the population, even to those who during the time of the attack were already in prisons or labor camps.

Instructions went out to the local NKVD's as well as to the chiefs of labor camps that "class enemies" (embracing more than half the prison population) were considered collectively responsible for Kirov's death. They were directly referred to as "Kirov's murderers." More often than not, additional hard labor was prescribed for these "enemies of the people" in order to atone for the "monstrous act." O. Feldheim later described the changes these instructions brought about in the labor camps of Russia:

As a result of Kirov's murder, the number of prisoners increased to such an extent that there just wasn't enough room in the old camps. Construction brigades were hurriedly sent in, cutting trees and immediately building barracks for "Kirov's murderers." . . . The chief called us out into the yard, where we were made to line up, and gave us a speech along the following lines: "You were the enemies of the people! You have just committed an atrocious crime [that is, Kirov's murder]. But despite all this you are now being given the chance to atone for your crimes against the Soviet state. You must redeem yourselves by heavy work, but you must be happy because the Soviet Government entrusts to you the construction of a railroad which will be of tremendous importance for the glorious future of our great country—the USSR! Hurrah!" [3]

This picture is typical of prisons and labor camps in 1935.

"No mercy for class enemies!" was again the slogan. "Class enemies" meant not only kulaks, capitalists, and Socialists but also a multitude of Communists guilty of betraying the party line. The structure of socialism in Russia, Stalin said, is completed in the rough, but these enemies must remember that socialism does not mean the abolition of compulsion on the part of the state. It is harmful to believe, Stalin maintained,

3. Feldheim in *Sovremennyye zapiski* (Paris, 1939), LXVIII, 418–422.

that freedom will increase in the Soviet state in proportion to the extent to which socialism is being achieved. Neither compulsion nor the state itself can be abolished.

Measures of compulsion and punishment must, on the contrary, be intensified. In October, 1937, the Central Executive Committee raised the maximum penalty for offenses against the state from 10 to 25 years: "Article 18 of the Fundamental Principles of Criminal Legislation of the USSR and the Union Republics is hereby amended to provide for a deprivation of liberty to not exceeding 25 years as a measure of criminal punishment." In 1938 the Penal Code reverted to the use of the term "punishment," which had been banned two decades earlier as a mark of capitalist ideology. In 1935, 17 years after its abolition, the term "prison" was again officially recognized. In August, 1936, new prisons were established for particularly severe punishment of inmates of labor colonies, who could be transferred to them for up to two years.

By the terms of the decree of April 7, 1935, children over 12 years, who had formerly been exempt from the death penalty and even from imprisonment, were now included under the general penal code. It was expressly stated that every penal measure was applicable to minors. How many children were actually executed under this decree remains a secret.

One of the central figures behind this flood of accusations and arrests was Andrei Vyshinski. His star was rising fast. The man allegedly chosen to restrain the former GPU leader, Yagoda, would soon outdo him in every respect, gain Stalin's confidence, and "liquidate" his rival.

Vyshinski, who had been a professor of law in the 'twenties, was not outstanding in either scholarship or politics. The absence of original ideas in his books and lectures was made up for by an abundance of quotations from Marx, Lenin, and Stalin—quotations that more often than not were utterly irrelevant to the subject in question but which always demonstrated loyalty to the supreme leader. Of Stalin Vyshinski spoke in superlatives of worship and adoration which at that time were still unusual in Moscow. His past (he had spent about 15 years in the Menshevik party) was a heavy burden, and he knew well that he had to atone for this sin by continuous genuflection and compliments to the powers-that-be. In his position any vestige of originality was dangerous. If any career was open to him, it was that of someone else's mouthpiece. Vyshinski has never been prepared to commit a crime unless he was sure of having Stalin's backing. On the other hand, Vyshinski has never shrunk from crime when he knew that Stalin wanted him to commit it. There is not much independence in the men around Stalin, but compared to Vyshinski any member of the Politbureau would appear a sovereign leader.

The murder of Kirov suddenly gave Vyshinski a chance to develop his abilities and inclinations and climb the ladder of power. Yagoda's branch of the NKVD in Leningrad, where Kirov had been murdered, was accused of laxity, and Yagoda himself was reprimanded. The investigation and the nation-wide "uprooting" of "Kirov's murderers" was entrusted to Vyshinski, soon afterward appointed Prosecutor of the Soviet Union. Waves of arrests and executions to avenge Kirov swept the country. Vyshinski carried out his assignment to the complete satisfaction of the Kremlin and was awarded the Red Banner of Labor "for the fight against counterrevolution."

For another year he collaborated with Yagoda in the Special Council of the NKVD. A few public trials and a multitude of sentences without trials marked the transition from the short-lived "liberalism" of 1934 to the peak of terrorism in 1937–38. Unbelievable as it may sound, Vyshinski soon managed to present Yagoda as lax, hesitant, and considerate to the enemies of the state. It was a feat to make of Yagoda—that monster of terrorism, the Soviet counterpart of the Nazi henchmen hanged at Nuremburg—a weakling and a liberal!

In September, 1936, Yagoda was ousted from his post; in 1938 he was tried by the Moscow Tribunal, sentenced to death, and executed. It is worth noting that he was skillfully included in a group accused of "rightist opposition"—those who had opposed the new upsurge of terror, collectivization, and the imposition of restrictions on the working class.

In September, 1936, N. I. Yezhov was appointed to replace Yagoda, and now the orgies of the purges had free rein. Yezhov had to collaborate with Vyshinski on the Special Council of the NKVD; he was a newcomer, a petty man in every respect, whereas Vyshinski was Stalin's confidant.

The utopian expectations of the 'twenties as to the abolition of compulsion on the part of the state and the growth of personal freedom were now declared to be treachery. Vyshinski was the mainstay of the new ideology. No flabby sentimentalism! he proclaimed in a widely publicized lecture, in March, 1937. He "exposed" Pashukanis, the Soviet authority on law, who—so Vyshinski said—was in reality a wrecker because he taught that courts in general, and criminal courts in particular, would have to disappear as soon as the capitalist psychology had gone. Therefore "Pashukanis is an enemy of the Soviet state and of Soviet law." Stuchka and other venerated fathers of Soviet law were found guilty of the same crimes. Even Nikolai Krylenko, People's Commissar and former Prosecutor, was found guilty by Vyshinski, who was mocking the old theory of "correction of offenders by labor." Punishment is not merely education, he said. "Punishment cannot be reduced to education, and let us not pretend that prisons are no different from schools!" To save his skin, Eugene Shirvindt, former Chief of Corrective Institutions, himself accused of sympathy with the "rightist deviation," insisted that "we must overcome the sugary liberalism and a sympathetic attitude toward the offender." [4]

Under these circumstances, after the brief relapse in 1934–35, the institution of forced labor took fresh growth. It reached its greatest proportions in the years immediately preceding the war. The pattern which had been set earlier was now being adapted to the network that extended all over Russia.

4. Shirvindt in *Sovetskaya yustitsiya* (1937), No. 21.

THE THIRD FIVE-YEAR PLAN

The GULAG was taken over by the NKVD from the GPU. Its official name is "Chief Administration of Corrective Labor Camps, Prisons, Labor, and Special Settlements of the NKVD." All corrective labor camps and colonies, and all places of detention were turned over to the GULAG in October, 1934. All exiles were included in its realm. Into the settlements of the GULAG the influx of exiles—special and voluntary migrants—continued in a steady stream, men and women never sentenced, not guilty of any crime, but for some reason deported to work under the NKVD. "Separatists" from the Ukraine and other national republics were sent to labor camps or, in some instances, to the settlements. Trotsky-ites and members of other Communist factions were deported with their families; thousands and thousands of men and women never connected with Trotsky or Trotskyism were included in this group of exiles. Kazakhs, Turkmen, and even Chinese were sent to labor camps in great numbers. Thousands of Greeks were deported from the Odessa region, Armenians and Georgians from the Caucasus, Finns and Poles from the border areas. Somewhat later the deportation of Germans got under way.

At least once, in 1937, the NKVD assigned to each of its local agencies a fixed quota of people to be arrested. The specified number was rather high in each case. The local chiefs immediately arrested all suspect persons, but in order to fill the prescribed quotas they had to go through their files and pick out those who had been considered dangerous or suspect long before and who had served their sentences five or ten years earlier. In this way peaceful citizens who for a long period of years had remained aloof from all political activity (or, for that matter, from all criminal activity) were arrested and frequently deported. If the quota was not filled, the agents of the NKVD would themselves be suspected of laxity and counterrevolutionary inclinations. By this sweeping action, the government attained two objectives: first, the elimination from the national community of potential enemies; and second, the filling of the gaps in the labor force in the camps caused by mortality, sickness, and other reasons.

The multitude of intellectuals arrested between 1935 and 1940 made possible the fulfillment of the economic, strategic, and other tasks of the GULAG. There were engineers, agronomists, and a large number of physicians among the newcomers to the camps, even where there were no hospitals and no medicine. The doctors needed for the entire network of labor camps have been and still are recruited mostly from among the prisoners.

Certain camps underwent considerable expansion during this period; for example, the Dalstroy, with its growing gold and other mineral output, and the camp at the Pechora River (in the northern Urals), which became so large that it had to be split into two systems—Ukhta and Pechora. A new city, Chibyu-Ukhta, became the capital of this new realm of the NKVD. Here coal was mined at the Vorkuta, oil wells sprang up at the Ukhta, a great electric power station was built near by, and new railroad lines were completed from Kotlas to Chibyu and from Chibyu to Ust-Kozhva.

Internal conditions in the various camps differed as they had before. Food improved to some extent in 1936–39 due to the good harvests. But the severity of the treatment did not abate. On the contrary, during the great purges acts of inhuman cruelty were often committed and later told by fugitives. Thus, in 1938, the NKVD dispatched a special commission from Moscow, under Lieutenant Kashketin, to visit the camps and determine whether the terms of punishment imposed under the "lenient" Yagoda were adequate. In Vorkuta, as a result, 3,000 "Trotskyites" were reported to have been summarily executed. The interrogation of this commission was frequently of such a nature that the prisoner soon after died. Having perpetrated acts of incredible barbarism, Kashketin's mission returned to Moscow, where, in their turn, the members were arrested.

The third Five-Year Plan, announced in 1939, again included a large number of projects assigned to the vast labor camps of the GULAG.

In his report outlining the third Five-Year Plan, Molotov indicated among the multitude of projects a considerable number of "mass works," in which forced labor had always played a major role. Two hydroelectric stations, "the greatest in the world," were to be constructed in the Kuibyshev region; power stations were to be built in Byelorussia, Soviet Azerbaidjan, and Armenia. Railroad construction was to be pushed for economic as well as strategic reasons: the northern Baikal-Amur Railroad was to be partially completed during the third five-year period; another line was to link Dzhulfa and Minzhevan, a third was to be built in Kazakhstan from Kant to Rybachye; the Black Sea Railway in Georgia was to be completed. A pipeline was planned for Kazakhstan; a so-called "Second Baku" was to emerge between the Volga and the Ural Mountains. A number of irrigation and river improvement projects were begun in various regions. Marshes were to be drained in Georgia. Peat was to be dug in Byelorussia. New metallurgical plants were to be erected in the Ukraine and around Magnitogorsk.

The plan was announced in March, 1939. Before the projects could be completed the whole Soviet economy began to be converted to war in June, 1940. Within another year all plans were upset by the German invasion, and the masses of forced labor were adjusted to the war needs.

XIV

The War and After (1940-1947)

The outbreak of the war in Europe in 1939 did not immediately affect Russian economy in general or its forced labor elements in particular; neither did the small-size war against Finland in the winter of 1939–40. The great changes came later, when mass deportations from eastern Poland began, and even more rapidly after June, 1940, when, after the defeat of France, the Soviet Government became aware of the menace of war in its direction and began mobilizing on a large scale. The maintenance of the army and the conservation of available food reserves for military needs automatically worsened living conditions in Soviet Russia. Conditions in the labor camps soon became very bad; during the Russo-German War they deteriorated steadily. The mortality rate, which rose alarmingly, recalled the terrible early 'thirties.

During the war the work of the labor camps was naturally geared to the requirements of war. Wherever possible, inmates were shifted to war production. Airfields and landing strips in the Soroka, Onega, Kargopol, North Dvina, northern Ural, and Pechora regions were built by forced labor. In the Kuibyshev area the camps were mobilized for building underground airfields. Prisoners worked on the erection of war plants and fortifications in the Don Basin and in the Stalingrad region. They built border defenses in the Bureya Camps near the Manchurian frontier. The Temnikov, Lower Amur, Far Eastern, and Kuznetsk Camps sent their men to build ammunition dumps and produce shells and ammunition cases. In Molotovsk prisoners worked in armament plants, and on the White Sea they expanded port facilities and worked as stevedores, unloading lend-lease goods. Strategic railroads were built by prisoners in the northern Caucasus and in the Caspian Sea regions. At a heavy cost in human lives, all these projects were carried out quickly and according to plan.

After 1940 non-Soviet citizens began to constitute an increasing proportion of the labor camps' population. There was a succession of Poles, Balts, Bessarabians, and then, during the war, of Germans, Italians, Rumanians, Hungarians, and Japanese. Another characteristic of the new situation was the increasing proportion of non-Russian Soviet citizens—Ukrainians, Tatars, Volga-Germans, Tadzhik, Ingush, and others.

The deportation of Poles from eastern Poland in 1940 proved to be the most important single act in this connection, both in magnitude and in the international repercussions it aroused. When the Soviet Government proceeded to integrate the newly acquired Polish provinces—and subsequently, also, the Baltic States and Bessarabia—into the Soviet Union, it intended to accomplish in a few months a task which had taken a decade to achieve in Russia—the liquidation of each and every actual or potential political opponent.

Within the course of a few months, many hundreds of thousands of men, women, and children were loaded on Soviet trains and transported to the northern and eastern provinces of Soviet Russia. They were picked up without warning, frequently shipped off without their belongings; and the journey—often taking two to three weeks—entailed such hardship and suffering that thousands of prisoners died on the way. About 25 per cent of the deported were sentenced by the NKVD to labor camps, while the rest went to special migrants' settlements. No precise figures are available. One source has estimated the number of persons deported as a result of sentences and as "ordinary" deportees at 880,000; that of persons recruited for labor in the USSR at 20,000; and that of prisoners of war captured in 1939 at 180,000; i.e., a total of 1,080,000.[1] Other Polish sources estimate the total of de-

1. Elma Dangerfield, *Beyond the Urals* (British League for European Freedom, London, 1946), p. 85.

portees from Polish provinces somewhat higher, at 1,470,000, of whom the special migrants accounted for 990,000, prisoners in labor camps for 250,000, and Polish prisoners of war for 230,000.[2]

Little did the Soviet authorities suspect, while the deportations were under way, that a year later an alliance with the Polish Government of General Sikorski would become imperative and that the hundreds of thousands of Polish prisoners would have not only to be set free but to be permitted eventually to leave Soviet soil; they certainly did not anticipate that this multitude of men and women would live to carry abroad eloquent and convincing tales of life in Soviet exile.

The amnesty for the Poles was signed on July 30, 1941, after the deportees had spent nearly a year in the various camps and settlements. The number of dead after two years has been estimated at 270,000 out of the total of 1,080,000.[3] Despite the amnesty considerable numbers were detained in the camps. Two years later, when diplomatic relations between the Soviet and Polish Governments were severed, new Poles began to pour into the prisons. Eventually, soldiers of the resistance movement, or "Home Army," and members of the underground arrived; as a rule they were sent to the eastern camps. In July, 1946, a report in the London *Polish Daily* gave detailed figures on 110,000 Poles in a number of Russian labor camps in 1946.[4]

The miracle of amnesty was for the Poles only, not for the other nationalities deported in the same year. From the three little Baltic republics, with an aggregate population of 5 million, about 200,000 Lithuanians, Latvians, and Estonians were deported. Essentially they belonged to the

2. Mora and Zwierniak, *La Justice soviétique*, pp. 86–87.

3. Dangerfield, *op. cit.*, p. 87. Other Polish estimates indicate a mortality rate of over 40 per cent for the same period.

4. Vorkuta, 11,000; Severonikel, 4,000; northern railroad camps, 3,200; Bezymenlag, 7,000 (including Lithuanians and others); southern camps, 4,900; Temnikov camps, 5,000 women; Tobolsk, 16,000; northern Ural camps, 1,500; Norilsk, 2,600; Novaya Zemlya, 1,000; southern Siberian camps, 8,000. In addition, 50,000 were reported living in five Far Eastern camps. *Polish Daily*, (London) July 30, 1946.

same political and social groups which were uprooted in Poland. The evacuation continued from 1940 to the eve of the war in 1941. About 200,000 persons were deported from Bessarabia before the German attack.

THE TECHNIQUE OF MASS DEPORTATION

We have in our hands 34 secret documents issued by the NKVD and NKGB—the People's Commissariats for Internal Affairs and State Security—pertaining to mass arrests, exile, and deportation to corrective labor camps from Lithuania in 1941. They are of considerable interest since—as is obvious from their contents and wording—they are typical of a number of similar "operations" carried out both earlier and later in connection with mass deportations of "disloyal elements" from various regions of Russia, Poland, the Ukraine, and the northern Caucasus.[5] All the documents are marked "Secret," "Top Secret," "Very Confidential," "Urgent," "Immediate Action," and/or "Personal." The most secret bear the notation at the bottom, "Return after Reading!"

The first thing that strikes one in these papers is their systematic, orderly, well-thought-out character. The instructions given in them cover not only essential matters of policy but also insignificant details. Orders are issued to prepare pencils, food for the personnel engaged in the operation; the number of rounds per revolver is specified. It is obvious that in Moscow there is a sizable contingent of highly experienced persons whose main occupation is—and for a number of years has been—the organization of such deportations for far-off regions.

The documents draw the special attention of the local organs to "agents' work." In the special terminology of the NKVD the terms "agents' work" and "agents' reports" always relate to the activities of secret agents and operatives, who, in line of duty, are members of underground organizations or at

5. Microfilms of these documents have been deposited with the New York Public Library.

least have personal contacts and enjoy the confidence of disloyal and suspect elements. Every time an unknown or potentially dangerous group is reported (for instance, when a group
scheduled for deportation hides in the forests), headquarters
orders the recruitment of a detail of operatives who are instructed to join the outlaws in order to assist in their liquidation. Reprimands are continually directed from above to the
local agencies, stating that the necessary number of "agents"
has not been recruited for the NKGB. All the documents confirm and reinforce the impression that such "agents" play an
essential role.

The national composition of the Lithuanian NKGB in
charge of the operation is interesting.[6] The reserves of trust-
worthy Lithuanian Communists were so thin that the Commissar for State Security for Lithuania was Gladkov, a Russian; and his subordinates (the documents contain over 100
names) were more than 90 per cent Russians. There were few
Lithuanians among them, and almost no Jews, despite the fact
that a sizable part of the urban population before the war was
Jewish. This contrast between show-case Lithuanian nation-
alism and actual subordination to Moscow is striking. Thus the
Lithuanian spelling of towns and counties is strictly adhered
to: Vilno is Vilnius, Kovno is Kaunas, Shauli is Sauliai; and at
the same time the defense of Lithuania's national interests is
entrusted to men with purely Russian names: Bykov, Bakulin,
Medvedev, Popov, Yudin, Koryagin . . .

The operation was carried out on June 6, 1941, i.e., some
two weeks before the German attack. The last phases of the
operation were still continuing, orders were being issued, and

6. Early in 1941 the former NKVD was divided into two "People's Commissariats"—the NKVD and NKGB. Deportations and similar activities passed to
the jurisdiction of the new NKGB, the People's Commissariat for State Security;
while the special armed forces remained under the NKVD. The administrative
division into two commissariats was of no political consequence; the two
agencies continued to work hand in hand, under Lavrenti Beria, member of the
Politbureau. In each of the 16 Union Republics one central NKVD and one
central NKGB headquarters were set up under the cloak of purely national
institutions; all of them actually were strictly subordinated to the Union organs
and carried out Moscow's orders to the letter.

frantic efforts were being made to arrest another few hundred suspects in hiding while German guns were already trained at Soviet targets and German fliers were climbing aboard their planes to bomb Soviet towns and villages. The last of the documents is dated June 21 and contains instructions for June 23.

On October 10, 1939, a Treaty of Mutual Assistance had been concluded between Lithuania and the Soviet Union. In it Lithuania was assured of unconditional Soviet abstention from all interference in Lithuanian affairs. Indeed, until June, 1940, the old parties and the old government remained at the helm. The day after the signing of the treaty, however—on October 11, 1939—the Moscow NKVD ordered its agents who by some means or other had begun to operate in Lithuania to start screening the population, so as to prepare a list of politically and socially dangerous elements *"regardless* of concrete data concerning their anti-Soviet activities." [7] This meant that the indices to be drawn up were to include not only politically active elements but also all those who by virtue of their position in the social life or in the economy might become opponents of the Soviet regime.

In August, 1940, the Baltic States were officially incorporated into the Soviet Union, and in November Moscow decided that a great operation was to be carried out throughout the area. Systematic preparations were immediately begun. On November 28 the Lithuanian NKVD issued orders to its local staffs concerning the compilation of these indices.

The orders included a long list of groups and persons termed dangerous.[8] It included of course all political parties except the Communists—from pro-tsarist to socialist and Trotskyite; all persons "expelled from the Communist party and the Communist Youth League"; all officers and émigrés, and a multitude of other groups. What was most significant, however, was the fact that even "shopkeepers, hotel and restaurant owners" were among the socially dangerous; even

7. Italics in original.
8. *Lithuanian Bulletin*, New York, 1946, No. 1.

"persons maintaining correspondence abroad" were to fall under the wide scope of the index.

Subsequent orders added to the list: Polish national organizations (the so-called OZON, the Non-party Bloc, and others), the leaders of the Polish Socialist and National Democratic parties, and others. The "Jewish counterrevolution" included a series of Zionist groups, the permanent contributors to Jewish-language newspapers, the "Bund," and "Jewish militarized-Fascist formations." There followed "White émigré formations," the Fraternity of Russian Truth, the Russian Military Union, the Russian Fascist Union, the National Labor Union of the New Generation, the so-called *mladorossy* ("Young Russia"), and various Ukrainian and White Russian organizations.

The schedule called for reports from the local agencies on the completion of indices by May 5, 1941; the entire job was to be finished by June 1. The operation itself was set for early in June. All those classified as anti-Soviet elements were to be deported to corrective labor camps, while members of their families were destined for exile into far-off regions. The instructions stressed, however, the imperative necessity to arouse no suspicion, to prepare quietly, and in doing so to make use of "agents' work."

Beginning on April 23, 1941, Gladkov, head of the NKGB in Kaunas, issued a stream of instructions, memoranda, orders, and reminders to his staffs in the various counties and cities of Lithuania. Then he and his subordinates began to prod for more rapid and efficient work. Gladkov was dissatisfied with the pace of preparations and his language became increasingly stern. His deputy, Bykov, reported in a "Top Secret" document, dated May 27, 1941, that "some chiefs have an irresponsible attitude and tolerate errors." He concluded with a threat: "I warn all chiefs and deputies of district staffs of the NKGB that those guilty of irresponsible compilation of material concerning counterrevolutionary and anti-Soviet elements will henceforth be held most strictly responsible." On May 29 Bykov reprimanded 17 local agencies for not having forwarded reports on persons to be indexed, nor a single summary report." The other phases of the preparatory operations were, according to him, no more satisfactory. "Failure to carry out directives in due time"—Bykov was once more menacing— "will be considered as a direct undermining of an operational combat assignment."

By the end of May the details of the forthcoming operation were fixed: in each district a "troika" (i.e., a leading team of three men) was established, consisting mainly of higher officials of the two departments of the Secret Police. Only in the two big cities, Vilno and Kaunas, were the "operational headquarters" larger. The troikas were made responsible for the proper execution of the deportation orders.

On May 31, 1941, the People's Commissariat of the USSR for State Security finally dispatched a brief communication, stating:

The People's Commissar for State Security of the Union of Soviet Socialist Republics, Comrade MERKULOV, HAS ORDERED:
Persons of anti-Soviet leanings engaged in active counterrevolutionary agitation are to be prepared for deportation into remote areas of the USSR.
Communicated for appropriate action.

The brief letter from Moscow also gave the official version of the political motives for the coming operation. It alleged that "mandatory grain deliveries to the state" were meeting opposition on the part of anti-Soviet elements.

All troikas assigned to the various districts were given "transcripts from the textbook of the NKVD of the USSR on operational action." The lengthy excerpt from the textbook contains little of general interest, but it confirms again the existence of secret texts for the forces of the NKVD. The transcript describes in detail how belongings found during searching operations are to be recorded in the protocols, the disposition of such belongings, how arrested personnel are to be registered, etc.

On June 4 Serov, the Deputy Commissar of the NKGB of the Union, sent out two further instructions. In order to determine the number of men needed for the operation, he instructed the local agencies (evidently on the basis of a standing order) to calculate on the following rule: "one operational official, one member of the NKVD, one soldier of the armed forces of the NKVD, and one representative of the local group of the Communist party." These men, Serov wrote, must "carry out the operation of two families."

He orders the selection of the party members for the operational teams in advance, but the nature of the operation must be kept secret from the men concerned. He further writes that the operatives are "to deliver the deportees to the railroad tracks, where they are to be met by auto transportation and brought to the railway station; to request in advance railroad cars on the ratio of at least 25 men per car." In general, he demanded "that the operation be carried out without noise or panic, so as not to permit any disorders or excesses whatsoever, not only on the part of the deportees but also on the part of a certain section of the neighboring population who have a hostile attitude toward the Soviet authorities."

On the eve of the operation, i.e., on June 5, a meeting of the members of each operational team took place, where for the first time the nature of the operation was revealed. All the personnel involved were informed of the "location of reserves of armed forces" in case they were needed, since "the deportees are enemies of the Soviet people, and hence the possibility is not excluded that they may offer armed resistance." "Arms must be kept in battle readiness. Weapons are to be loaded but not cocked." Orders going into every detail established the rule that husbands and wives must be separated. Even the weight of personal effects permitted the "migrants" was prescribed in order not to tax the available freight space. The very pretexts used for arrests were standardized in order not to frighten the exiles' families, and to let them believe they were being transferred to a near-by colony:

. . . Care must be taken that the operations are carried out without disturbance and panic, so as not to permit any demonstrations and other trouble not only on the part of those deported but also on the part of a certain section of the population hostile to the Soviet administration.

. . . Operations shall be begun at daybreak. Upon entering the house of the person to be deported, the senior member of the operative group shall assemble the entire family in one room, taking all necessary precautionary measures against any possible trouble.

. . . After completion of the search the deportees shall be notified that by a government decision they will be deported to other regions of the Union. The deportees shall be permitted to take with them household necessities not exceeding 100 kilograms in weight. . . .

If inhabitants of the village begin to gather around the deportee's house while operations are in progress, they shall be called upon to disperse to their own homes and crowds shall not be permitted to form.

. . . The delivery of the deportees from the village to the meeting place at the railway station must be effected in daylight; care, moreover, should be taken that the assembling of every family shall not last more than two hours. In all cases throughout the operations firm and decisive action shall be taken, without the slightest excitement, noise and panic. . . .

In view of the fact that a large number of deportees must be arrested and distributed in special camps and that their families must proceed to special settlements in distant regions, it is essential that the operation of removal of both the members of the deportee's family and its head should be carried out simultaneously, without notifying them of the separation confronting them. . . .

The convoy of the entire family to the station shall, however, be effected in one vehicle and only at the station of departure shall the head of the family be placed separately from his family in a car specially intended for heads of families. During the assembling of the family in the home of the deportee, the head of the family shall be warned that personal male effects must be packed in a separate suitcase, as a sanitary inspection of the deported men will be made separately from the women and children.

. . . Red Army men of the convoying forces of the NKVD shall surround the entrainment station. . . . After the railway car has been filled with the necessary number of families, it shall be locked. After the people have been taken over and placed in the deportation train, the chief of the train shall bear responsibility for all persons handed over to him and for their delivery to their destination. . . .

The operation took place as scheduled. The secret had been well kept, and the population was taken unawares. In the former capital of Lithuania the "operational report," dated June 19, 1941, stated that by and large the operation proceeded according to plan; there was virtually no resistance, and whatever incidents there were were due to "inexperience and inefficiency of the operational personnel." There was hardly any shooting, and only one man was wounded. On the other hand, the report notes, "in the course of the operation, the following comrades made an outstanding showing, defying time and fatigue"—and there follow six names, evidently recommended for promotion or decoration. In the course of the operation in Kaunas 23 persons hid and one escaped; besides, 122 were absent from their homes at the time of the action.

The deportees were loaded into trains routed as follows:

From Lithuania, chiefly to stations along the Krasnoyarsk, Karaganda, Tomsk, and Moscow-Kiev Railroads;

From Latvia, into the Altai region, to Kotlas (Gorky R.R.), and Starobelsk (Moscow-Donbas R.R.);

From Estonia, to various stations of the Gorky, Tomsk, Moscow-Donbas, and Moscow-Kiev Railroads.

On June 21, 1941, i.e., a few hours before the first German raid, Commissar Gladkov directed another secret memorandum to his subordinates. In the course of the operation, he explained, a part of the "enemy elements subject to arrest and deportation" had managed to escape, passing to an outlaw status. They were reported hiding in the forests, and would henceforth be referred to as "bandit groups." In some instances they were said to have arms. Gladkov instructed his subordi-

Отбирать какие-либо вещи выселяемых, за исклю-
чением оружия, контрреволюционной литературы и валюты, а также
пользоваться продуктами питания выселяемых – категорически вос-
прещается.

Предупредить всех участников операции о строжай-
шей судебной ответственности за попытку присвоения отдельных ве-
щей выселяемых.

5. Порядок разделения семьи выселяемого от главы.

Ввиду того, что большое количество выселяемых
должно быть арестовано и размещено в специальные лагеря, а их
семьи следуют в места специальных поселений в отдаленных облас-
тях, поэтому необходимо операцию по из"ятию, как выселяемых
членов семьи, так и главы их, проводить одновременно не об"яв-
ляя им о предстоящем их разделении. После того, когда проведен
обыск и оформлены соответствующие документы для личного дела, в
квартире выселяемого, оперативный работник заполняет документы
на главу семьи, вкладывает их в личное дело на него, а документы, оформленные на членов семьи, вкладываются в личное дело вы-
селяемой семьи.

Сопровождение же всей семьи до станции погрузки
производится на одной подводе и лишь на станции погрузки главу
семьи помещают отдельно от семьи, в специально предназначенный
для глав семей вагон.

Во время сбора в квартире выселяемых предупредить главу семьи о том, что личные мужские вещи складывал в
отдельный чемодан, так как будет проходить сан.обработка выселя-
емым мужчинам отдельно от женщин и детей.

Reproduction of page 5 of the original instructions of the NKVD concerning the arrest and deportation of persons destined for forced labor camps and exile. Separation of head of family from other members, entrainment procedure, confiscation of belongings, search, etc.

nates how to combat such "bandit manifestations." The principal means consisted in dispatching agents-provocateurs to the "bandits":

. . . From among former Shauliites, kulaks, officers, etc., in areas of manifestation of banditry, organize the passing of agents to an "illegal" status as well as escapes into the forests, under pretense of wishing to escape persecution by organs of the NKGB, so as to have these operatives assimilated into bandit groups, expose them fully, and liquidate them. Every such combination is to be carried out only after receipt of my approval. . . .

7. Carry out the recruitment of agents from among village mayors, who on account of their functions know all local residents individually and can inform you of cases of suspicious gatherings, absence of some inhabitant from the village, appearance of suspect persons preparing to pass to an illegal status, etc.

As already stated, all the operations in the Baltic States yielded a catch of about 200,000 [9] of whom 50,000 to 60,000 went to the labor camps, while the rest were resettled in exile. This series of operations was on a moderate scale, far from the largest of the NKVD's deportations—just an ordinary, unexciting, everyday event.

THE WAR

With the outbreak of war in 1941, and especially after the great retreat of the Soviet armies, the old slogan of "mercilessness" was again revived. "Stop liberalism in the practice of the courts," wrote the official law publication.[10] I. Golyakov, president of the Supreme Court, urged the renewed application of the severe law of August 7, 1932, providing the death penalty for "pillage of Socialist property."

Then the government took the next spectacular step—it

9. E. M. Kulischer, *Displacement of Population in Europe* (New York, 1946), pp. 62–64. A detailed study carried out by the Baltic Humanitarian Association in Sweden reaches the conclusion that the number of "killed, arrested, and deported amounted to 60,973 Estonians, 34,250 Letts, and 38,450 Lithuanians"—a total of 133,673, besides those voluntarily evacuated to Russia. *The Baltic Refugees* (Stockholm, 1946).

10. *Sotsialisticheskaya zakonnost'* (Socialist Law), 1942, No. 2.

reintroduced the very term "katorga" (penal servitude), which had been abolished "forever" in the first months of the Soviet regime.

On April 19, 1943, the Presidium of the Supreme Soviet decreed that collaborators with Germany may be sentenced to death by hanging (this too was a restoration of prerevolutionary law, since only death by shooting had been permitted since 1917) or, in lesser cases, to exile to katorga for 15 to 20 years. The decree was immediately applied. A part of the defendants in the Krasnodar and Kharkov trials were sentenced to terms of forced labor, now appearing under the name of katorga; the same was true long after the war in the convictions of the Semionov group in 1946. The reform completed the reversion to old Russia in the terminology of penal law.

The deportation of Soviet citizens during the war involved, first, politically unreliable elements who were still at liberty at the outbreak of the war; and second, and mainly, large groups from the "disloyal" nationalities. These constituted the main object of the large-scale punitive operations during the war years.

The first among these were the Germans of the Autonomous Volga–German SSR, to which groups of German origin residing in other regions of Soviet Russia were added. A decree of August 28, 1941, abolished the Volga–German Autonomous Republic for alleged diversionist activities. The 1939 census had shown it to have a population of 605,000. A considerable part of this population was now resettled in the east, in the Altai region of western Siberia, and in other areas.

After the German retreat from the northern Caucasus and Crimea it was found that many Chechens and Ingush of the Caucasus and Tatars of the Crimean ASSR had collaborated with the invader. Despite the fact that the majority of these nationalities could not be made responsible for acts of treachery, they were accused of failure to resist and prevent the disloyal activities of certain of their nationals and officials. The deportations started as soon as the German armies were driven out. These two autonomous republics ceased to exist;

their territory was, in the main, incorporated into the Russian SSR. But not until June 25, 1946, did the Supreme Soviet of the Russian Republic make the formal decision on this painful purge. The "law" abolishing the two republics said that during the war against Germany

many Chechens and Crimean Tartars, upon the instigation of German agents, joined voluntary formations organized by the Germans and, together with the German forces, engaged in armed warfare against the Red Army. Following German instructions, they organized diversionist bands to fight the Soviet regime behind the lines. The basic mass of the population of the Chechen-Ingush and Crimean ASSR's did not demonstrate any opposition to these traitors to the fatherland. In connection herewith, the Chechens and Crimean Tartars were resettled in other regions of the USSR, where they were provided with land, given the necessary assistance by the state for their economic organization. . . . The Chechen-Ingush ASSR was abolished, and the Crimean ASSR reorganized into the Crimean Region.

Finally, the residents of the Kalmyk ASSR and of the Karachayev Autonomous Region were also considered to have demonstrated a lack of loyalty to their fatherland and their national units were likewise liquidated during the war, all or part of their population being deported.

It is impossible to calculate even the approximate total of these deported elements. The population of the five regions in question amounted to 2,798,000 in 1939 [11] but of course not all were deported. Officially nothing has been told of the fate of the deportees. The NKVD undoubtedly worked in conformity with its traditional pattern of sending the most suspect and active elements of these nationalities to corrective labor camps, while the rest, in the absence of individual convictions, were forced to move to "free settlements" in which,

11. Volga-German ASSR   605,000
    Kalmyk ASSR   220,000
    Chechen-Ingush ASSR   697,000
    Crimean ASSR   1,127,000
    Karachayev Region   149,000

willy-nilly, they had to become pioneers in farming and cattle-breeding.

The resettlement of peasants has always been a difficult task in Russia, both before and after the Revolution, although it never reached dimensions as great as in recent years. Soil must be made arable, buildings erected, and the necessary tools, horses, and cattle provided. The most strenuous efforts are necessary to create a new village in hitherto uninhabited areas. During the war, however, the huge stream of compulsory movements of population into the forests and tundras took place without any preparation, at a time when the government had its hands full elsewhere and was in no condition to supply the migrants with even the barest essentials. Their fate was therefore tragic. Essentially the movement of population represented a repetition of the mass deportation of kulaks in the early 'thirties, with all the ominous consequences. Those who survived the hardships of the war years now live in their new settlements and toil under the vigilant eye of the MVD.

By the end of the war and immediately thereafter, new groups of forced laborers began to flow into the labor camps. Again there were two sources of supply of this manpower: foreigners and Russians.

Among the foreigners the main new source consisted of prisoners of war. The Soviet Government has never announced the number of prisoners captured by the Russians. The number of German prisoners has been estimated at from 3 to 4 millions; in addition, smaller groups of Rumanians, Hungarians, Italians, and Finns have been in Soviet captivity. At the Moscow Conference of Foreign Ministers in March, 1947, Mr. Molotov stated that, while 1,003,974 Germans had been repatriated, only 890,532 still remained in Russia. Even assuming a high mortality rate among German prisoners of war, these figures are susceptible to considerable doubt on all counts. In August, 1945, the Soviet armies' drive through Manchuria resulted in the capture of Japanese prisoners who were subsequently transferred to Siberia. Their number is estimated at 900,000.[12]

From a purely legal point of view, the compulsory employment of prisoners of war is normal and justifiable. In the case of the Soviet Union, however, no limitations are placed on such employment, since the Soviet Union does not adhere to the Geneva Convention; nor does the International Red Cross have any influence on Russian authorities in regard to the treatment of the prisoners. At a time when even the free population of Russia had to live on rather meager rations, the diet of prisoners of war was just as near the subsistence minimum as that of Russian forced labor in the camps of the NKVD.

A detailed report in the *Continental News Service* (London, August 26, 1946) says that during their first period of captivity prisoners were sent from one "transient camp" to another and consequently obtained a comprehensive picture of the camp system. In Odessa, for example, where there were 24 comparatively small camps, the prisoners were employed in rebuilding the port and factories. New concrete coastal fortifications and ammunition stores were erected. The port itself was enlarged and electric cranes installed. At another camp, No. 188, at Rada, near Tambov, the daily death rate was reported to be 15 for a total of 4,000 to 5,000 inmates. Camp No. 270, at Boroviche, about 250 kilometers southeast of Leningrad, was divided into two subcamps, one for senior officers and one for the lower ranks, each containing 5,000 to 6,000 prisoners; 90 per cent of the inmates were Poles, members of the resistance movement. The camp was situated on marshy ground and the prisoners were employed in cutting peat and felling trees. In Leningrad and its suburbs there were altogether 30 camps containing over 200,000 people, some of them women.

There were also many show camps, inhabited by specially selected prisoners, such as Krasnogorsk, near Moscow, where the privileges accorded the prisoners gave rise to many fabulous stories among the other camps about good food, pleasant

12. *New York Times*, December 20, 1946.

living conditions, and no work. Among the inmates of this camp were Marshal Paulus, General Seydlitz, and some prominent Spanish "Reds." Another of these privileged camps was No. 150, situated in former monastery buildings in the Urals and containing only high-ranking German officers. This was a part of the "Win Germany" technique pursued during the war.

As for living conditions in most camps, such as those of Odessa or Leningrad, the premises consisted of dilapidated buildings, surrounded by barbed wire and sentry boxes. In camps situated in the forests, prisoners lived in wooden huts or even in tents. They usually slept on the ground, without mattresses or even straw, and with only one blanket. They had no soap, towels, or medicaments, not even iodine, and they were infested with lice. The food was insufficient, though there was no starvation. The prisoners were given potato soup three times a day, 600 grams of bread daily, and *kasha* with melted soya fat twice a week. They got no meat, animal fats, or vegetables.

The prisoners worked 10 to 12 hours a day six days a week. Technicians and skilled workers of all kinds received preferential treatment. In theory the prisoners were to be paid one ruble a day for eight hours' work and 25 kopeks for every hour of overtime. They rarely received their wages, however, and it was openly said in the camps that the money was paid out by the authorities in Moscow but found its way into the pockets of superintendents and local agents.

There was a great deal of sabotage, particularly in the factories. To combat this the authorities were compelled to post armed guards in every factory. Propaganda lectures were held at least once a week in each camp. Mobile film units sometimes visited the camps to show propaganda films. German prisoners were encouraged to join the "Antifa" [anti-Fascist] organization, and the most reliable were sent to special courses, on completion of which they were to return to their own country as Communist agitators.

Among the projects carried out by the labor of prisoners

of war the outstanding one is a great new railroad leading from the vicinity of Kuibyshev on the Volga to Taishet, west of Lake Baikal in Siberia. This railway, begun before the war, will be about 2,500 miles long and is to connect the eastern part of European Russia with the new and projected industrial centers of Magnitogorsk, Akmolinsk, Pavlodar, Kulunda, Barnaul, and the Kuznetsk Basin. In Taishet, which is located on the old Trans-Siberian line, the new South Siberian Railroad will link up with the Baikal–Amur line, under construction in the 'thirties and 'forties as a second road from European Russia to the Pacific Ocean. According to Soviet sources, 3 million Axis prisoners of war were occupied on these tremendous projects in 1946; among them were about 2 million prisoners from Germany, Italy, Finland, and Hungary, and about 800,000 Japanese.[13]

The Italian Government reported in the Constituent Assembly on February 27, 1947, that only 12,513 prisoners of war had returned from Russia out of a total of 60,000. The mortality rate, due to epidemics, was particularly high in the Turkestan concentration camps; here it reached 94 per cent. The liberal newspaper *Risorgimente Liberale* reported that "the Russians showed bestial carelessness, contempt for human life, and no respect for international agreements regulating the treatment of war prisoners." [14]

The postwar Russian occupation of large territories in Europe and Asia gave the Soviet military and police authorities arbitrary and unquestioned power over all sections of the native population, particularly in the defeated nations, and the suppression of oppositionist movements led to frequent deportation to Russia of individuals and groups. Soviet military tribunals acted in Germany as well as in other former Axis countries as political agencies of the Soviet Government. The greatest number of deportees has been reported from the Soviet zone of Germany. Men accused of anti-Soviet activities

13. *Irkutskaya Pravda*, quoted in the *New York Times*, December 17, 1946.
14. *New York Times*, February 28, 1947.

or of pro-Fascist sympathies have been sentenced to up to 20 years of forced labor in Russia. It has been reported that up to 20 per cent of German youths in the Soviet zone have been arrested, interned at the concentration camp of Ferch, near Potsdam, and sent from there to Russia.[15] This percentage may be exaggerated; but there is no doubt that measures of this kind have been fairly extensive.

German prisoners of war, released by the Western Powers and repatriated to the Russian zone, were often arrested and deported to Russia for forced labor. Not less than 4,000 officers and an unknown number of enlisted men were taken to Soviet camps in Germany and then shipped to the East. Soviet authorities were especially rigorous with those German officers who had "graduated" from American "courses in democracy" and were supposed to constitute an important means of democratic regeneration in Germany.[16]

Thus, while certain contingents of former prisoners of war have been returned to Germany from Soviet captivity, there has been a stream of foreign labor moving in the opposite direction, from west to east.

RUSSIAN PRISONERS OF WAR

In the meanwhile millions of Russians were returning to the Soviet Union. The two most numerous categories among them consisted of Russian laborers, men and women, forcibly dragged to work in Germany; and Russian prisoners of war, for the most part captured during the Russian retreat in 1941–42. From the second group the Germans had attempted to organize "labor battalions" of the men who were considered unreliable and unfit to bear German arms; and Russian military formations (General Vlasov's army and other units) with Russian officers but under German control. In addition, individual Russians entered the German service.

15. Report by Max Januszewski to the British military authorities in Germany, based on his personal experiences in the concentration camps of eastern Germany. *Neue Volkszeitung,* June 1, 1946.

16. *New York Journal American,* January 24, 1947.

Now this huge mass of humanity was returning home. Real
traitors made up but a negligible fraction of them. But their
experiences abroad—the standard of life they had seen and
their contacts with Allied troops—made them a danger in the
eyes of their government. They were carrying home germs
of criticism. They had become politically unreliable in their
own country.

Screening of repatriates therefore became a rule. All Russians returning from German captivity or German slavery had
to pass through camps, surrounded by barbed wire and closely
guarded by armed detachments, and every one of them—especially prisoners of war—was subjected to detailed interrogations. The whole investigation was carried out by the NKVD
in accordance with strict and detailed instructions from Moscow. The very fact of his captivity was the accusation leveled
against every Soviet prisoner of war. According to a Soviet
principle of long standing, a member of the Red Army is forbidden to fall into enemy hands under any circumstances. A
war waged by the Soviet Union is considered different from
all other wars between nations: it is a sort of holy war, a cru-
sade in which no individual may surrender. Soldiers and officers of the Soviet Army were instructed to follow these principles: if surrounded by the enemy without hope of escaping,
fight to the finish, kill as many as possible before getting killed;
if wounded do not let yourself be captured; commit suicide
rather than surrender alive. These maxims had important im-
plications in more than one sense. The Soviet Union never adhered to the Geneva Convention concerning the treatment of
prisoners of war. It remained indifferent to the fate of Red
Army men who had fallen into enemy hands. A Soviet prisoner of war is an outcast—so the theory went—he is not
worth the attention and aid of his country. The frightful mortality rate among Russian prisoners of war in Germany was a
consequence of this attitude.[17]

17. "In regard to the rules concerning prisoners of war the Government of the
USSR does not consider itself bound by any international agreements whatsoever. At the present time the penalty for premeditated surrender into captivity
not necessitated by combat conditions is death by shooting, according to Par. 14

It also played a considerable part during the first 18 months of the war when Soviet morale was low and masses of Russian soldiers were easily taken prisoners by the Germans. The terrible fate of Russian prisoners in Germany was persuasively utilized in the Soviet campaign of exorting the Red Army to resist.

And now, after the war, the concept of a "holy war" was made use of in screening the masses of prisoners and deportees to replenish the contingents of forced labor.

While American and British prisoners of war were returning home as honored citizens and were received with general sympathy and compassion for the hardships they had sustained, Soviet soldiers, from private to colonel, had to undergo a humiliating procedure. They were often stripped of their clothes and given German rags to wear; officers' shoulder straps were torn off; they were given the lowest food rations, less than the bulk of the Soviet Army received. And everyone was made to answer dozens of questions asked by NKVD investigators—as to why he had failed to take his life at the last moment, how he had spent the years of imprisonment in Germany, and so on. Executions were infrequent; only those who had served in a commanding capacity with the Germans were shot. Members of the Vlasov army and other pro-German formations were usually given terms of 15 to 25 years of corrective labor. The great majority of prisoners, however, who had remained loyal to their country, were likewise sent off to hard labor, with the exception of old men and some of the women, who were permitted to return home. And in the files of every Russian returning home the entry "Socially dangerous" was made.

A multitude of reports confirm this peculiar treatment of Soviet repatriates and add eloquent details to this over-all picture. Here, for instance, is what Lieutenant G. Dlinnykh tells

---

of the Regulations on Military Offenses." *Great Soviet Encyclopedia*, XIV, 285. Also Penal Code, par. 193[22]. "Decree No. 270" of 1942 declares a prisoner captured alive by the enemy ipso facto a traitor; it provides for the loss of allowances by the prisoner's family and for severe punishment of the prisoner's family in the case of officers.

of his experiences, in an as yet unpublished manuscript received from France. He was put to work by the Germans in a plant near Berlin, was wounded by an exploding mine, and was in a hospital when the Red Army occupied the area.

After my recovery [he relates] I was sent to a screening camp and thence to a construction battalion. In the screening camp all the Russians who had been in Germany had to appear before a commission of the NKVD. A detailed interrogation takes place—How, why, and when did you get to Germany? Why didn't you join the Partisan movement? Where and with whom did you work in Germany, and so forth.—Beatings are frequent. All those suspected of collaboration with the Germans (be it only on the basis of denunciations and hearsay) are sent to separate camps and then appear before the Revolutionary Tribunal in Frankfurt-on-the-Oder, where after a brief trial they are sentenced to various terms of forced labor in concentration camps—usually more than five years.

Those whose records are "clean" have a notation made in their records: "SO" [i.e., socially dangerous], and then the younger men and part of the women are sent to construction battalions and work details with the army, while the older men, part of the women, and the children are sent home. There the adults must report to the local offices of the NKVD, are entitled to remain home only one month, and then must serve two years in special labor camps. The terms of those remaining in Germany—with the army and work details—are not known.

Former Vlasovites were at first shot without much ado, but now they are usually sentenced to 15 to 25 years. . . .

The repatriates are depressed, especially those who had been in the American and British zones. They are forbidden to attend higher schools or occupy responsible positions for a long time. In general they are treated as "second-class" citizens.

Another lieutenant of the Red Army gave an account of his deportation to a labor camp in Siberia and his miraculous return to Western Europe, which was published in the *Svobodnoye slovo* (Free Word) in Paris under the title "Judge Me!"

I have been a member of the Communist Youth League since 1934; from 1941 on, I served as liaison officer in the Red Army. My older brother is a member of the party, the head of a workshop in a big plant; my other brother was also a party member and a major in the Red Army: he was killed during the "liberation" of Poland in 1939. My father was secretary of the party committee in a remote district until his death in 1938. All our family had always been loyal to the Soviet regime, consciously and out of profound conviction. I did not at all share the defeatist mood, when in the first months of the war the majority of our soldiers and a part of the officers desired to surrender to the Germans. I did not believe in the German idea of "liberation."

After capturing three heavy German tanks I was wounded in the battle of Orel. I was awarded the Order of the Red Banner "for valor and bravery in action." In October, 1941, our entire unit was surrounded and captured after a desperate fight. A bomb tore off three of my fingers. How it happened that I, an officer, a candidate for party membership, failed to shoot myself as instructed, and how I let myself be taken prisoner, I cannot explain. Perhaps the acute pain in my hand held me back, or else perhaps the awareness of having fought to the last; or maybe the utter exhaustion after 11 days of uninterrupted fighting had rendered me completely apathetic and indifferent to my future. Besides there were 2,000 other soldiers and officers sharing my fate. I cannot describe my horror when a few days later I became fully aware of being a prisoner, nor the abhorrence of the German treatment of the prisoners, whom they were shooting for disobedience, starving to death, killing the sick and exhausted who were unable to march on. My experiences and emotions of those days defy the boldest imagination.

I was sent to work near Katowice in Silesia, where I was required to toil under hard conditions despite my crippled hand. I shall not describe the working conditions there. That was one of the gloomiest aspects of German captivity, I believe. Within four months I had become a blood-spitting invalid with swollen legs. In May, 1944, in view of my inability to perform hard labor, I was transferred to the Hannover region to work in a plant producing spare parts. At the same time I was again approached with an offer to join the Vlasov army, but I preferred to die an honest man in the eyes of my fatherland.

I continued to work until the Americans arrived and freed the Russian prisoners and deportees. There were many among us who did not wish to return home. To me this attitude seemed absurd, unreasonable, pathological. . . . I was then in command of a group of over 400 persons who wanted to return home immediately. I counted the days, anxiously looking forward to the happy moment of going home.

We took leave of those who had decided not to return in a mood of mutual hostility. I considered them ungrateful and erring sons of our fatherland and they frankly called us fools.

. . . We have reached the Russian zone. A few minutes after the departure of the American trucks that had brought us there we were ordered to line up. I was disagreeably surprised by the great number of armed soldiers who guarded us on all sides. At last an officer showed up and without greeting ordered us to tear off our shoulder straps in terms little suited for the ears of the women and children present. Then addressing the entire group he proceeded to tell us that we were traitors, that we had gone over to the enemy on purpose, that we had volunteered for work in Germany, and that the women had only catered to the basest instincts of the enemy.

They took us—a small group of former Red Army officers—to an unspeakably filthy empty hut. We received no food. Two days went by in waiting. Then two of our comrades were called out and taken away. One of them soon returned but refused to answer our questions; the other one never came back. Late in the night I was summoned. The examining officer—a strange character, highly nervous, with a constantly twitching body—instead of interrogating me began to heap accusations on me. Why had I let myself be captured? Why hadn't I escaped? Why had I consented to work for the Germans? Why had I failed to engage in sabotage? Why had I failed to kill any Germans while in prison? Why had I failed to do anything to liquidate any of those who joined the Vlasov army? I asked him when and to what army unit I would be directed. He smiled and said that first I would have to expiate my guilt and air out my infected ideology. At this I got mad: I who had fought bravely to the last, who had been wounded twice, whose hand had been crippled, who had experienced all the torment of captivity and forced labor, who had refused to join the Vlasov army, who had never done anything disreputable in my life—was I to be accused of treason and deprived of decorations won in battle? Was this justice? I said I would complain to Marshal Zhukov and demand a thorough investigation. To this he replied with a torrent of profanity. When I pointed out that for two days I had had nothing to eat and asked him to have my belongings returned to me, he said we had feasted long enough on American rations and it would do us good to go hungry for a while and that our luggage had been confiscated.

By the next morning our group had shrunk: 12 comrades—almost half of us—had not returned from the interrogation. They were shot immediately in the garage, which had been specially arranged for this purpose. About 60 of our whole convoy were liquidated in this fashion. I knew the story of every one of those who had arrived with me, I knew how and why they had found themselves in Germany, and I knew that they all had a clear conscience and were eager and happy to go home.

. . . One day we were taken to another hut and made to undress and exchange our American outfits for old German uniforms, tattered and filthy, that seemed to have been taken off corpses . . .

Dirty, unshaven, in our ragged German uniforms and broken shoes, we presented a pitiful picture. The distress of the men whose wives and children had been deported to an unknown destination the day before can easily be imagined. We were all deeply troubled by the question: why all this? What had we done to deserve it? . . . We started off under an impressive escort. We marched until nightfall with hardly any food. After four days we were loaded in a freight train with tightly closed windows. There were 62 persons in our car. There was no room to stretch out; we had to take turns sitting down. The train had no less than 50 cars, and all of them were filled with people like us. Some died on the way. Twice the doors of the car were opened to let us watch the shooting of several deportees who had attempted to escape.

At last the whole transport was unloaded, some 30 to 40 kilometers from Omsk, as we learnt later. Again we marched, reaching a cluster of newly built huts after dark. There were a good many such huts, but communication between them was strictly forbidden. Inside there were bunks in two tiers and nothing else. The next morning those of us who knew foreign languages were called up. I was sent to a German camp a few miles away to serve as translator.

I do not know the total number of camp inmates, but I estimate that there must have been several hundreds of thousands in our huts, people of various nationalities and from many countries. They were all engaged in building vast industrial plants for which the equipment was brought from Germany. We christened the project "New Germany." The entire personnel, engineers, technicians, as well as craftsmen, clerks, and medics, was recruited from among the prisoners. Everyone had experience in his field. The organization was admirable. "Don't spare any human beings: carry out the task according to plan."

The mortality was high. This was due to the lack of proper working clothes, the terrific cold, the speed-up and the competition, the bad food and the shortage of medical supplies. No distinction was made in any respect between Germans and Russians like myself. One had the impression that the destruction of the human beings concentrated here was being carried out on directives from Moscow. Suicides were frequent.

One day there arrived a routine commission of inspectors. In one of them I recognized a cousin of mine. He passed me twice without a sign of recognition. The next time I saw him I went up to him with some question concerning my work. He recognized me but still gave no sign. For two days we met constantly; I felt his eyes resting on me—but that was all. And this from a cousin, almost a brother, a childhood playmate, my closest friend for nearly ten years! I decided then and there to make an end to this wretched and hopeless life. I had a rope in my possession and intended to hang myself that very night. But late that night I was summoned to the office of the commission, where I found my cousin by himself. He asked me some questions concerning my work, then sent the guard away, locked the door and—we were alone. We hugged and kissed each other in the boundless joy of our reunion. . . . He begged me to tell him frankly what had brought me here, and I told him the whole story. He wept while listening to me.

From him I learnt many interesting things. My fate, he told me, was that of all those returned from German captivity or deportation, including women. As a result of the purges conducted by the Red Army in occupied territories, hundreds of transports were daily being directed to the various places where the "New Germany" was under construction. Thousands of "religionists" were being brought there from the areas liberated from the Germans. My cousin explained to me the significance of the appointment of a patriarch by the party. I learnt that in the model towns, which were to be shown to visiting foreigners, churches had been opened and fine shops with a superabundance of excellent high-priced foodstuffs had been established. But nothing similar could be found in places remote from the center, and the idea of opening churches in provincial towns would have seemed absurd, and those who dared advance it soon would have found themselves among the builders of "New Germany."

It was interesting to hear from him about the people's exultation over the victory. Everyone believed that an easier life could now be expected, that the ceaseless feverish work of 12 to 13 hours a day would come to an end and the half-starved population would be given food. They hoped that the NKVD would relax its vigilance and cease suspecting everybody of being a wrecker and traitor. My cousin told me that not only the "common man," the rank-and-file soldier, but also the higher-ups, including the marshals, live in constant fear, and that he himself—a party official of high standing, possessor of many decorations won in the war—enjoyed neither peace of mind nor a sense of security. . . .

It is impossible for me to tell here the story of my "reincarnation," with false documents bearing a strange name, of the Red Army uniform which I wore, and the journey which brought me in an official capacity to one of the zones of occupation in Germany, where I discarded my Red Army uniform. . . . With a feeling of deep pain I reflect on my shattered life, on the undeserved disgrace which was the sole reward I received for my boundless love of my country. And now do I not still love my country? At the first call of my people I shall return to serve it—the people, but not those leaders who cling to their power and are ruthlessly destroying our helpless misguided people. . . .

Now judge me! Pass judgment on me and tell me what I am guilty of! My conscience is clear, my will is unbroken and—despite everything I have been through—I have enough strength left to fight for the real liberation of my enslaved and terrorized but still magnificent people!

COMPULSORY REPATRIATION TO FORCED LABOR

At the end of the war every belligerent nation assumed that all displaced nationals would be anxious to return home as soon as possible. No government considered compulsory measures necessary to force repatriation—except the Soviet Union.

Besides Russian prisoners of war, millions of other Soviet citizens were in western Europe by the end of military operations in 1945. There were Russian laborers, men and women, "imported" into Germany and German-occupied countries during the German reign; thousands of Russians had joined the anti-Nazi underground in France and other countries; there were remnants of Vlasov's Army and other Russian military formations who had fought against the Soviet Army; and there were German "labor battalions" recruited from Russians. While demanding the wholesale and compulsory return home of all these groups, the Soviet authorities began to prepare the "cases" for the NKVD. The decision to screen each and every individual of this huge mass was soon carried out. If a man had worked in a German plant or on a German farm, had he gone by his own will when labor was being lured to Germany, or had he been dragged away by force? In the former case, he was a traitor and therefore subject to severe punishment. If he was a Russian partisan in France, was he not trying to hide his previous collaboration with the Germans? And if he had been a member of any Russo-German military formation, he was sure to be punished either by death or a sentence to katorga.

In 1944 the Soviet Government began diplomatic negotiations with the aim of compelling its allies to send home all Soviet citizens in their zones, regardless of their wishes. At first this desire met with some reluctance on the part of the Western Allies, but they gave in. These proceedings were not revealed in the official communiqués, since the American and British authorities apparently wished to avoid public discussion of a measure that actually condemned to great hardship not only persons guilty of treason but also thousands of innocent men and women.

Compulsory shipment of Soviet citizens back to Russia began in 1944 and was not terminated until 1946. The question had been raised at the Yalta Conference of the Big Three and had been settled in accordance with Soviet wishes. The President of the United States and the British Prime Minister could not have been unaware of the real significance of Stalin's demands. The tendency toward cementing friendship with Stalin at almost any price in more than one instance induced the unconditional acceptance of his demands by the Western Allies. But in this case the violation of elementary rules of morals and humaneness was flagrant. The "friendship"— which after all was not achieved—was paid for with the blood of thousands of Russians.

Russia, like every other country, was naturally entitled to judge its own citizens for their behavior during the war. Yet there has been a perennial distrust of the NKVD system of justice, of its inclination to wreak vengeance, of the ease with which it pronounces and carries out its rigorous sentences. If it had been revealed before the conscience of the world, the British and American consent to Stalin's demand would certainly have provoked vigorous protests. The agreements remained secret until March, 1947.

As soon as the war in Germany ended, the Yalta decisions were put into effect. Millions of Soviet citizens were soon repatriated from Germany and other countries. On the other hand, many thousands of Russians, prisoners of war and civilians alike, refused to return; thousands crossed the German border into Switzerland, France, Belgium, and Holland. It soon became known that those who had been repatriated were screened and, where any doubts arose, were placed in "transient camps" controlled by the NKVD.

Nothing was ever reported in either the Soviet press or radio about the fate of Soviet "traitors" after the war. In order not to disclose the extent to which Russians had waged war against the Soviet Union, and in order to sustain the wartime legend of the unanimous support accorded the Soviet Government by its people during the war, the matter of repatriates was passed over in silence within Russia. Only once, in 1946, a short dispatch appeared about the trial of General Andrei Vlasov and his aides, who were convicted of treason, sentenced to death, and executed.

It happened, however, that more facts became known abroad. American troops in Germany were obliged to comply with the order to load the interned Russian soldiers and displaced persons onto trains and convoy them to the Soviet zone; no protests on the part of those shipped back were of any avail. A few of them managed, however, to return from the other side of the demarcation line and they told of the impending trials and threatened punishment. The summer and fall of 1945 witnessed a real struggle between the American authorities in Germany and Austria and the interned Russians; it took clubs, rifle butts, and bayonets, and shooting over the prisoners' heads to usher them into the box cars that were to bear them to Russia.

In January, 1946, 10 Russian soldiers in Dachau committed suicide by cutting their throats, while 21 others were saved after attempting suicide with razor blades. Though threatened with rifles and carbines, they refused to leave the shelter, begging GI guards to shoot them rather than carry out the extradition order. Although no mention had been made of their destination, they appeared certain of the preparations and determined to die rather than obey. The next day, in another barrack, the Russians tore off their clothing in a vain effort to frustrate the guards and, linking their arms, resisted pushing and shoving. When the guards finally rushed the building, some prisoners were dead, having cut their own throats, while others had used pieces of clothing to hang themselves.[18] It was a humiliating assignment for the United States Army!

In order to have French prisoners of war repatriated from the Soviet-occupied zone of Germany—their number was over 300,000—the French Government had to make a sig-

18. *New York Times*, January 20, 1946.

nificant concession in return, namely, to allow Russian NKVD commissions to go to France and operate freely against the *nevozvrashchentsy* ("nonreturners," a term applied to this special category of Soviet citizens). In accordance with the secret agreement, the NKVD established its own concentration camp on French soil, at Beauregard, near Paris. NKVD men in uniform and in plain clothes, aided by hired agents, gathered intelligence about Soviet citizens in hiding, raided their domiciles, rounded them up and sent them to Beauregard, whence they were forcibly sent back to Russia.

An artillery officer with a long record of guerrilla warfare, who had likewise been a prisoner of the Germans and had been detained on Alderney Island, where 1,200 of 2,000 Russian prisoners had died, tells his ordeal after the liberation of France in these words:

In the fall of 1944 I was taken to Camp Beauregard near Paris. This was one of the many collection points for Soviet citizens who had been German prisoners or deportees. There were about 3,000 persons in Beauregard at the time. The administration consisted of former prisoners of war like us under the control of the Military Repatriation Commission.

At first we had a free and easy life. We came and went as we pleased. The administration carefully avoided any show of strict discipline in order to allay our suspicions and attract as many people as possible. But Soviet people aren't so easily duped. We were visited by Bogomolov [the Soviet Ambassador to France], Guzovski, and other officials of the Embassy and military mission; they made speeches about our fatherland forgiving us and awaiting us; they said that the guilty and the innocent were equally dear to our country, and that once we were home each individual case would be examined, with the result that some would be rewarded and others punished. One such speech was enough for us. We knew what was meant by "examining things once we were home" and "forgiving everything." Anyway, what did they mean by "forgiving" a man who had suffered endlessly at the enemy's hands? We were to be encouraged to go home, and once there we would be punished as "traitors to our country" for having let ourselves be captured alive. All our hopes for changes and an evolution of the Soviet regime in the years of war were shattered with one blow at our first contact with the "authorities." A "Soviet atmosphere" pervaded the camp. People began to fear one another, they were afraid of speaking out loud, denunciations began, people were being shadowed and investigated: the agents of the NKVD were at work.

One evening Comrade Guzovski came to the camp. That day the whole camp had been drunk, and the intoxicated guards, who did not know Guzovski, refused to admit him. This incident resulted in such a response and such threats on the part of Guzovski that our last doubts were dispelled about the fate that awaited us in our country. The next day Bogomolov came out to the camp to try to alleviate the distressing effect of Guzovski's pronouncements, but to no avail. Many officers of the Commission while drunk had hinted at the fate of "traitors to our country," and their words spread with lightning speed throughout the camp. Most of the inmates had but one thought: escape. Everybody who had connections outside the camp tried to obtain false documents and shelter. Of course not many succeeded in this.

As the date of our departure approached our spirits were desperately low. Disorders and drunkenness could no longer be restrained, robberies were rampant in the vicinity of the camp. Everyone wanted to be free and do as he pleased for the last time.

In July, 1945, the first transports left for Russia. Others followed all through the summer. And as men left, others were brought in from all over the country. The camp was surrounded by armed guards and we could no longer go to town.

Escapes were frequent. When the critical moment arrived, I too, escaped . . .[19]

A Ukrainian, forcibly deported to Germany under the occupation, had been put to work in a German machine repair shop. After the liberation, he says,

he decided to reconcile himself to his fate and return to Russia with his group. They were being sent off well, with speeches, music, and banners, on trucks. . . . They were driven to a collecting point near Leipzig and placed behind barbed wire. Instead of music, there were loaded machine guns. The welcoming speech

19. From an unpublished manuscript of a former Red Army officer, written in Paris in May, 1946.

was full of curses and threats. Then interrogations began: this was no longer the army, this was the NKVD. They asked an endless number of questions, and after each reply the interrogator would shout: "You liar!" The food was atrocious. Nor did the conversations among the men sound very comforting; there was talk of the horrible fate of the preceding parties. The returnees were told that all those suspected of sympathizing with the Germans and having done good work for them were immediately segregated and placed in a separate camp for "Vlasovites"; there the conditions were no better than they had been in German camps for Russian prisoners of war. It was said that groups of returnees were even sent off by foot to the [Soviet] border. . . .

After his freer life in France, our mechanic was greatly depressed. One day, while still in this camp,

. . . he found himself in front of a convoy of American trucks that had just brought in a new group of men. "Like a feather I jumped into one and hid under a bench. I lay there without daring to breathe. It was dark already. I didn't care what might happen." After half an hour the truck, driven by an American soldier, left the camp without inspection. At the first stop the driver chased off his stowaway, but this was already in the American zone, near a railway station. From there he made his way back to France—without money, without a ticket, without papers. . . .[20]

Bloody and hair-raising incidents were reported in the French press, and public opinion was soon aroused against the doings of the Soviet agents in France and their methods. For a long period the French Government did not dare oppose this Russian activity since it was based on a previous official commitment. Not until May, 1946, did M. le Troquer, Minister of Internal Affairs, tell Soviet Ambassador Bogomolov how great was the indignation in France and demand the cessation of the MVD's activities there.

Similarly in Sweden considerable excitement resulted from the disclosure of the Soviet demand for the forcible return of 157 citizens of the Baltic states, who had escaped from Germany. It became known that by a secret agreement the Swed-

20. *Novyi zhurnal*, XIV (New York, 1946), 243–244.

ish Government had recognized the Soviet annexation of the Baltic nations back in 1940. Living in constant fear and under pressure from the Soviet Government, Sweden finally yielded and returned the unfortunate doomed refugees.

In the United States the repatriation of Russian prisoners of war seized in France and Germany proceeded silently even before the end of the war, but dramatic events were revealed only after the armistice. On Ellis Island, at Fort Dix, N.J., and at Camp Ruston, La., as well as on the West Coast many Russians due to be repatriated committed suicide. Others jumped overboard after leaving American soil. The number of those shipped to Russia has not been made public.

On October 4, 1945, General Eisenhower tried to abrogate this article of the Yalta Agreement and ordered the discontinuance of forcible repatriation of Russian nationals. At that time 26,400 Soviet citizens were still in American custody. The spokesman for the Supreme Allied Commander explained that "we are not going to risk the lives of American soldiers to make them [the Russians] go." The State Department, however, overruled Eisenhower's instructions and ordered the completion of the repatriation program.

As a result of this large-scale action of the Soviet Government and strong pressure brought to bear on its allies, Soviet Russia gained great masses of manpower and a new source for the replenishment of forced labor camps. How many of the millions of Russian repatriates have wound up in labor camps it is of course impossible to tell. Together with Germans and other prisoners of war working in Russia and along with the remaining inmates of the forced labor camps, they lend an unusually heterogeneous character to the body of forced laborers. From the industrial Don Basin, for instance, a report states:

Rumanians, Yugoslavs, Poles of German origin were deported to the Don Basin to work in the mines. There are also at work there German, Hungarian, and Rumanian war prisoners, as well as a certain number of Italians. Likewise Soviet citizens returned from captivity are immediately dispatched to this region, where they are subjected to a rather severe discipline, having to work under the provisions of the labor draft and being deprived of the right to return to their families. Another category of the workers consists of Soviet citizens who served with the German Army or collaborated with the Germans. These have been sentenced to forced labor in the coal mines. Their terms vary from 10 to 20 years. A certain number of these forced laborers were pardoned in September, 1945, on condition that they remain in the Don Basin and have their families transferred there.[21]

Two kinds of purges went on in Russia after the end of the war and both supplied new contingents of forced labor. The first took place in former enemy-occupied regions and involved unreliable and suspect Soviet elements. On the basis of various evidence and denunciations, the MVD deported considerable groups of men and women to camps in the north and east, the proceedings and sentences never being mentioned in the press. This action was taken in accordance with a decree of April, 1943, reintroducing "penal servitude" for collaboration with the enemy.

The second purge started in August, 1946, and dealt primarily with Soviet officials found guilty of embezzlement, incorrect reporting, inefficiency, and other Soviet delinquencies. A few trials and sentences have been reported officially, as a warning to the population. The purging process was obviously intended to last for a considerable period; its results cannot but benefit the depleted manpower reserves of the labor camps.

In the meanwhile, the new Five-Year Plan for 1946–50, which stresses rehabilitation of industry, agriculture, transportation, and waterways, was announced. Among its projects a great many are in the group traditionally carried out by forced labor.

The peat output is to be increased 39 per cent over prewar figures. The rebuilding of power stations must be conducted at great speed. Hydroelectric stations are planned in a number

21. *Sotsialisticheski vestnik* (1946), No. 10.

of new locations. The petroleum industry in the Volga area is to be increased 2.4 times; new petroleum fields are to be developed in the Tatar Republic, and the Saratov, Kuibyshev, Urals, Ukhta, and Sakhalin regions; a large liquid fuel industry is to be created in eastern Siberia, the northern Caucasus, and the Leningrad region. New railroads are to be built to a total of 7,230 kilometers; secondary tracks to a total of 12,500 kilometers are to be built or restored. On existing railroads 50,000 kilometers of new rails are to be laid. The Stalin White Sea–Baltic Canal is to be rebuilt and work is to begin on the Mariinsk waterway. Inland water transport systems are to be restored and wharves and ports are to be rebuilt on the Dnieper, Pripet, Don, Kuban, Neman, western Dvina, and Svir rivers, and on lakes Ladoga and Onega. The "felling of trade timber shall increase by 59 per cent" over the prewar figures.

The timber-felling area shall be increased, chiefly where the timber can be brought down for floating in the following river basins: the northern Dvina and its tributaries, Pechora, Kama, Vyatka, Kilmez, Unzha, Vetluga and Belaya; the felling of timber shall be increased in western Siberia and the Far East. In the five-year period 17,500 kilometers of timber transport roads for mechanical traction, 6,500 kilometers of narrow-gauge railway, 2,500 kilometers of tractor roads, and 8,500 kilometers of motor roads shall be built in the lumber regions, mainly in the northern and northwestern regions and in the Urals (Kama Basin).[22]

The fulfillment of this great plan is, under present Soviet conditions, contingent upon the existence and expansion of the system of forced labor.

22. Voznesenski's report to the Supreme Soviet, March, 1946.

XV

The Reappearance of Old Russia?

> "My father chastised you with whips but
> I will chastise you with scorpions."

"There will come a time when sentences will not impose years and months of imprisonment but days and hours of forced labor. . . . Prison work is the most effective and rational mode of criminal repression." These are not the words of a Soviet leader, of the bearer of great and new ideas about punishment and correction. It was the tsarist Minister of Justice, Nikolai V. Muraviov, who, in 1902, told a congress in St. Petersburg about this vision of his. The congress was considering problems of convict labor, and Muraviov was neither a Socialist nor a liberal. He became rather prominent as State Prosecutor in the case of the revolutionists Zhelyabov, Perovskaya, and others who were accused of assassinating Tsar Alexander II and who were later executed. Muraviov was also the father of the formula of "self-supporting prisons" which later became immensely popular with Soviet professors of criminal law and with molders of penal policy in the late 'twenties.

Nor was it a Communist spokesman who, in 1912, visited the Prison Exhibition, inspected a workshop, and stated with emphasis: "This is a very important business." It was Tsar Nicholas II himself.

During the three centuries preceding the Revolution the employment of convict labor and exiles had become a tradition in Russia. In no other country has the utilization of forced labor in the economy of the state itself played as significant a role as in the history of Russia. Slave labor has been employed to a much greater degree by the state than by individuals. This characteristic phenomenon of Russian history—the prevalence of the state in colonization, transportation, and, to some extent, industry—appeared also in the economic use of prison labor.

In France, Colbert had introduced the galleys as a substitute for the death penalty, and not until sails replaced oars in the navy did galley slavery disappear. In fiction and in literature the oarsmen chained to the boats and suffering inhuman privations during the long cruises have remained the most vivid symbol of enslavement down to our day.

In Russia, the naval forces constructed by order of Peter I in the Sea of Azov were manned by convicts, whose sentences read: "Condemned to the galleys." A galley was called katorga in Russian. While naval galleys soon fell into disuse, katorga, like galley, came to mean the worst possible prison punishment coupled with hard labor. The word was later officially adopted and figured in penal codes and court sentences until the day of the Revolution.

Early in the eighteenth century a part of the galley slaves were transferred to St. Petersburg and Baltiiski Port to do construction work there. Because of a scarcity of workers— the periodic curse of Russian industrial development, so paradoxical in a highly populated country, and prevalent both before and after the Revolution—not only the worst criminals but even minor offenders and insolvent debtors were ordered to construction jobs. When founding his new capital, Peter I gave instructions to gather the required contingent of forced laborers in these words: "to assemble a few thousand thieves for next summer all over the provinces and cities."

The use of compulsory labor soon became widespread. It was employed in the salt mines of the Ural Mountains, in the building of fortresses, in the construction of the ports of Riga, Taganrog, and Reval. By the middle of the eighteenth century, prisoners were working in silver and iron mines in the Urals and in Siberia. At that time the katorga was not merely a means of punishing criminals, it was rather forced labor required by the government. "In addition to convicts, the group of compulsory laborers included persons unable to pay taxes and private debts and who had to pay them off in labor. Certain people were assigned to specific jobs: artillery and admiralty employees, factory workers." [1]

A milder form of compulsory labor was employed by the state in the colonization of sparsely populated regions, particularly along the eastern periphery of the empire. For this purpose persons sentenced to exile, rather than more serious offenders, were utilized. The deportation of exiles attained considerable proportions in the seventeenth and eighteenth centuries. Sent away to wild and uninhabited areas with harsh climates, without outside assistance, and virtually abandoned there, they often perished in droves. With characteristic disregard for the suffering and lives of prisoners and exiles, the state could be satisfied that the ones who remained alive constituted a nucleus of Russian influence and the first line of defense against neighboring states. Exile served the Russian state as an inexhaustible source of labor wherever it was needed for civilian and military tasks, for the peopling and fortifying of borders. . . . "The exiled perished in masses, their blood was shed in streams, but exile served its purpose and rendered a great service to the Russian state." [2]

The colonization of Siberia and, in particular, of the Far East, was to a certain extent accomplished through the use of prisoners and exiles. While many new settlements sprang up, the price paid in human lives was tremendous. Early in the nineteenth century 1,500 men were settled to the east of the Baikal Sea. They soon lost all their belongings and were forced to wander the roads begging alms. In the Urals a police official, Loskutov, created a colony that existed only so long as this local tsar was able to terrorize his subjects into obedience by means of whipping and wholesale corporal punishment. When Loskutov was arrested, a large part of the population dispersed.

One hundred and fifty thousand men and women, guarded

1. Ivan Foinitski, *Ucheniye o nakazanii* (Penal Law), p. 269.
2. N. Sergeyevski, *Nakazaniye v russkom prave 17-go veka* (Punishment in the Seventeenth Century), (1887), p. 257.

and accompanied by their children, plodded from Moscow to Siberia along the famous Vladimir Track during the two decades from 1826 to 1847. To prevent escapes, chaining was introduced, and all exiles' heads were shaved.

With the abolition of serfdom in the 1860's the use of slave labor diminished considerably for a few decades, since, in a sense, prison work was the industrial counterpart of agricultural serfdom. In the mid-'eighties it again began to expand—rather slowly at first, more rapidly after the turn of the century. The value of work performed by prisoners was reported to amount to 111,000 rubles in 1885, 1,250,000 in 1906, and 8,200,000 in 1915. These figures are misleading, however, since they appear to cover only work done within prison walls. The main tasks of the prisoners were performed outside the prisons—stone quarrying; coal mining; gold mining in Siberia; construction of ports, prisons, buildings, and highways. In 1896 the Amur Highway was built; the descriptions of its building strangely and vividly resemble the stories of the corrective labor camps of today. The work was so hard, the treatment so severe, and life under the local bosses so terrible, that "people cut their own fingers and toes off, stuck iron crowbars into their own and each other's backs." [3] Official prison reports often mentioned instances of self-mutilation.

The number of inmates in katorga prisons was

5,790 on January 1, 1906
7,779 on January 1, 1907
12,591 on January 1, 1908
22,649 on January 1, 1909
28,060 on January 1, 1910
32,000 on January 1, 1912
29,352 on January 1, 1914 [4]

The large increase occurring between 1906 and 1914 is due, to a certain extent, to sentences imposed for political offenses.

3. A. Tipunkov, "O Tom chto bylo" (What Used To Be), in G. N. Chemodanov, *Nerchinskaya katorga* (Moscow, 1924), p. 131.
4. Vyshinski, ed., *Tyurma kapitalisticheskikh stran*, pp. 61, 143.

Nevertheless, the maximum of approximately 30,000 on the eve of the first World War should be the yardstick for evaluating the role of prison labor in old Russia.

Another rise in the incidence of prison labor occurred in 1915–16 and was due to the war. Prison workshops produced linen, shoes, and clothing for the armed forces; prisoners worked in the munitions industry and made hand grenades; they loaded and unloaded ships, did forestry, mining, and railroad construction. The number of working prisoners thus rose to about 50,000 during the first World War.

In 1900 the Russian delegate to the International Prison Congress, Solomon, proudly told a congress of prison officials in Brussels:

"The Middle Ages left Russia with a heritage of torture, knout, and exile. The eighteenth century abolished torture, in the nineteenth the knout was done away with, and the first day of the twentieth century is the last day of the penal system based on exile."

Solomon was profoundly mistaken. His own government soon proceeded to expand the old penal system, and then—a quarter of a century later—a new government came to resurrect and employ, on an unexampled scale, methods and measures that Mr. Solomon had prematurely buried as vestiges of a shameful past. In addition to the prerevolutionary prisons, hundreds of concentration camps were now opened. Instead of the 30,000 convicts doing hard labor in 1914, there were now many millions of forced laborers. The exile system reached proportions hitherto unknown anywhere in the world. Numerically, it far outdid Hitler's concentration camps. Today the system of prison and exile of old Russia appears merely as a seed which under new conditions has yielded a rich harvest.

To many a superficial observer the present evolution of Russia presents itself as a gradual reversion to her historic pattern, to habits, feelings, and policies of prerevolutionary times.

They note the reëmergence of a pan-Slav philosophy, of military insignia and officers' epaulettes, of knout and *nagaika;* they see a drive for the Dardanelles and Port Arthur; they take cognizance of dozens of manifestations of similar tendencies—and they are happy to conclude that the Soviet Government itself is "discarding Communism" and gradually reverting to the ways of old Russia. In their eyes the resurrection of the old Russia makes the prevailing political system "national" and "rooted in the past." They hope that a *modus vivendi* can be reached more easily with the traditional, "national Russia," and are therefore prepared to acquiesce in many of the foul and base deeds if they are reminiscent of eastern traditions and clothed in historical formulae.

They are doubly wrong, these peculiar optimists. It is not true that the Soviet Government is discarding Communism from its philosophy and policies. Rather it sponsors, fosters, and kindles it both inside and outside of Russia by all and any means—including some that are vestiges of the past. What it fosters and kindles, however, is not the soft, lofty, and dreamy philosophy of Communism of bygone decades; it enforces a reality of unlimited coercion, of serfdom, slavery, and penal servitude.

Nor is it true that Russian history is a sequence of murder, torture, violence, and cruelty, as it so often appears to a superficial student. Besides knouts and katorga, the history of Russia—more perhaps than that of many other nations—abounds in humanitarian and liberative movements, idealism and self-sacrifice for the cause of human liberty and the rule of law. Glorious pages of world history have been written in Russia throughout a century of struggle against the degradation and enslavement of man. For a century the aspiration of Russia's greatest thinkers was a free nation in which human rights would be secure.

The terrible truth is that out of Russia's rich historical past the Soviet leadership, after prolonged vacillations and against opposition from within, has chosen to revive the harshest, most cruel and barbaric features, enhancing them greatly, while crushing under its heel the growths of freedom and humanism which had slowly appeared from beneath the surface during the course of the past century and which are equally a part—the noblest, proudest part—of the legacy of Russia.

LITERATURE ON FORCED LABOR
IN RUSSIA

Literature on Forced Labor in Russia

The literature on Russian labor camps and forced labor in general is more abundant than is commonly assumed. Since the early 'thirties quite a number of books have been published, especially in the United States, Britain, France, and Germany, dealing exclusively with this subject; there are even more which devote one or more chapters to the issue.

Five books in English are "musts" for anyone wanting to understand modern Russia; no student of Russian affairs and no intelligent person in general should overlook them. In the chronological order of the period they deal with they are:

Red Gaols (London, 1935) is the memoirs of a woman whose name could not be revealed at the time (apparently the daughter of a prerevolutionary diplomat), who was arrested in 1923 during the antireligious campaign, spent over eight years in prisons, concentration camps, and labor camps, including the Solovetski Islands and the Belomor Canal Camps, was freed in 1932, and left Russia in 1935. The narrative is startling but truthful.

Vladimir Tchernavin, *I Speak for the Silent Prisoners of the Soviets* (Boston, Ralph T. Hale & Co., 1935). The author is a Russian scientist who in his youth took part in scientific expeditions to Altai and Mongolia; later he led expeditions exploring Central Asia and the Far East, and subsequently became a recognized authority on ichthyology. In 1925 he was appointed Director of Production and Research of the Northern State Fishing Trust. Arrested as a "wrecker," he was sent to the Northern Camps and there witnessed the transformation of the concentration camps into economic institutions. This highly readable book contains one of the most penetrating analyses of the early period of the forced labor system. While a prisoner, Tchernavin was given the assignment of organizing the use of forced labor in the fishing industry, and in line of duty had to travel along the northern coast. After arranging a meeting with his wife and son in the far north, he escaped with his family to Finland. The dramatic story of their flight, during which they spent about three weeks in endless forests under conditions of extreme privation, was told by the author's wife, Tatiana Tchernavina, in *Escape from the Soviets* (London, 1933).

George Kitchin, *Prisoner of the OGPU* (New York, 1935). The author is a Finnish citizen who went to Russia as the representative of a number of American companies under the NEP. Having refused to furnish the GPU with information on Finland, he was accused of espionage and sentenced to four years of deprivation of liberty. The fact that he served in the supply department of a corrective labor camp saved his life. His book was published soon after he left Russia, and he died a short time later as the result of the long imprisonment.

Lilian T. Mowrer, *Arrest and Exile* (New York, W. Morrow & Co., 1941). With a foreword by Olga Kochanska. Mrs. Kochanska, a violinist, is the widow of Waclaw Kochanski, a famous Polish musician. After the death of her husband Mrs. Kochanska—a native of Chicago, Ill.—was recognized as a United States citizen, and this circumstance saved her after her deportation from Poland to a settlement of the NKVD. She reached this country in 1941, by way of Siberia and Japan. As is the case with many foreigners who before their imprisonment and exile knew neither Russia nor the Russian people, the author is often not only anti-Communist but anti-Russian in general. Despite this feature the book is highly informative and useful.

The Dark Side of the Moon (New York, 1947). Introduction by T. S. Eliot. In a short preface Helena Sikorski, the widow of the Polish Premier, recommends the unnamed author of this book as "a woman of scrupulous integrity and fairness." Upon instructions of the late General Sikorski the author was given access to official material and documents. Her book is based on a multitude of firsthand reports of Poles, men and women, deported to Russia in 1940, released in 1941–42, and then permitted to leave the Soviet Union. The actual life in Soviet labor camps and settlements is presented vividly and objectively. Some mistakes concerning Russian history have been made; Russian names have been misspelled; but these errors do not diminish the value of the book so far as the factual material is concerned. In fact, it is one of the most important books of our day.

Other books in English that are of value to anyone interested in a more thorough study of the problem of forced labor in Russia are the following:

S. A. Malsagoff, *An Island Hell* (London, 1926). The author escaped in 1925 after more than a year in the Solovki.

Allan Pim and Edward Bateson, *Report on Russian Timber Camps* (London, 1931); *Out of the Deep* (London, 1933), with an introduction by Hugh Walpole; and *Forced Labour in Russia* (London, 1931), published by the *British-Russian Gazette and Trade Outlook*, deal with the "dumping problem" discussed in Chapter XI of this book. The last-mentioned volume presents the Soviet viewpoint, while Messrs. Pim and Bateson report on the findings of the British Anti-Slavery Society. The second book contains letters from inmates of Soviet timber camps and has a preface by Sir Bernard Pares, who recommends the volume with the words: "I have seen the originals of the letters; I have no doubt of their authenticity."

Duchess of Atholl, M.P., *Conscription of a People* (New York and London, 1931). This serious, scholarly volume on the early stages of industrialization and collectivization in Russia reveals a good understanding of the forced labor system as an integral part of the Five-Year Plans.

Ivan Solonevich, *Russia in Chains* and *Escape from Russian Chains* (both London and New York, 1938). The author served in various capacities in Russia, was arrested and sentenced, together with his brother and son, to a term in the Northern Camps. Together the three escaped to Finland, later settled in Bulgaria, and eventually went over to the most extreme pro-Hitler elements among Russian émigrés. The two books, strongly pervaded by passion and bitterness, are nevertheless important sources of information.

Julia de Beausobre, *The Woman Who Could Not Die* (New York, 1938). A quiet and objective book written by a woman who was sentenced to five years of corrective labor for "terrorism." Because of serious illness she was freed before the expiration of her sentence and permitted to go to England. The author tries to portray everyone, even the prison chiefs, humanely. It is probably this trait that makes the overall impression especially gloomy and full of horror.

Belomor (New York, 1935), is an abbreviated translation of the beautiful and luxurious Russian volume, *Baltiisko-Belomorski Kanal imeni Stalina*, edited by Maxim Gorky. The book contains the official and highly optimistic Soviet version of the use of forced labor in the construction of the White Sea–Baltic Sea Canal.

Ada Halpern, *Conducted Tour* (New York, 1945; also published in London under the title, *Liberation—Soviet Style*), is a well-written and illuminating story of a Polish woman deported to NKVD settlements in Central Asia in 1940–41.

Elma Dangerfield, *Beyond the Urals* (London, British League for European Freedom, 1946), with a preface by Rebecca West, also gives the story of the deportation of Poles to Russia. The booklet contains valuable data.

Eugene Schirvindt (Yevgenii Shirvindt), *Russian Prisons* (London, 1928). This small pamphlet by the former chief of Soviet prisons sketches the ideological approach to crime and punishment in the early Soviet period and the blueprints of penal organization and living conditions in the prisons.

Eve G. Grady, *Seeing Red* (New York, 1931); Essad-Bey (Leo Noussimbaum), *Plot against the World* (New York, 1933); John D. Littlepage, *In Search of Soviet Gold* (New York, 1937); Anton Ciliga, *The Russian Enigma* (London, 1940); Freda Utley, *The Dream We Lost* (New York, 1940); John Scott, *Behind the Urals* (New York, 1942); William L. White, *Report on the Russians* (New York, 1945);

and Victor Kravchenko, *I Chose Freedom* (New York, 1946) all contain chapters on Soviet forced labor or references to it.

The following books in French are worthy of attention: Yuri Bessonov, *Mes 26 prisons et mon évasion de Solovki* (Paris, 1928). Bessonov was an officer of the old army who was imprisoned and deported to the Solovetski Islands. He escaped from the camp of Kem.

Senator Frédéric Eccard, "Le Travail forcé en Russie soviétique," in *Revue Hebdomadaire*, April 25, 1931, contains letters written by British and Norwegian sailors who had been in the Russian north; also letters from Russian prisoners, former officers, and priests.

"Les Camps de concentration de l'URSS," by an unnamed author in *Etudes*, March 20, 1934. Life in a prison camp in Karelia.

Joseph Czapski, *Souvenirs de Starobielsk*, 1945, deals with the fate of Polish officers in Russia in 1940; it also contains a report of the author's visit to the chief of the GULAG, General Nasedkin.

One of the most important books ever to appear on Russian prison camps is *La Justice soviétique*, published in French in Rome, 1945. Its authors, Sylvester Mora and Peter Zwierniak, are two Polish officers who have written on the basis of their personal experiences as well as of a great many firsthand reports. The first part of the book deals with the general picture of Soviet criminal law, exile, and the corrective labor system; the second part contains a large collection of personal reports on living conditions in the labor camps. The map attached to the book is of great interest and value.

A considerable number of books on Russian labor camps were published in Germany, almost all of them after 1932 under the National Socialist regime. Many of these publications are worthless, serving only primitive propaganda purposes. The Soviet labor camps are attacked not because they are concentration camps but for racial reasons; both the administration and the government are depicted as Jewish institutions which make use of the labor camps to oppress and destroy a host of Russian people. Facts are often distorted to create the desired impression. The Nibelungen-Verlag particularly indulged in the publication of books of this caliber.

Among the better volumes is Alexander Schwarz, *In Wologda's weissen Wäldern* (In the White Forests of Vologda) (Altona, 1937). The author, a Volga-German deported to an NKVD settlement in the north, accurately reports on the living conditions of the exiles, on their attempts to get help from relatives in Germany, their illnesses, and the great number of casualties.

Karl I. Albrecht, *Der verratene Sozialismus* (Socialism Betrayed) (Berlin, 1939). This large volume was written by a German forester with a strange background. A German soldier in the first World War, he fought against the Communist insurgents in Bavaria, then became a Communist himself and went to Russia in 1924. He spent ten years there and climbed high on the Soviet ladder of success. Enjoying the full confidence of the party leadership, he was instrumental in the organization of the lumber industry in the north and became Chief of the Lumber and Chemical Department of the Central Control Commission of the Communist party. A lengthy article appeared in *Pravda* under his name (September 5, 1931) recommending the mechanization of the northern lumber industry. According to Albrecht, this was the content of a paper read by him before the Politbureau. Arrested in June, 1932, he was sentenced to death by the Revolutionary Tribunal, but due to the intervention of the German Government (he had managed to keep his German citizenship), he was later turned over to the Gestapo, which at first put him under arrest. His description of this last phase of his Soviet career is incomplete and obviously insincere. The book contains a large number of interesting photographs and for a reader able to distinguish between fact and fiction there is valuable information in it.

Alexandra Anzerova (probably a pen name), *Aus dem*

Lande der Stummen (From the Land of the Silent) (Breslau, 1936). The author, who lived in Russian prisons from 1924 to 1933, describes the lot of women, practices of self-mutilation, and other aspects of life in the labor camps.

Andrei Russinow (pseud.), *Die grosse Täuschung* (The Great Illusion) (Berlin, 1936). The author lived in Archangel and had a chance to observe the life of prisoners and deportees.

Peter Nikolajew (pseud.), *Bauern unter Hammer und Sichel* (Peasants under the Hammer and Sickle) (Berlin, 1936). The writer as a prisoner went through various labor camps—Volga, Karelia, and others.

J. Rempel, *Der Sowjethölle entronnen* (Escaped from Soviet Hell) (Kassel, 1935). The life of exiles in Archangel. Often confused and inaccurate.

Olga Dmitrievna, *18 Jahre der Sowjetherrschaft* (Eighteen Years of Soviet Rule) (Vienna, 1938). The book is an enlarged edition of *Red Gaols*, listed above.

At the lowest level are books like Ernst Kluge, *Wahrheit über Sowjetrussland* (The Truth about Soviet Russia) (Leipzig, 1932); Hermann Greife, *Zwangsarbeit in der Sowjetunion* (Forced Labor in the Soviet Union) (Berlin, 1936); Lorenz Kamphausen, *Unter Arbeitern und Bauern* (Among Workers and Peasants) (Berlin, 1938), and others.

Soviet literature on criminal law and especially on corrective labor camps is voluminous. It is of course uniformly favorable and presents the official concept of correction by labor, "reforging," and cultural achievement. For a reader familiar with the Soviet manner of writing and presenting facts these books are an important source of information. Besides the volumes on Soviet law in general and on criminal law in particular, a number of books and magazine articles deal with the labor camps and exile; more often than not the authors are high officials of the NKVD or of the Commissariat of Justice.

Sovetskaya yustitsiya (Soviet Justice) is the most important publication on law, the courts, and penal institutions. Its volumes have for more than two decades contained pertinent articles by Stuchka, Krylenko, Shirvindt, Vyshinski, and others.

Y. Shirvindt and B. Utevski, *Sovetskoye penitentsiarnoye pravo* (Soviet Penal Law) and M. Isayev, *Osnovy penitentsiarnoi politiki* (Bases of Penal Policy) (Moscow, 1927), contain the early liberal version of reforming and reforging prisoners.

A. A. Gertzenson, *Bor'ba s prestupnostyu v RSFSR* (The Fight against Crime in the USSR) (Moscow, 1928), contains factual and statistical material on the development of criminality during the 'twenties.

Sotsialisticheskaya zakonnost' (Soviet Law), publication of the Ministry of Justice, the Supreme Court, and the Office of the Prosecutor of the USSR (since 1935).

Sovetskoye gosudarstvo i pravo (Soviet State and Law), organ of the Law Institute of the Academy of Science, a periodical publication.

Ot Tyurem k vospitatel'nym uchrezhdeniyam (From Prisons to Educational Institutions) (Moscow, 1934), edited by Andrei Vyshinski, is a collective work by a number of writers and government officials, as is another volume, *Tyurma kapitalisticheskikh stran* (Prisons in Capitalist Countries) (Moscow, 1937).

Semion Firin, *Itogi Belomorstroya* (The Balance Sheet of the Belomor) (Moscow, 1934). Firin was Deputy Chief of the GULAG and Chief of the Dmitrov Labor Camp.

I. L. Averbakh, *Ot Prestupleniya k trudu* (From Crime to Labor) (Moscow, 1936).

Bolshevtsy (The Colonists of Bolshevo) (Moscow, 1936) a collective work edited by Maxim Gorky.

A play by Nikolai Pogodin, *Aristokraty* (The Aristocrats) (Moscow, 1935).

For a discussion of the final stage in the transformation of prisons and the stabilization of the corrective labor camps, see: B. Utevski, *Sovetskaya ispravitelno-trudovaya politika*, (Soviet Corrective Labor Policy) (Moscow, 1935); Andrei

Vyshinski, *K polozheniyu na fronte pravovoi teorii* (On the Present State at the Front of Legal Theory) (Moscow, 1937), two lectures delivered before the Moscow Academy of Law; and a number of articles in *Sovetskaya yustitsiya*, 1936–39.

Among the Russian émigré publications the following are of special value:

N. I. Kiseliov-Gromov, *Lageri smerti v SSSR* (The Death Camps in the USSR) (Shanghai, 1936). Written by a former officer of the White Army who later entered the service of the GPU and escaped in 1930.

General I. M. Zaitsev, *Solovki* (Shanghai, 1931). This book is dedicated to the Anti-Comintern and written in a spirit of complete devotion to prerevolutionary Russia; it contains some interesting factual material on the Solovki camps.

M. Z. Nikonov-Smorodin, *Krasnaya katorga* (Red Katorga) (Sofia, 1938). The author was a land-surveyor who played a leading role in local anti-Soviet peasant uprisings during the Civil War and succeeded in escaping arrest for eight years, was then sentenced to death, and had his sentence commuted to ten years in labor camps. After six years of imprisonment he fled to Finland.

Olaf Feldheim, in *Sovremennyye zapiski* (Contemporary Notes), Paris, Vols. 65–69, 1937–39. The author is a Finn who was employed as a "specialist" in Soviet industry from 1924 to 1929, was arrested in 1929, and sentenced to five years for "counterrevolution." He spent two years in the Vishera camps, was then transferred to Siberia and imprisoned in the 9th Division of the *Siblag*.

Other important émigré publications have been translated into English and are listed above among books in English.

The chapters of this book dealing with northeastern Siberia and the Dalstroy are based on information drawn from several sources, which can be listed as follows:

Detailed information on the general conditions of life in the region is found in the extensive geographical literature of

Russian scientists and explorers. In the prerevolutionary era authoritative works were written by Middendorff, Bulychov, Cherski, and others. Among the Soviet works on the subject one may list as especially important: *Vvedeniye v izucheniye rastitel'nosti Yakutii* (Introduction to the Study of Plants in Yakutia) by V. L. Komarov, Member of the Soviet Academy of Sciences; *Vechnaya merzlota* (Perennial Frost) by M. I. Sumgin, Member of the Soviet Academy of Sciences; *Sovetskaya Yakutia* (Soviet Yakutia) by G. Kolesov and S. Potapov; *V nevedomykh gorakh Yakutii* (In the Unknown Mountains of Yakutia) by S. V. Obruchev; *V predgoryakh Indigirki* (In the Foothills of the Indigirka) by M. Krotov; and also the official handbook *RSFSR: Administrativno-territorial'noye deleniye* (RSFSR: Division into Administrative Territories), 1942. With the same group of works must be classed the numerous memoirs published by political exiles under the old regime who visited Kolyma and the adjoining regions, such as those of Tan-Bogoraz, Seroshevski, Nogin, Tsiperovich, Zenzinov, and others.

Some information on the present conditions at Magadan and in the Dalstroy territory is found in the Soviet periodicals of recent years. In this literature, meager both in quantity and in content, the following articles deserve mention: "Smena landshafta" (Change of Landscape) by N. Mikhailov, in the almanac *XXII God* (The 22d Year), (Moscow, 1939); "Kolyma—strana skazochnykh chudes" (Kolyma—the Fabulous Land) by N. Zagorodni, a series of reports on a journey to Magadan and the Kolyma published in *Izvestia* in September, 1944; "Na krainem severe—Magadan, Indigirka" (In the Extreme North—Magadan, the Indigirka) by S. Boldyrev, published in *Ogoniok*, No. 32, 1946; report of a speech by I. F. Nikishov, head of Dalstroy, reprinted in *Russki Golos*, New York, February 12, 1946. This literature naturally presents only that side of Dalstroy's operations which can be treated for display.

Information about the present prisoners in the Kolyma region and the actual conditions of work on the construction projects of Dalstroy is available only in the literature published outside the borders of the Soviet Union. The most detailed factual material is found in the reports of the Poles who, taken prisoner in 1939, spent 1940–41 in the prison camps of the Kolyma region. Many such reports have appeared in various Polish publications, and some of them have been included in the books, *La Justice soviétique* and *The Dark Side of the Moon*, both mentioned above. Information from Russian sources is scattered in the Russian émigré press. Of special interest is the story of a Soviet seaman who took part in several voyages to Magadan (*Sotsialisticheski vestnik*, New York, December, 1945).

In addition to the published material the writers of these chapters have been able to draw on the private information of persons who have a firsthand knowledge of the conditions in the Kolyma region.

Index

G

GELFGOT, A. P., 178
Geneva Convention of 1929, 278, 282
Georgia, Georgians, 16, 38, 259, 261
German, monk, 168
Germany, Germans, 5, 16, 23–25, 38, 44, 47, 50, 86, 93, 98, 153, 197, 212, 213, 222, 231, 254, 259, 263, Chap. XIV, 314
Gertzenson, A. A., 158 n., 160 n., 162 n., 316
Gestapo, 25, 314
Gizhiga, 70
Gladkov, 266, 268, 272
Goebbels, Joseph, 86 n.
Golyakov, I., 274
Gorelik, Meier, 180 n.
Gorky, Maxim, 95, 189, 213, 225, 231, 237 n., 242–243, 312, 316
Gorky (city), 216, 272
— (region), 67
Gorski, 199
GPU. See MVD
Grady, Eve G., 229, 312
Great Britain, 153, 169, 181, 197, 212, 218–219, 221–222, 225, 230, 283–284, 290
Great Northern Sea Route. See Arctic Ocean
Greece and Greeks, 92, 94–95, 259
Greife, Hermann, 315
Gropper, Roberta, 315
Guards. See Vokhra
Gubarevo camp, 70
GULAG, 157 n., 208–210, 240, 244–245, 247, 259–261, 313, 316
Guriev, 175
Guzovski, 294

H

HAITI, 96 n.
Halpern, Ada, 47 n., 312
Hannover, 285
Hausschild, Hilde, 25
Henderson, Arthur, 219, 222
Hitler, Adolf; Hitlerism, 25, 29, 31, 32, 47, 50–51, 92, 98, 140, 223, 231, 254, 303, 312, 313–314
House of Commons, Great Britain, 219, 222
House of Representatives, U. S., 220

Hungary, Hungarians, 5, 181, 263, 277, 280, 296

I

IGARKA CAMPS, 58, 69
Illarion-Troitski, 175
Indigirka (River), 110, 111, 135, 139, 318
Informers. See ISO
Ingash camp, 69
Ingush, 263, 275–276
Internal Affairs, Commissariat and Ministry of. See MVD
Irkutsk (city), xiv, 69, 280 n.
— (region), 69
Isayev, M., 157 n., 164 n., 316
ISO, 15–16, 235, 245–246
"Isolator." See Solitary confinement
Italy and Italians, 59, 95, 222, 263, 277, 280, 296
ITL. See Corrective labor camps *and* GULAG
Ivan the Terrible, 169
Ivanitski, 179
Ivanov (prisoner), 186
Ivanovo region, 66
Ivdel camps, 61, 67
Ivory Coast, 119
Izhma. See Ukhtizhma
Izvestia, 130, 134, 180, 200, 250

J

JANUSZEWSKI, MAX, 281 n.
Japan and Japanese, 114, 118, 131, 222, 263, 277, 280, 310
Jews and Jewry, 5, 32–34, 38, 52, 135, 266, 268, 314
Judiciary Collegium of the GPU, 250
"Jumpers," 195
Justice, Commissariat and Ministry of, 49, 150–152, 154, 156–159, 163–164, 203, 206, 210–211, 214, 240, 244, 299, 315–316

K

KABARDIN SSR, Kabardinians, 67
Kakolin, 144
Kalmyk ASSR, 276
Kama (River), 298
Kamchatka camps and Peninsula, 61, 70, 135
Kamenskaya, 214

Kamphausen, Lorenz, 315
Kandalaksha, 63
Kansk, 69
Kant, 261
Kara Sea, 66
Karachayev region, 276
Karaganda, *Karlag*, 23–24, 58, 61, 68, 72, 214, 272
Karelia, 52, 58, 101, 168, 197, 208, 219
Karelo-Finnish SSR, 63, 71 n.
Karelo-Murmansk region, 51
Kargopol camps, 61, 63, 262
Karjalainen, 227
Karkaraminsk, 58, 71 n.
Karnashov, Trofim, 229
Kashketin, Lieutenant, 260
Katanian, 180
Katowice, 285
Kaunas, 266, 268–269, 272
Kazakhs, Kazakhstan, 5, 16, 26, 45, 52, 68–69, 259, 261
Kem, 58, 168–169, 171, 173, 179, 181–189, 212, 224
Kemerovo camps, 68
Khabarovsk, 70
Kharkov, 229, 275
Khibinsk, 58, 63, 212
Kholmogory, 168, 171–172, 200
Kiev, 272
Kikshozero, 212, 224
Kilmez (River), 298
Kirghiz, 5, 46
Kirillovski, 186–187
Kirov, Sergei, 252, 254–255, 257
Kirov region, 67
Kiseliov-Gromov, N. I., 52, 190 n., 317
Kitchin, George, 58 n., 226–228, 241 n., 310
Klinger, A., 175 n.
Kluge, Ernst, 315
Kochanska, Olga, 46, 310
Kocharovski, Georgi, 180 n.
Kola Peninsula, 63
Kolesov, G., 318
Kolyma camps and region, 3, 62, 70–72, Chap. VI, 216, 318–319
Komarov, 318
Komi SSR, 3, 66
Komsomol. *See* Communist Youth League
Komsomolsk, 69, 70, 71, 73
Kond Island, 52, 174
Kopman, Dr. Arthur, 220, 221 n.

Korea and Koreans, 6, 16
Kosariov, Alexander, 22
Kosogor, 214
Kotlas, 3, 33–34, 58, 61, 62, 66, 72, 214, 227–228, 260, 272
Kotova, Elizaveta, 180 n.
Kozin, 22
Krashennikov, A. N., 196
Krasikov, 180
Krasnodar, 3, 275
Krasnogorsk, 278
Krasnoyarsk camps, *Kraslag*, 61, 69, 73
— region, 69, 272
Krasovski, Vladimir, 173
Kravchenko, Victor, 84, 313
Kremlin, 22, 109, 230, 257
Kronstadt Revolt, 170
Krotov, M., 318
Krylenko, Nikolai, 105, 150–152, 202, 203, 232, 258, 316
Kuban, 122, 298
Kuibyshev, Valerian, 215
Kuibyshev region, 67, 261, 262, 280, 298
Kulbak, M., 33
Kuloi, *Kuloilag*, 61, 63
Kulischer, E. M., 274 n.
Kulunda, 280
Kungur, 58, 68, 188, 214
Kurilko, 189
Kuznetsk, 42, 58, 215, 262, 280
KVCh, 13–14

L

LABOR, COMMISSARIAT AND MINISTRY OF, 193–199
Ladoga, Lake, 173, 298
Ladoga camps, 63
Latvia and Latvians, 116, 188, 264, 272, 274 n.
Laurion, 94
Le Troquer, 295
League of Nations, 97, 222
Lebedev, Leonid, 180 n.
Lena (River), 135
— camps, 59, 69
Lenin, V. I., 146, 149–151, 155, 158, 203, 254, 256
Leningrad (city), 44, 73, 84, 128, 171, 175, 187, 214, 257, 258, 300
— (region), 63, 214, 298
Leninogorsk, 69
Lenkoran, 61
Lianozovo-Kryukovskaya, 164